The Great Disappearing Act

The Great Disappearing Act

Germans in New York City, 1880–1930

CHRISTINA A. ZIEGLER-McPHERSON

Rutgers University Press

New Brunswick, Camden, and Newark, New Jersey, and London

Library of Congress Cataloging-in-Publication Data
Names: Ziegler-McPherson, Christina A., author.
Title: The great disappearing act: Germans in New York City, 1880–1930 /
    Christina A. Ziegler-McPherson.
Description: New Brunswick: Rutgers University Press, [2022] | Includes bibliographical
    references and index.
Identifiers: LCCN 2021010329 | ISBN 9781978823181 (paperback) | ISBN 9781978823198 (cloth) |
    ISBN 9781978823204 (epub) | ISBN 9781978823211 (mobi) | ISBN 9781978823228 (pdf)
Subjects: LCSH: German Americans—New York (State)—New York—History—
    20th century. | German Americans—Cultural assimilation—New York (State)—
    New York—History—20th century. | German Americans—New York (State)—
    New York—Social conditions—20th century. | New York (N.Y.)—History—20th century.
Classification: LCC F128.9.G3 Z54 2022 | DDC 305.893/107471—dc23
LC record available at https://lccn.loc.gov/2021010329

A British Cataloging-in-Publication record for this book is available from the British Library.

References to internet websites (URLs) were accurate at the time of writing. Neither the
author nor Rutgers University Press is responsible for URLs that may have expired or changed
since the manuscript was prepared.

♾ The paper used in this publication meets the requirements of the American National
Standard for Information Sciences—Permanence of Paper for Printed Library Materials,
ANSI Z39.48-1992.

www.rutgersuniversitypress.org

Manufactured in the United States of America

For the victims of the *General Slocum* disaster,
June 15, 1904

Contents

Illustrations

Figures

Tables

The Great Disappearing Act

Introduction

• •

In early spring of 1902, the United States hosted Prince Albert Wilhelm Heinrich of Prussia, the younger brother of Kaiser Wilhelm II. The second European royal to visit the United States, Heinrich (or Henry) arrived in New York City on February 22 and spent six of his seventeen days in the country meeting with and charming the city's politicians, socialites, the press, German American clubs, business leaders, and "captains of industry."[1] He attended the Metropolitan Opera, the German-language Irving Place Theater, several formal dinners, and many informal breakfasts; visited Columbia University and several elite social clubs; and launched his new yacht, the *Meteor*, built by an American shipbuilding company. In addition to New York City, Henry visited Washington, DC, Philadelphia, Chicago, Milwaukee, Chattanooga, and Boston before sailing back to Germany on the Hamburg-America ship, the SS *Deutschland*, on March 12. The trip was viewed by both the U.S. and German governments to be a diplomatic triumph.

The excitement of Henry's visit and the positive attention Americans showered on the German prince highlighted the high socioeconomic status and success German immigrants and German Americans had achieved in the United States—and New York City—by the turn of the nineteenth century. In 1902, German immigrants and their children and grandchildren were a highly visible part of New York City daily life. For nearly one hundred years, German businesses, churches, social clubs, schools, theaters, and newspapers had marked the social, cultural, and economic landscapes of the city. Germans and German Americans were politically integrated, economically successful, upwardly mobile, and confident about their community's place in the city's history and social structure.

But within twenty years, New York City's German community lay shattered. Traumatized by anti-German xenophobia during World War I, German New Yorkers sought to hide in plain sight by denying their heritage, abandoning their language and any visible aspects of their culture, and disappearing into Anglo American society. By 1930, New York's once highly visible German community had become virtually invisible.[2]

How this successful, confident immigrant group could be brought so low and then disappear within a few decades is the key question of this work. The German experience in New York City between 1880 and 1930 can tell us much about the nature and structure of immigrant communities, as well as the processes by which immigrants and immigrant communities adapt and change over time in reaction to prejudice and other external pressures.[3]

Although Germans had similar motivations to assimilate as other immigrant groups—prejudice against their status as an ethnic and linguistic minority, desire for socioeconomic upward mobility, generational tensions, and so on—there were several factors that made the German immigrant experience in the United States unique: the massive size of this immigration (more than 5.8 million people during 1830–1930); the long period of continuous immigration and cultural replenishment; and German communities' high degrees of social organization and self-segregation. Anglo Americans' favorable attitudes toward German culture and German immigrants were also distinctive.[4] These factors allowed German immigration to change American society in significant ways that the migration of other groups did not. Finally, German immigrants were alone in experiencing the xenophobia of World War I, when the German language and culture were demonized and community institutions were attacked at all levels of society, from the presidency on down.

Assimilation is the processes by which a society becomes more homogeneous through such means as political incorporation, socioeconomic interaction, residential settlement, intermarriage, a common lifestyle, and shared identity and values.[5] Integration—often defined as participating in mainstream social, political, and economic institutions and adopting the majority's cultural practices—is only one stage of assimilation. The presence and absence of prejudice and discrimination against a group are also key elements in determining whether or not that group has assimilated.[6]

In the nineteenth century, Americans had a vague understanding of what assimilation was and how it happened. But most people had confidence in the ability of American institutions and culture to incorporate diverse European groups into one national culture and society dominated by a white, English-speaking Protestant majority. But this faith in the positive power of assimilation was limited to European immigrants. Nineteenth-century white Americans had no interest in encouraging the assimilation of Black Americans, American Indians, or Asian immigrants and took aggressive steps to prevent interactions that would lead to any kind of assimilation by these groups. Jim Crow segregation, American Indian reservations, and Chinatowns were all consequences of white Americans' efforts to maintain a racially pluralistic society that encouraged the assimilation of desirable European immigrants, primarily through the offer of citizenship, the vote, and other political rights.[7]

German American community activists entered into this not-particularly rigorous philosophical debate about assimilation with a very different vision of American society than that held by white, English-speaking Americans. Already integrated politically and economically, German Americans rejected embracing the English language and Anglo American cultural practices and instead argued for a pluralistic understanding of American society in which the preservation of the ethnic group and its language, culture, and institutional structure was understood as a societal benefit that should be promoted and defended.[8]

These German Americans asserted that to be a true American, one had to exemplify American ideals, especially the idea of liberty. To be an American was a state of doing, not of being, and the best way of expressing one's freedom as an American was to be true to one's ethnic heritage. For these German American activists, being a good American meant being a good German: speaking good German, being active in German social and cultural groups, and displaying the positive characteristics of German immigration and German culture to other groups.

These German American thinkers believed that they could pick and choose which aspects of American culture they wished to adopt and still be considered fully American by the larger society. Therefore, Germans would be politically incorporated as citizens but not residentially integrated; they would participate in the mainstream economy and be as socioeconomically upwardly mobile as Anglo Americans but maintain their language and not marry outside of their group; they would define themselves as both German and American but still expect to be accepted by other Americans as true Americans, without prejudice or discrimination against their Germanness. In short, German Americans believed that they could assimilate into American society on their own terms, not the terms of the larger, Anglo American English-speaking Protestant majority.[9] The main proponents of this theory of pluralism were the leaders of pan–German American organizations, such as the National German-American Alliance, that sought to overcome long-standing divisions among German immigrants and consciously create a national German American community and identity.[10]

This philosophical debate between German American intellectuals and English-speaking American elites about the nature and process of assimilation in American society came to an abrupt end during World War I. It was during the mobilization for war that the idea of "100 percent Americanism" erupted as the primary way of defining American society. In "100 percent American-ism," an individual could only be American—100 percent—and nothing else; the "hyphen," as in "German-American" or "Irish-American," was unaccept-able. The concept of 100 percent Americanism was most aggressively promoted by those of English heritage who no longer defined themselves as English Amer-ican but solely as American. This hostility to the so-called hyphen was used to attack German Americans and other immigrant groups that opposed Ameri-can entry into the war, particularly Irish Americans.

But 100 percent Americanism was not simply a large stick with which Anglo Americans could beat opponents in a political debate about foreign policy; it was the measure by which Anglo Americans sought to measure the assimila-tion of other groups, particularly German Americans. As the dominant eth-nic group in the country, Anglo Americans asserted their right to be the exclusive arbiters of "Americanism," and in World War I, this was measured by one's adoption of Anglo American cultural values and practices, as well as support for a pro-British foreign policy.

Before World War I, German Americans had been the ethnic group best positioned to promote alternative visions of American society and theories of assimilation, and the United States had countless large and small German com-munities where this alternative understanding of pluralism was developed and lived on a daily basis. Germans were the largest immigrant group in the United States, with 5,875,571 Germans immigrating to the United States between 1830 and 1930.[11] Although this immigration ebbed and flowed, Ger-mans consistently composed one-quarter to one-third of all immigrants to the United States in the nineteenth century, with high points being between 1850–1859 and 1880–1889. It was not until the 1890s that German immigration began to slow and decline, and immigration from southern and eastern Europe increased in both numbers and overall percentages.[12]

German immigrants in the United States came from thirty-nine states and city-states that composed the German Confederation and then, after 1871, the German Empire. Other German speakers came from Austria, Switzerland, Luxembourg, Belgium, Denmark, the Alsace region of France, Bohemia (then a part of Austria-Hungary, now in the Czech Republic), South Tyrol in Italy, Poland (especially Silesia), Lithuania, Russia, Ukraine, and Transylvania (now part of Romania). Although for the purpose of this study, "German" is under-stood to be those people who emigrated from what is now Germany, the pres-ence of many other immigrants who either understood themselves to be ethnically German and/or who spoke German meant that the German Amer-ican community was much larger than the immigration statistics suggest.

German-speaking immigrants settled across the United States, although Germans tended to be more urban than native-born Americans and tended to concentrate in the Midwest and certain areas in the Northeast. In addition to

New York City, there were large German communities in Chicago, Philadelphia, Milwaukee, St. Louis, Cincinnati, Baltimore, and Buffalo, and in these and many other cities, Germans were the largest (or second largest) immigrant group. Each German community in the United States reflected the different migration streams of German immigration, with immigrants from certain German states clustering in certain American cities and avoiding others.[13] And while there were many German communities in the United States, these communities differed considerably in structure, and there was no one model for community development.

In Cincinnati, for example, geography played the primary role in the development of that city's German community, as German immigrants and their children and grandchildren concentrated in a dense neighborhood known as Over the Rhine. Between the 1830s and 1890s, Over the Rhine developed into a geographically and culturally isolated but class diverse neighborhood where German speakers from all over Europe lived and established businesses, churches, and a wide range of social organizations. But when community elites assimilated into the larger city by moving out of the neighborhood into English-speaking areas in the late nineteenth century, Over the Rhine degenerated into a poor ethnic enclave where former residents returned only to attend social events deemed essential to being German.[14]

In Milwaukee, the city with the highest percentage of German immigrants in the United States, Germans also formed a large, diverse, and geographically segregated community that was largely economically and socioculturally independent of the larger English-speaking city before the Civil War.[15] In St. Louis, another large midwestern city where Germans were the pioneering founders, German clubs (*Verein*, plural *Vereine*) were the foundation of a community that was geographically disbursed and continued to be so as Germans moved farther west in the late nineteenth century.[16]

In New York, the German community was defined by both geography and cultural-social institutions. Located in the Eleventh, Tenth, Thirteenth, and Seventeenth Wards on the southeastern side of Manhattan Island, below East 14th Street, Kleindeutschland (Little Germany) developed as the United States' first ethnic enclave in the 1830s and 1840s as German immigration to the United States surged.

Why and how the neighborhood received this name, Kleindeutschland (versus Kleinbaden or Kleinbayern, for example) is not known. The name was definitely in circulation in the German-language press by 1870, and residents believed that it reflected their community in all of its diversity. The journalist Caspar Stürenburg wrote of the neighborhood in 1885: "Klein-Deutschland; . . . ein Eiland [*sic*] von ächter deutscher Kleinstädterei . . . mitten in dem großstädtischen Häusermeer" (an island of real German small town in the middle of the great city's sea of houses).[17]

By 1880, there were 549,142 German immigrants and their American-born children in New York City, composing nearly half of the city's 1.2 million residents.[18] In addition to Kleindeutschland, German immigrants formed satellite communities in other neighborhoods in Manhattan, Brooklyn, and Queens, as well as across the Hudson River in Hudson County, New Jersey.[19] Although Milwaukee was the most German city in terms of percentage of population, New York City had more Germans total and was the third largest German-speaking city in the world, after Berlin and Vienna.[20]

The majority of German immigrants in New York City came from the south and west of the German-speaking states—Hesse, Baden, Württemberg, and Bavaria—and then, after the 1860s, from the northern and eastern states of Prussia, Brandenburg, Hannover, and Mecklenburg. Virtually all immigrants from the port cities of Hamburg and Bremen settled in New York City.[21]

Institutions, particularly social clubs, or Vereine, were the glue that held New York City's German community together. Although Kleindeutschland appeared to English speakers to be a linguistically and ethnically homogenous and geographically distinct neighborhood, it was, in fact, very diverse and stratified in terms of religion, class, German state of origin, and time of immigration. It was thus, through participating in Vereine, that German New Yorkers expressed and defined their community, or *Deutschtum* (state of Germanness).[22]

Kleindeutschland emerged as an immigrant community at the same time as distinct neighborhoods defined by class and ethnicity were developing in New York City. It was through the development of Kleindeutschland and then other immigrant communities that New Yorkers, and then Americans in general, came to understand ethnicity as an important factor in defining neighborhoods as something more than geographic space.[23]

In the eighteenth and early nineteenth centuries, New York City was a city of diverse neighborhoods in which people of different classes, occupations, ethnicities, and religions lived in close proximity to one another in residential areas shaped by different sectors of the local economy. Most people needed to be within walking distance of work if they did not live above or in front of their workplaces, and so occupational groups tended to cluster in certain neighborhoods: maritime workers near the east and west side docks; clerks and other white collar workers near the banks and other financial institutions downtown; tailors, seamstresses, and other garment workers east of Broadway; and so on.[24]

But immigration in the nineteenth century changed the socioeconomic geography of the city. Immigrant groups brought different types and amounts of social capital with them, creating a close relationship between occupation (especially between skilled and unskilled labor) and ethnicity that, in turn, affected the character of a neighborhood. It was in the mid- to late nineteenth century, as new housing and new methods of public transportation were developed, that New Yorkers began to segregate themselves by socioeconomic class. The eighteenth-century city had had rich or poor streets within a particular area, whereas the nineteenth-century city had wealthy neighborhoods that were overwhelmingly ethnically and religiously homogeneous (i.e., native-born white Anglo Saxon Protestant) and poor neighborhoods that were ethnically and religiously diverse. The markers and boundaries of these transformed spaces were clear to everyone in the city.[25]

Kleindeutschland was the first example of an ethnically defined neighborhood in New York City and was the product both of native-born English-speaking Americans refusing to live near immigrants and German-speaking immigrants choosing to live with people "like" themselves.[26] But unlike homogeneous middle- and upper-class white American neighborhoods in the city, Kleindeutschland was never more than 65 percent German in the nineteenth century, and many other immigrant groups—especially other Central Europeans—lived in the neighborhood.[27] Thus, Kleindeutschland was homogeneous in terms of socioeconomic class but diverse in terms of language, ethnicity, and religion.

Kleindeutschland was a community in transition and flux in the late nineteenth century, as German immigrants and their American-born children and grandchildren—aided by public transportation—began moving out of the Lower East Side uptown and to the Bronx and Brooklyn in search of better housing. This uptown and outer-borough movement was in full force by the time of the *General Slocum* disaster in 1904 and was nearly complete by World War I. By 1917, most German immigrants and German Americans lived in Yorkville, Harlem, and the Bronx, with few remaining in what was then known simply as the Lower East Side.

Although Italians and eastern European Jews had immigrated to the United States in large numbers in the early 1900s, Germans were still the second largest immigrant group in New York City before World War I, after Russian Jews. German New Yorkers were prosperous, well established in the city's business community, and proud of their community's many cultural and social institutions and traditions. Germans and German Americans vigorously defended Germany's actions in World War I, loudly lobbied for American neutrality, and firmly rejected the idea that Americanism was equal to being English speaking and taking the side of Great Britain in foreign policy.

Believing firmly in their constitutional right to lobby their government, Germans and German Americans were therefore shocked by the strength and fury of the anti-German movement during World War I. The experience of having their language and cultural traditions attacked as "un-American," being declared "alien enemies," and, in many cases, losing jobs and being forced to move because of wartime restrictions was traumatic for German New Yorkers, who had long believed that they were among the pioneers who had built New York City into the great city that it was.

After World War I, many German institutions continued to exist but had changed their names to English and more "American-sounding" ones and/or had adopted English as the language of business. Smaller organizations ceased to function as members drifted away, not willing to associate themselves with visibly German organizations. German bars, restaurants, and beer gardens, where many Vereine had met, were the most affected by this institutional decline and by Prohibition, which became federal law in 1919.

By 1930, German immigrants in New York City were divided into two groups: those who had immigrated before World War I and those who had immigrated after. For both groups, the war had been a traumatic experience, but the nature and depth of that trauma were radically different. Germans and German Americans in the United States had suffered the demonization of their ethnic group but had experienced little actual violence beyond the occasional street harassment. They were residents—and often citizens of—one of the victorious powers. German immigrants who had survived the war in Europe had experienced the military defeat and then occupation of their country, the dramatic change in their system of government from monarchical empire to democratic republic, and the near collapse of their economy, in addition to the horror of having lost an entire generation of young men (nearly 6 million dead and wounded). Between 1920 and 1929, 386,634 people emigrated from Germany to the United States to escape the political and economic turmoil of the Weimar Republic, many of them settling in New York City.

These two groups viewed the war in totally different ways based on their very different experiences. Germans who immigrated in the 1920s held more favorable views toward the prewar German Empire, were more skeptical of democracy, and, by the end of the decade, were more likely to support fascist groups (such as the German American Bund) and other authoritarian organizations (such as the Ku Klux Klan) than Germans who had immigrated before the war.[28]

The question of whether World War I "caused" Germans in the United States to rapidly assimilate cannot be answered, because what German American identity would have looked like in the 1920s without the war is unknown. But Germans in many different cities were apparently already assimilating according to such variables as residential integration, lifestyle practices, and speaking English.[29]

On the other hand, German immigrants and German Americans continued to prefer to marry people like themselves, and cities with large German populations, such as New York City, had low rates of intermarriage with non-Germans because of the large marriage pool.[30] Many German Americans, especially those active in German churches, also valued bilingualism more than other Americans and only reluctantly gave up speaking German.[31] In addition,

Germans' opposition to alcohol prohibition was not simply a question of the personal freedom to drink beer or wine but was the foundation of Germans' understanding of recreation and relaxation and was tightly bound up in rituals of socializing, or *Gemeinschaft und Gemütlichkeit* (community and coziness), that were very different from Anglo American attitudes about alcohol and leisure time.

American society continued to be dominated by native-born white Anglo Saxon Protestants for most of the twentieth century, and American culture still retains many powerful elements of the United States' English and British heritages: the dominance of the English language, English common law tradition, puritanical morality, individualism, litigiousness, proclivity toward conspiracy theorizing and witch-hunting, and so on.[32]

But it is clear is that the American society and culture that Germans assimilated into by the 1930s had itself been profoundly shaped by one hundred years of German immigration.[33] In the case of Germans, "assimilation" did not mean absorption into an unchanging, static American culture dominated by white English-speaking Anglo Saxon Protestants but rather was a process of creating a new society and culture through the interactions of English speakers and German speakers, with each ethnic group becoming more like one another and, in turn, changing the larger society's understanding of what it was to be an American.

German immigrants introduced new foods (lager beer, hot dogs, pretzels, etc.), new forms of recreation, new educational methods and systems (the kindergarten, the high school, the research university, physical and vocational education), holiday traditions (the Christmas tree, Santa Claus, gingerbread houses, nutcrackers, Advent calendars, the Easter Bunny and Easter egg hunts, etc.), and new forms of social and labor organization to the United States. The concept of "the weekend" as a time of leisure and personal free time versus church attendance and Bible reading was itself a product of the German-dominated labor movement and its campaign for an eight-hour workday, beginning in the 1880s.[34]

As Germans assimilated into American society, they changed that society through the force of their numbers and the attractiveness of their cultural practices.[35] But this was not always an easy or comfortable process, and there was often resistance on the part of the Anglo American majority to accept aspects of German culture, especially in the 1910s and 1920s.

The irony was that by helping to create a new American culture, Germans had fewer ways to distinguish themselves from non-Germans besides language, and each new generation had fewer fluent German speakers. The wartime demonization of the German language, in particular, and bilingualism, in general, further encouraged German Americans to drop the German language altogether. Meanwhile, Prohibition struck a death blow to the ritual of drinking beer or wine in a bar or beer garden with friends and family (at least until 1933).

When Prince Henry disembarked from the North German Lloyd liner, the SS *Kronprinz Wilhelm*, on February 22, 1902, and entered New York City, German New Yorkers were already largely assimilated in many significant ways. The appearance of a large, well-organized, and distinctly separate German community masked the fragile brittleness of Kleindeutschland, which was soon to be overwhelmed during the war. But in the decades between the Civil War and the prince's visit, New York's German community was large, diverse, dynamic, and concentrated in one clearly identifiable neighborhood: Kleindeutschland.

1

A Snapshot of
Kleindeutschland in 1880

••••••••••••••••••••••

A German immigrant traveling to New York City in 1880 would have sailed on a Hamburg-America or North German Lloyd steamship from either Hamburg or Bremen and arrived about ten days later. After being ferried from the companies' piers in Hoboken, New Jersey, to the Castle Garden Emigrant Landing Depot at the Battery, he would have been screened for disease and obvious disability and then admitted into the country.[1] From Castle Garden, he would have been able to take a (horse-drawn) streetcar to Kleindeutschland, a neighborhood well known in German-speaking Europe.[2]

This newcomer, or "greenhorn,"—one of 457,000 Germans who immigrated to the United States in 1880—would have found a large, well-organized community. More than 370,000 German immigrants and Americans of German descent lived in New York City, most of them in Kleindeutschland.[3]

Packed into four hundred blocks between the Bowery and the East River and 14th Street and Division and Grand Streets, more than 309,000 people lived on the Lower East Side of Manhattan Island. The neighborhood's population density of nearly 214,000 people per square mile was more than four times that of the density of the city as a whole.[4] The Bowery, the western border of the neighborhood, was the entertainment center, while Avenue B served as the main shopping street of the district. Tompkins Square Park—bounded on the north by East 10th Street, on the east by Avenue B, on the south by East 7th Street, and on the west by Avenue A—provided much needed open space for public meetings and relaxation.

Table 1.1
Origins of German Immigrants in New York City
(Manhattan), 1880

Total New York City population	1,206299
Total number of foreign born	478,670
Total number from the German Empire	163,482
From:	
Prussia	39,001
Bavaria	17,990
Baden	10,611
Württemberg	7,798
Hannover	7,282
Hesse	3,993
Saxony	3,954
Hamburg	1,589

SOURCE: Bureau of the Census, 1880, 538–540, table 16. 69,797
German immigrants did not state their state of origin or else simply
noted "Germany" as place of birth.

Upon arriving in Kleindeutschland, our newcomer would have needed to find a place to live. But this decision would have been determined in large part by which part of German-speaking Europe from which he had come.

Germans were more highly self-segregated than other European immigrant groups in New York City in the nineteenth century, and German New Yorkers strongly preferred to live with or near people from the same region in German-speaking Central Europe.[5] Thus, although the majority of Kleindeutschland residents were from the south and west (Bavaria, Hesse, Baden, and Württemberg), the Prussians in the neighborhood clustered in the Tenth Ward, which was 50 percent Prussian by 1880. Hessians, Hannoverians, and Badeners concentrated in the Thirteenth Ward, while Württembergers settled the Seventeenth Ward. Bavarians and other southern Germans, particularly Badeners and Württembergers, were found in large numbers in all of the wards, except for the Prussian Tenth.[6]

German-speaking Jews had their own subcommunity within Kleindeutschland in the Tenth Ward, especially on Grand, Stanton, Ludlow, and Pitt Streets, where about a dozen synagogues could be found.[7]

This clustering reflected long-standing prejudices, rivalries, and even outright hostilities between German states long independent but now mostly corralled together in the new German Empire, established in 1871. Just as northern Germans and southern Germans disdained one another socially in Germany, so did they residentially in Kleindeutschland.

FIG. 1.1 Trow Company, Map of New York City, 1880–1889. (New York Public Library.)

There were two factors at work in this self-segregation: the desire to live with or near people like oneself and the desire to live far from certain other groups. In the case of Germans in New York City, as important as it was to live near people from one's home state, it was equally—if not more—important to not live near Irish Catholics.[8] German Protestants shared English-speaking Protestants' distain for the religion of the Irish, while German Catholics resented the Irish's control of the American Catholic Church and their austere, unfamiliar traditions.[9] Germans of all faiths looked down on Irish immigrants for their poverty and perceived social dysfunction.

The size and steady flow of the German immigration (2.9 million during 1830–1880 and another 1.4 million in the 1880s) meant that German immigrants could be selective in deciding where and with whom to live, because there were nearly always enough people from a particular German state or region to form a residential cluster.

Although the nuclear family formed the basis of the German community, German immigrants were more likely to live in extended families (with adult siblings and their children living in the same building or next door to one another), and New York City's dense urban environment of multifamily apartment buildings encouraged this.[10] For instance, the piano manufacturer William Steinway's twenty-one-year old nephew Fred lived with Steinway and his family just outside of Kleindeutschland on East 20th Street in 1880.[11]

But regardless of where our newly arrived immigrant lived, he almost certainly would have lived in a multifamily apartment building, or tenement, like the one the Baden tailor Lucas Glockner built at 97 Orchard Street in 1863: a five-story brick building with four apartments per floor and shop space on the first floor and in the basement. Outdoor toilets were in the rear yard.[12]

Although about one-third of the residents of the neighborhood were not German, Kleindeutschland was still a largely self-contained community, with stores, clubs, bars, beer gardens, music halls, theaters, churches and synagogues, and schools that catered to German speakers. One measure of the self-sufficiency of a community is whether it can provide all of the social, cultural, economic, and spiritual needs of its members without their having to leave the community and/or rely on outside institutions. In Kleindeutschland, a German immigrant could buy German food and other household items at thousands of German grocery stores, delicatessens, butcher shops, and bakeries; drink German-style lager beer in more than five hundred *Lokals* (bars); drink beer and listen and dance to German music at eight hundred beer gardens; see a classical German play or new vaudeville skit at three theaters; read more than twenty German-language newspapers and magazines; buy German-language books at Westermann and Company or Ernst Steiger's or borrow them from the Astor Library; participate in thousands of clubs, fraternal orders, and labor unions; exercise and play sports at two gymnasiums; bank at the Germania

Bank, Sender Jarmulowsky's bank, the German Savings Bank, the German American Bank, or the German Exchange Bank; receive unemployment, injury, or funeral assistance from thousands of mutual benefit societies; and on Sunday, choose from thirty-three churches and synagogues that conducted services in German. Only the public schools in the neighborhood were controlled by outsiders, and even here, some New York City public schools offered instruction in German. Parents could also choose from eleven private German-language schools for their children.

Reinforcing German New Yorkers' distinctiveness from English-speaking Americans and other immigrants was their high degree of social organization. A very important cultural practice—and one still maintained in Germany today—is the organizing of social clubs, or Verein. Besides language, Vereine were the foundation of Kleindeutschland as an immigrant community. German immigrants organized Vereine based on German state of origin, class, occupation, religion, and time of immigration, resulting in the duplication of many associations.[13] But the basic purpose of all Vereine was the same: to meet regularly to engage in an organized group activity.

There were several different types of Vereine that can be classified by both purpose and function. First, there were Vereine that reflected aspects of German culture that immigrants brought with them. These included music Vereine, particularly choirs but also bands and orchestras; *Schützenvereine* (shooting clubs); and *Turnvereine* (gymnastics clubs).

The second type of Vereine were those that immigrants developed to meet their needs as foreigners living in a new country. These included *Unterstützungsvereine* (mutual benefit societies), *Landsmannschaften* (homeland societies), and *Gewerkschaften* (labor unions).

By 1880, New York City's German community contained a large working class, a small but growing middle class, and an emerging upper class all within the same geographic space. Of the few Vereine to have elite pretensions, only the Deutsche Gesellschaft (German Society, a charitable organization founded in 1784 that provided social services to newly arrived immigrants) and the Gesellschaft Harmonie (Harmony Society, an exclusive Jewish men's club that charged one hundred dollars as membership dues) were located outside of the neighborhood: the Deutsche Gesellschaft downtown, at 13 Broadway, close to the Castle Garden immigrant station, and Gesellschaft Harmonie at 45 West 42nd Street.[14] Most other Vereine were located where most Germans lived, in Kleindeutschland.

The *Gesangvereine* (singing societies) were among the most important and long-lasting German societies. Fulfilling the cultural stereotype of musical Germans, German immigrants founded nearly sixty-five musical societies in New York City by 1870, most of them based on the Lower East Side and most dedicated to singing.[15] These choirs sang a mix of traditional German folk songs and opera and gave regular performances, as well as benefit concerts to raise money for various charities and in response to disasters, such as fires and epidemics. For example, in April 1880, the Liederkranz singing society performed Hector Berlioz's *The Damnation of Faust* as a benefit for St. Francis Hospital.[16]

The Liederkranz, Arion, and Beethoven Männerchor were the largest men's choruses in New York City and reflected how seriously German immigrants and German Americans took music as an expression of their culture.

Founded by twenty-five men in 1847, the Liederkranz had more than fifteen hundred members in 1880, with most members being upwardly mobile businessmen and politicians who paid thirty dollars for the privilege of networking at concerts organized by the piano manufacturer William Steinway, who also regularly sang with the choir. (Members who sang in the choir paid only twelve dollars per year.)[17] Not just a group of men who liked to get together to sing, the Liederkranz's *Männerchor* (men's choir) had its own clubhouse at 25 East 4th Street and a professional conductor, Agriol Paur. Besides conducting the men, Paur managed a singing school for ladies and conducted the *Damenchor* (women's choir) and an orchestra.[18]

The Liederkranz's close connection with Steinway (who frequently served as president of the Verein) meant that the Liederkranz's choruses often performed at Steinway Hall at 109 East 14th Street, which the Steinway Piano Company had opened in 1866 as a combination showroom and recital hall.[19]

Arion (which had split from the Liederkranz in 1854) had more than one thousand members who met at the society's clubhouse at 21 St. Mark's Place.[20] The Beethoven Männerchor remained more "exclusive" with only five hundred members and had its clubhouse at 210 East 5th Street.[21]

While upwardly mobile men sought to join the Liederkranz, Arion, or Beethoven Männerchor, working-class men organized their own choruses. There were enough German labor union choirs to form the Arbeiter-Sängerbund (Workers' Singing Association) in the 1880s, and the New York City area was home to more than forty anarchist singing societies in the late nineteenth century, as well as the Arbeitersgesangverein Vorwärts (Workers' Singing Society Forward), the Sozialistisches Liedertafel New York (Socialist Singing Society of New York), and the Karl Marx Singing Society. Anarchists enjoyed music as much as capitalists, and the Gesangverein Lassallea-Ottensen (Lassallea-Ottensen Singing Society) and Herwegh-Männerchor (Herwegh's Men's Choir), both anarchist choirs, each had more than two hundred members. For those who could not sing but still enjoyed music, the Fritz Sundersdorf Orchestra regularly performed at German anarchist festivals in the 1880s.[22]

German music and German-born and trained musicians dominated New York City's music scene, and one-third of the city's 3,151 professional musicians and music teachers in 1880 were German immigrants.[23] A very German part of the city's labor movement were the musicians' Vereine and Gewerkschaften.

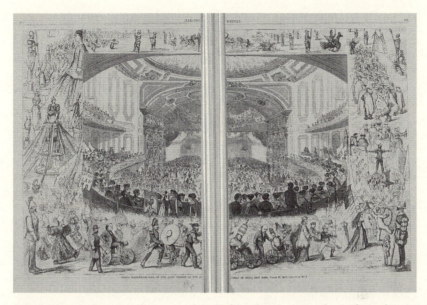

FIG. 1.2 Thomas Nast, *Grand Masquerade Ball of the Arion Society at the Academy of Music, New York, March 27, 1867, Harper's Weekly,* 11, no. 537 (April 13, 1867): 232–233. (Library of Congress.)

The most important of these was the Aschenbroedel Verein (Cinderella Club), a German American professional orchestral musicians' social and benevolent association with three hundred members and a clubhouse on East 4th Street. Among its many members were the conductors Carl Bergmann, Theodore Thomas, and Walter Damrosch, as well as all of the members of the Theodore Thomas Orchestra and most of the members of the New York Philharmonic Orchestra.[24] At least half of the members of another musicians union, the Musical Mutual Protective Union (MMPU), were German.[25] Band leaders and musicians, such as George Maurer and August Schneider, made a decent living (ten to fifteen dollars per week) playing concerts and accompanying theatrical performances and Verein balls.[26]

Another important German cultural import to the United States was the Turnverein (gymnastics club). Founded in 1811 in Berlin as part of the city's resistance against Napoleon's invasion of Prussia, the Turners combined exercise and radical politics, and used gymnastics as part of their paramilitary training.[27] The Turners introduced physical exercise as recreation to the United States and built two *Turnhalle* (gymnasiums) in the neighborhood, the first at 27–33 Orchard Street and the second at 66–68 East 4th Street. The new Turnhalle featured a restaurant on the first floor; bowling alleys in the basement; meeting rooms, classrooms, dancing, fencing, and locker rooms on the second floor; a ballroom and stage on the third floor; and the gymnasium, finally, on the fourth floor.[28] The Turners even had a school that educated more than six hundred students in the late 1870s.[29] The Turnhalle's multifunctional space was a central meeting place for a variety of Vereine in Kleindeutschland and hosted many different types of social gatherings.

But 1880 began tragically for New York's Turnverein, when a fire broke out at the new Turnhalle early on the morning of January 5, after the hall had hosted a Jewish wedding and a Verein meeting. Seven people were killed, and five others, seriously injured. The Hebrew Orphan Asylum (located in the rear of the Turnhalle) and Primary School No. 6 (at 15–17 Third Street) were also threatened by the flames. The victims were the manager, William Winckel; several of his extended family; servants; and waiters who lived in the building. An estimated ten thousand people lined 5th Street the next day for a funeral for several of the victims, with music being provided by the Aschenbroedel, the Turner Liedertafel singing society, and the Gesangverein Schillerbund. So many people wished to attend Winckel's funeral at the Arion Society on January 14 that tickets were given out to control the crowd. Hundreds of members of the Vereine that met at the Turnhalle escorted Winckel's coffin to Woodlawn Cemetery in the Bronx.[30]

Schützenvereine, which had been very popular in the 1850s and 1860s, were becoming less so after the Civil War. But clubs such as the Deutsche Amerikanische Schützen Gesellschaft (German American Shooting Club), the Germania Schützen Bund (Germania Shooting Federation), and the Independent Schützen Corps were still sites of socializing and recreation for many German men. This was the case especially because rifle ranges were increasingly located outside the city, in Ridgewood, Queens, and in North Bergen, New Jersey, thus giving men and their families an excuse to get out of the urban jungle.[31]

The Unterstützungsvereine (mutual benefit societies) were less visible than some of the other Vereine but were no less important to the average German immigrant. These social welfare organizations were developed by and for mostly working-class immigrants living in a foreign country that provided little to no social safety net in case of illness, accident, or sudden death. For a small monthly payment (between twelve and twenty-five cents) members received small sums if they became sick or disabled, and the Vereine contributed funds for a funeral if a member died. From these Vereine came the principles and practices of the American insurance industry.

Most Unterstützungsvereine were organized around particular occupations or trades and provided similar functions as trade unions in the 1850s. But in the 1860s, more and more Unterstützungsvereine were organized on the basis of home origin, as immigrants found it easier to trust funds to a fellow immigrant from the same region versus a stranger holding the same job.[32] The Teutonia Benefit Society, based at 295 Bowery, was one of many such Unterstützungsvereine in 1880.[33]

Landsmannschaften, which grouped people according to German place of origin, were among the first Vereine Germans organized after immigrating because they built on the existing networks of friends and friendly acquaintances that immigrants used to emigrate and then find housing and jobs. These homeland societies performed a similar social welfare function as Unterstützungvereine (providing members support in times of illness, injury, and death), but they also organized regular meetings, dances, and picnics to celebrate the history and culture of the regions of Germany from which people had emigrated.[34] Landsmannschaften combined to sponsor annual *Volksfeste* (celebrating the culture of a particular German state or region), *Maifeste* (May Day celebrations), *Turnfeste* (gymnastic competitions), and *Sängerfeste* (singing contests) attended by thousands of people at picnic grounds in Hoboken, New Jersey; Jones's Wood in upper Manhattan; and at concert halls, theaters, and rented halls around the Lower East Side.

The Plattdeutschen Volksfest—first held in 1875 to celebrate the culture of northwestern Germany—attracted 150,000 people to Schützen Park in North Bergen, after a huge parade in which the participants marched across the city from Kleindeutschland to the Hudson River ferry on the west side of the island. Once in New Jersey, the festivalgoers ate, drank, danced, and listened to music and speeches celebrating their region's traditions.[35] The Bremer Verein, which was organized by people from the port city of Bremen, recreated that city's Freimarkt festival, which has been held in October since 1035, in the new homeland.[36]

To raise money to put on these large festivals, the homeland societies sold tickets and souvenir programs that featured not only the description of the planned event but also dozens of advertisements from local businesses announcing their support and giving best wishes to the Verein for a successful event.[37]

German immigrants also brought with them their trade unions, or Gewerkschaften. German Gewerkschaften had a great deal of influence on the American labor movement, particularly in the development of trade or craft unions and their focus on organization, collective bargaining, and acceptance of industrial capitalism, in part because German immigrants made up a large minority of skilled workers in the United States. The first president of the American Federation of Labor (AFL), Samuel Gompers, grew up in Kleindeutschland in the 1860s and was influenced at an early age by the organization of German Gewerkschaften and Vereine. Gompers later applied many of these organizational principles and values to the organization and structure of the AFL.[38]

Another type of Verein that was hugely popular in Kleindeutschland were fraternal orders, or "secret societies." (These societies were called "secret," even though their locations and leadership were listed in city directories, because their rituals were secret.) The mid-nineteenth century was the period in which secret societies flourished in the United States, and many Germans organized German-language fraternal orders, such as Hermanns Söhne (Sons of Hermann), Vereinigte Deutscher Brüder (United German Brothers), the Freiheitssöhne (Freedom's Sons), and the Order of Haru Gari, as well as German-speaking lodges of the Masons and many other fraternal orders. The first German Masonic lodge in New York was established in 1819, as an extension of the Grand Lodge in Prussia. By 1871, there were eighteen German Masonic lodges in New York, and nearly all of these German fraternal orders had their lodges in Kleindeutschland.[39] As with their English-speaking counterparts, German fraternal orders were places where men socialized, networked, and raised money for charity. Although secret societies were for men, most fraternal orders had women's auxiliaries, and many German women were active in these parallel groups.

Although most Vereine were secular, there were also religious Vereine attached to the three main faiths: Catholicism, Judaism, and Protestantism. Catholics made up the majority of German immigrants in the city, and German Catholic priests and devout laymen tried to create a parallel German Catholic community within Kleindeutschland to provide alternatives to Protestantism, socialism, and radical atheism.[40] German Catholics organized themselves into several lay religious societies, such as the Cazilien Verein, the Archconfraternity of the Holy Family, the Archconfraternity of the Immaculate Heart of Mary, and the Archconfraternity of the Holy Rosary.[41] Herman Ridder—the publisher of the *Katholisches Volksblatt* and later the influential *New Yorker Staats-Zeitung* newspaper—was very active in the Society of St. Alphonsus Church.[42]

Most German Jews were unaffiliated with synagogues and organized themselves into secular fraternal organizations, such as B'nai B'rith (founded in New York City in 1843) or the Free Sons of Israel (organized in 1849).[43] In 1876, the Society for Ethical Culture was founded by Temple Emanu-El's head rabbi Samuel Adler's son, Felix Adler, with the motto "Deed, not Creed," and this society attracted many secular German Jews. German Jews also founded the Hebrew Relief Society at 46 Exchange Place and the Hebrew Sheltering Guardian Society at First Avenue and East 57th Street.[44]

Although Jewish Germans often had their own Vereine, they were part of the German community. Of the city's twelve rabbis serving German Jewish congregations, nine preached exclusively in German, and all had been trained in Germany. Some Jewish newspapers, such as the *Israelitische Press* and *Jüdische Volkszeitung* (Jewish People's Newspaper), also published in German (versus Yiddish).[45]

By 1880, class divisions in Kleindeutschland's Vereine were clearly apparent, as more successful immigrants and German Americans made their Vereine more exclusive through charging higher initiation and membership dues, requiring sponsorship for membership, and building clubhouses, which often had caretakers and other permanent staff. Yet these increasingly elite Vereine remained flexible enough to include both immigrants and second- and third-generation German Americans, meeting the social and emotional needs of both groups.

The construction of Verein clubhouses could be seen all over Kleindeutschland in the late nineteenth century and provided work for many German carpenters, masons, and other construction workers. They were also an important source of revenue and pride for German-born architects, such as August H. Blankenstein, Weber & Drosser, William C. Frohne, Marc Eidlitz, De Lemos & Cordes, and Maynicke & Franke, who often used architectural features that were popular in Germany at the time.[46]

Smaller, more middle- or working-class Vereine that could not afford real estate continued to take advantage of the many halls and assembly rooms that could be rented out for meetings and events. Besides the Turnhalle, smaller Vereine regularly used the Germania Assembly Rooms at 42 Avenue A, owned by George Sauer; Concordia Hall, at 20–30 Avenue A, owned by the Hungarian immigrant Hugo Kladivko; Harmonia Hall at 139–145 Essex Street, owned by Lawrence Lang; and Walhalla Hall at 52–54 Orchard Street.

Although many Vereine organized themselves according to fraternal structures and followed fraternal procedures—such as having charters or constitutions, using meeting guides (such as Robert's Rules of Order), and keeping minutes—Vereine were not simply German versions of American fraternal orders. Music, theater, and athletic Vereine were transplants from Germany, and craft-based mutual aid societies were modeled on older European guild traditions and practices. Only the Landsmannschaften emerged out of and in reaction to the American context. After all, people in Hamburg, for instance, did not need to create a homeland society, but immigrants from Hamburg—seeking to find and support one another among all of the Bavarians and Badeners in Kleindeutschland—did.

There were thousands of Vereine in New York, and it was common for a person, especially a man, to be a member of several: a Landsmannschaften to remember and celebrate the homeland, an Unterstützungsverein for financial assistance in case of emergency, a Gewerkschaft for work, a fraternal order or two for networking and socializing, and a music or sports Verein for recreation.

Among successful German immigrants, a large Verein membership was socially and professionally de rigueur. If a man was not particularly involved in clubs, this obvious failure of Germanness was attributed to the person being particularly devoted to family life. In the case of the furniture and chandelier manufacturer Henry Iden, an immigrant from Duvenstedt near Hamburg, it was explained that "he was not a club man, his leisure moments being spent quietly at home with his family." Another common explanation for a lack of Verein membership was made about the advertising pioneer Albert Frank, who was from Breslau, Silesia: "He did not belong to many clubs, but to a large number of charitable organizations."[47]

This rich type of associational life was not limited to just German immigrants, but the large number and wide variety of organizations was one thing that made New York City's German community distinctive. Since most mid-nineteenth-century Jewish immigrants came from German-speaking regions, Jewish Vereine closely resembled German Vereine.[48] Irish immigrants, the other large immigrant group in New York City, did not create the same number or type of social clubs as Germans. Since the Roman Catholic Church opposed Freemasonry, Irish Catholics created their own fraternal orders, while politically oriented Irish immigrants established organizations devoted to supporting Irish independence from Great Britain. But poorer Irish immigrants did not develop a similar club tradition as Germans.[49] Fraternal orders were very popular among native-born Americans of all backgrounds, but English-speaking Americans also did not create the variety of clubs that Germans did.[50]

Another aspect of life in Kleindeutschland—and one that was often remarked upon by non-Germans—was the location of all of this socializing: the bar or saloon. Socializing with alcohol in Lokals and beer gardens was central to Verein life in Kleindeutschland. The concept of *Gemeinschaft und Gemütlichkeit* (community and coziness) were important German cultural attributes that transcended regional, religious, and class divisions in both Germany and in New York City. Since all New Yorkers, both German and non-German, worked a six-day work week, German immigrants attended their Vereine meetings in the evenings and on Sundays, usually in bars, and the accompanying alcohol consumption—particularly in the presence of (and with the participation of) women and children—was shocking to Anglo Americans (not to mention, illegal in New York State and New York City). Attitudes toward alcohol—and how, when, and with whom one drank—were the biggest cultural differences between Germans and Americans of British heritage.[51]

Despite the Puritanism of many Anglo Americans, New York City was a drinker's paradise. The city had more than 7,000 saloon keepers and bartenders in 1880, 3,235 of them German born.[52] The temperance advocate Robert Graham documented 9,075 places that sold liquor in New York City in 1883, including 4,819 hotels, 3,722 bars that only sold beer and ale, and 534 grocers and druggists licensed to sell alcohol. Graham estimated that another 1,000 establishments illegally sold alcohol without the required license. He claimed that there was a saloon for every 125 persons in New York City.[53]

But the geographic distribution of these more than 10,000 bars was uneven, and Kleindeutschland had a larger percentage than many other neighborhoods.

A sixty-three-block section of the Lower East Side between the Bowery and Norfolk Street and East Houston to Division Streets (the Tenth Ward) had 423 lager-beer saloons and another 137 establishments selling undefined liquor in the early 1880s.[54]

John Schneider's saloon at 97 Orchard Street—which opened in November 1864 and was a fixture on Orchard Street until 1886—was a typical German Lokal. Schneider had emigrated from Bavaria in 1842 at the age of twelve and had grown up in Kleindeutschland. Schneider's wife, Caroline Dietman, had emigrated from Prussia in 1849, when she was fourteen; their marriage was unusual, in that Bavarians and Prussians did not normally mix, much less marry one another. On November 12, 1864, the Schneiders announced in the largest German-language newspaper, the *New Yorker Staats-Zeitung*, that they had bought Schurlein's saloon at 97 Orchard Street and would be open that day for business, offering a lunch of pretzels, sausages, pigs' feet, and sauerkraut, all cooked by Mrs. Schneider. For the next twenty years, Caroline Schneider would daily cook a mountain of traditional foods that would be made available to customers, who could enjoy a free lunch with the purchase of a drink.[55]

For those who did not want to patronize Schneider's, there were three other bars on that block of Orchard Street alone in the early 1880s: John Kneher's saloon at 98 Orchard Street, Gustav Reichenbach's saloon at 94 Orchard Street, and Dederick Speh's place at 111 Orchard Street.[56]

For those who did not want to drink in a bar, there was the beer garden. New York City had more than eight hundred beer gardens in the nineteenth century, and the Bowery was home to some of the largest establishments: the Atlantic Garden (at 50 Bowery and at one time the largest restaurant in the country, with seating for fourteen hundred); the Deutscher Volksgarten (at 199 Bowery); the National Garden (at 104 Bowery); and the Pacific Garden (at 54 Bowery). These and many others in the neighborhood served German-style lager beer and German food, accompanied by live music.[57]

Unlike the traditional Anglo American bar—which was exclusively for men and only tolerated women as prostitutes—the beer garden was recognized by German immigrants to be a family-friendly environment, and a visit to the beer garden in the afternoon or evening was a common way German families spent their Sundays. As the Unitarian minister and writer Matthew Hale Smith reported:

> The Germans visit these gardens to spend the day. They are eminently social. They come, husband and wife, with all the children, brothers and sisters, cousins and neighbors; nor are the old folks omitted. The family bring with them a basket of provisions, as if they were on a picnic. Comfortable rooms are provided for their entertainment. They gather as a family around a table. They exchange social greetings, and enjoy to their bent the customs of their

FIG. 1.3 *A German Beer Garden in New York City on Sunday Evening*, 1859. (New York Public Library.)

fatherland. They play dominoes, cards, dice; they sing, they shout, they dance; in some places billiards and bowling are added, with rifle shooting. The room and entertainment are free to all. A welcome is extended to every comer.[58]

The phrase "garden" conjures up images of outdoor space, but most beer gardens were indoors, although some had outdoor space (with covered patios in case of rain). Sulzer's Harlem River Park and Jones's Wood were legitimate outdoor venues and very popular with German New Yorkers, but these open spaces were also a considerable distance from Kleindeutschland.[59]

The Virginia-born writer James Dabney McCabe visited the Atlantic Garden in 1872 and observed:

The true beer-garden finds its highest development in the monster Atlantic Garden, which is located in the Bowery, next door to the Old Bowery Theatre. It is an immense room, with a lofty curved ceiling, handsomely frescoed, and lighted by numerous chandeliers and by brackets along the walls. It is lighted during the day from the roof. At one side is an open space planted with trees and flowers, the only mark of a garden visible. A large gallery rises above the floor at each end. That at the eastern or upper end is used as a restaurant for those who desire regular meals. The lower gallery is, like the rest of the place, for beer-drinkers only. Under the latter gallery is a shooting hall, which is usually filled with marksmen trying their skill. On the right hand side of the room is a huge orchestrion or monster music-box, and by its side is a raised platform, occupied by the orchestra employed at the place. The floor is sanded, and is lined with plain tables, six feet by two in size, to each of which is a couple of benches. The only ornaments of the immense hall are the frescoes and the chandeliers. Everything else is plain and substantial. Between the hall and the Bowery is the bar room, with its lunch counters. The fare provided at the latter is strictly German, but the former retails drinks of every description.

During the day the Atlantic does a good business through its bar and restaurant, many persons taking their meals here regularly. As night comes on, the great hall begins to fill up, and by eight o'clock the place is in its glory. From three to four thousand people, mainly Germans, may be seen here at one time, eating, drinking, smoking. Strong liquors are not sold, the drinks being beer and the lighter Rhine-wines. The German capacity for holding beer is immense. An amount sufficient to burst an American makes him only comfortable and good humored. The consumption of the article here nightly is tremendous, but there is no drunkenness. The audience is well behaved, and the noise is simply the hearty merriment of a large crowd. There is no disorder, no indecency. The place is thoroughly respectable, and the audience are interested in keeping it so. They come here with their families, spend a social, pleasant evening, meet their friends, hear the news, enjoy the music and the beer, and go home refreshed and happy. The Germans are very proud of this resort, and they would not tolerate the introduction of any feature that would make it an unfit place for their wives and daughters. It is a decided advantage to the people who frequent this place, whatever the Temperance advocates may say, that men have here a resort where they can enjoy themselves with their families, instead of seeking their pleasure away from the society of their wives and children.

The buzz and the hum of the conversation, and the laughter, are overpowering, and you wander through the vast crowd with your ears deafened by the sound. Suddenly the leader of the orchestra raps sharply on his desk, and there is a profound silence all over the hall. In an instant the orchestra breaks forth into some wonderful German melody, or some deep-voiced, strong-lunged singer sends his rich notes rolling through the hall. The auditors have suddenly lost their merriment, and are now listening pensively to the music, which is good. They sip their beer absently, and are thinking no doubt of the far-off Fatherland, for you see their features grow softer and their eyes glisten. Then, when it is all over, they burst into an enthusiastic encore, or resume their suspended conversations.[60]

In 1880, the audience would have been listening to the Damen Elite Kapelle or the Vienna Elite Lady Orchestra, a well-respected ensemble of a dozen female musicians who performed at the beer garden for decades from the 1870s to the 1890s.[61]

For people who wanted to get "out of the city," or who were already living uptown in Yorkville, the outdoor beer garden at the Terrace Garden Theater at East 58th Street between Third and Lexington Avenues quickly became popular after it opened in 1866, and the opening of the Third Avenue elevated train line in 1878 made this beer garden even more accessible. The Terrace Garden was part of a larger theater complex sometimes known as the Lexington Opera House that offered theatrical performances, dancing indoors in the ballroom or outside in the garden, bowling, and restaurant dining. The beer garden and theater were connected on the ground floor, and theater patrons could easily visit the beer garden during intermissions for a quick drink. The Terrace Garden was also a popular place for Verein meetings.[62]

The concept of the beer garden became so popular among non-German New Yorkers that the Liederkranz conductor Theodore Thomas performed with his orchestra regularly at the Central Park Garden at Seventh Avenue between West 58th and West 59th Streets, just south of Central Park.[63] Unlike most beer gardens, where admission was free—with the expectation that visitors would buy food and drink—here visitors were charged fifty cents admission, which, in turn, attracted a higher class of patron who could afford the price of a couple of steak dinners just for admission.

Besides Vereine, Lokals, and beer gardens, German New Yorkers also had their own German-language theaters, newspapers, schools, and churches and synagogues that allowed immigrants to maintain their language and culture and perpetuate it among their children and grandchildren.[64] The large size of the German immigrant community and the continuous immigration from German-speaking countries and regions for most of the nineteenth century made the development and sustenance of these many cultural institutions possible.

Among New York's many theaters were several devoted to German-language theater: the Thalia Theater, which opened in 1879 at 46 Bowery; the Stadt Theater also on the Bowery; and the Germania Theater, which was based at Tammany Hall in the 1870s.[65] Operating in a competitive business, these theaters offered a mix of traditional German classical theater, especially Goethe and Schiller, and more contemporary comedies, melodramas, and musicals.

The Thalia Theater was located next door to the Atlantic Garden and was owned by William Kramer (born Wilhelm Kraemer in Prussia), who cut an opening in a wall on the second floor of the theater to connect the galleries and the beer garden to allow theatergoers to have a drink during intermissions.[66]

The Stadt Theater was, according to James Dabney McCabe, "exclusively a German establishment."[67] It was originally located at 37–39 Bowery and was the first German theater in New York, opening in 1854. A new building was built in 1864 at 43–47 Bowery that could house 3,500 people and also included a hotel. Performances at the Stadt Theater included German-language productions of Shakespeare's *Othello*, *The Merchant of Venice*, and *Richard III*, as well as Goethe's *Faust*. The Stadt Theater's manager, Otto von Hoym, also presented opera, and Richard Wagner's *Lohengrin* was performed for the first time in the United States at the Stadt Theater in 1871.[68]

German-immigrant and German American entrepreneurs also were an active part of New York City's growing entertainment/recreation areas outside of the city. Brighton Beach, Brooklyn—in particular, Coney Island—was the site of several hotels, restaurants, and beer gardens built by German immigrants, including the Coney Island hotdog vendor Charles Feltman's Garden (also called Feltman's Ocean Pavilion), Paul Bauer's Brighton Beach Hotel, and the Kaisergarten, a replica of a beer garden/entertainment complex in Munich. These hotels, restaurants, beer gardens, and other forms of entertainment attracted large numbers of German Americans (and other New Yorkers of various ethnic backgrounds).[69]

Beer gardens and theaters were the sites of major cultural clashes between Germans and English-speaking Anglo American Protestants in the 1870s and 1880s. Although state laws against the sale of alcohol were rarely enforced by New York City police, there were occasional crackdowns, as police responded to pressure from Anglo American Protestant religious reformers, who strongly objected to Germans' and others' violation of Sabbath laws.[70] Atlantic Garden owner William Kramer got around the city's laws against alcohol sales on Sundays by selling lower alcohol content *Weissbier*, along with Wiener schnitzel, pigs' knuckles, and sirloin steak.[71]

But beer garden operators—such as Paul Falk, the owner of the Volksgarten and then the Tivoli Garden, and the brewer John Eidlong of the Pacific Garden—were often arrested and fined for violating the city's excise laws against selling alcohol on Sundays. The fines, which could be $250 or higher, were an important source of revenue for the city, and corrupt police officers supplemented their meager pay with bribes from saloon keepers and beer garden owners to stay open on Sundays.[72]

Another New York City ordinance prohibited "the performance of any tragedy, comedy, opera, ballet, farce, negro minstrelsy, negro or other dancing, wrestling, boxing with or without gloves, sparring contests, trial of strength, or any part of parts therein, or any circus, equestrian or dramatic performance or exercise, or any performance or exercise of jugglers, acrobats, club performances or rope dancers on the first day of the week [Sunday]."[73] Theater owners found evading this law very challenging, but beer garden operators (who were sometimes also theater owners, as in the case of Kramer) attempted to get around the Sunday performance ban by offering "sacred concerts" on Sundays. Since the Episcopal, Roman Catholic, and Lutheran Churches allowed instrumental music (e.g., organ) to be performed in their religious services, the city could not ban all music performances on Sundays, and the beer garden owners' claims that their Sunday musical offerings were spiritual in nature infuriated Sabbatarians. Gustav Lindenmüller, the owner of the Odeon Theater and beer saloon at 49 Bowery, pushed the envelope even further by calling his saloon "Lindenmüller's Shaker Church."[74]

Less controversial than the theaters and beer gardens but no less important to the maintenance of German immigrants' culture and sense of community were the many German-language newspapers. An extensive foreign-language media industry existed in New York City in the nineteenth century, with German dominating as the main foreign language appearing in print. New York had approximately twenty German-language newspapers being published either daily or weekly in the 1870s, and several of the larger daily papers also printed separate weekly editions with circulations in the tens of thousands. The most prominent and long-lasting of these publications were the conservative Democratic paper, the *New Yorker Staats-Zeitung*, edited by Oswald Ottendorfer in the 1860s–1900 and still publishing today; the socialist *New Yorker Volkszeitung*, established in 1878 by the educators Adolph Douai and Alexander Jonas; and the social-democratic paper the *New Yorker Abend-Zeitung*, edited by Friedrich Kapp. These papers covered issues and events in the community that the English-language press was either unaware of or did not consider important enough to be citywide news, albeit from the different political perspectives of their editors and publishers. They also reprinted articles from German-language European-based newspapers and either reprinted or covered news from other German communities in the United States.

Smaller publications, often devoted to various political causes, included the *Volks-Tribun*, a paper devoted to advocating for land reform and socialism; *the Soziale Republik*, edited by Gustav Struve and supported by the Workers' League; the labor paper, *Der Hahnruf*; and the early Marxist papers, Gottfried Kellern's *Reform* and Joseph Weydemeyer's *Die Revolution*. F. Schedler's *New York Demokrat* attempted to compete with Ottendorfer's *New Yorker Staats-Zeitung und Sonntagsblat* (Sunday page).

German New Yorkers also read Rudolph Lexow's *New Yorker Criminal Zeitung und Belletristisches Journal*, which combined crime coverage and literature; the *Literarischer Monatsbericht*, a monthly literary magazine; a German edition of *Leslie's Illustrated Weekly*; the *Deutsche Illustrierte Familien Blätten* (German illustrated family pages); the *Gartenlaube* ("Garden Arbor," an illustrated magazine), and *Puck*, the first successful humor magazine, published by the Austrian immigrant and illustrator Joseph Keppler and German immigrant Adolph Schwarzmann.[75] Keppler, Thomas Nast, and Friedrich Graez were among a growing number of German-born artists and cartoonists who influenced American political opinion through their illustrations.[76]

There were also a wide variety of publications targeting niche markets. Franz Sigel's *Revue* marketed itself to German military companies, Turnvereine, Schützenvereine, and Gesangvereine. The *Deutsch-Amerikanische Wein Zeitung* (German American wine newspaper), founded in 1871, appealed to oenophiles.[77] Other specialty publications included the *Farmer-Zeitung*, the *Lutheranische Herold*, the *Handels Zeitung* (trade newspaper), and the *Musik Zeitung*. The *Nachrichten aus Deutschland und der Schweiz* (News from Germany and Switzerland) provided what its name advertised. People interested in fashion could read the *Die Mödenwelt* (Fashion world).[78]

For more serious readers, the two main German-language bookstores were the New York branch of the Braunschweig firm Westermann and Company, which had opened in 1848 and was at 838 Broadway, and Ernst Steiger's store, located at 25 Park Place.[79] Steiger's advertised itself as "the largest German book concern in America" and sold school texts, periodicals, and contemporary books from Germany and other European countries, imported two or three times per week. Steiger's also had a circulating library for those who could not afford to buy new books.[80]

Another source of German (and other foreign language) books was the Astor Library at 425 Lafayette Street. This reference and research library opened to the public in 1854 and had a collection of 80,000–90,000 books paid for by the German immigrant John Jacob Astor, then the richest man in the United States. The German-born architect Alexander Saeltzer designed the building in the *Rundbogen* style, which was the prevailing style for public buildings in Germany in the mid-nineteenth century.[81]

German bookstores and library books were useful in preserving language, but the most effective way of maintaining German language skills was education. To ensure that their children were educated in the German language and according to German educational methods, German immigrants established several private schools. August Gläser's Deutsche Bildungsschule für Knaben und Mädchen (German School for Boys and Girls) had been at 141 Chrystie Street since 1846; the Deutsche Bürgerschule (German Citizens' School), directed by E. Feldner, was at 191 William Street, while Rudolf Dulon's German-American School was at 11–13 Mark Street. The famed early childhood educator Adolph Douai had two private German schools, one for boys and the other for girls. There was also the Freie deutsche Schule (Free German School) at Otto von Hoym's Stadt Theater on the Bowery; the Deutschamerikanische Akademie (German American Academy) at 649 Third Avenue; the Freie deutsche Volkschule (Free German People's School) on Fourth Street, managed by Franz

Straubenmüller; A. Harr's German School at 421 East 9th Street; the German-American Institute, headed by Peter Stahl, at 244 East 52nd Street; and the Turners' school.[82]

But private schools could be expensive, especially for working-class parents, and so increasingly German immigrants began demanding German-language instruction in the public schools. They were somewhat successful in these efforts. In 1870, the New York City school system began offering German as part of the regular elementary curriculum, and in 1873, nearly 20,000 students were enrolled in the city's 464 German classes, most of these in Kleindeutschland.[83]

However, the goal of city school officials was not to have bilingual education, per se, but to attract German students away from private and parochial schools into public schools, where they could be assimilated into an English-speaking, Protestant culture. Thus, German-language instruction was not to be the foundation of public education in New York City schools but rather a means to transition immigrant children to English.[84] In fact, as German public school attendance increased, German-language offerings were pushed back into the higher levels of grammar school beginning in 1875.

German parents thus found themselves on the losing sides of both democracy and New York City power dynamics. Although Germans were a large minority in the city, they were still a minority, and an even smaller voting bloc, because many immigrant men were not citizens and women could not vote. In addition, the New York City School Board's Commissioners of Common Schools were primarily English Americans, while many of the teachers and principals were Irish American. New York City had only 367 German-born teachers in 1880 (7 percent of the total number of teachers), and most of them taught in the German private schools.[85]

Even in Kleindeutschland, German parents struggled to get German-language instruction into their neighborhood schools. Of the twenty-seven public schools in the Tenth, Eleventh, Thirteenth, and Seventeenth Wards, nearly all had English American or Irish American principals and vice principals.[86] Thus, Germans' inability to control the New York City school system, as they did in smaller communities (such as Hoboken, New Jersey), meant that German would always be a foreign language, not the primary language in New York City schools, even in schools where German students predominated.[87]

Parochial schools that offered or taught in German were an option for German parents who wanted their children to at least be bilingual, and an estimated 11,000 children attended German Catholic and Lutheran and other private German-language schools in the mid-1870s.[88] But German Catholic parents found themselves with even less of a voice in the city's Irish-controlled Roman Catholic Church than in the public school system, where at least men could vote for and lobby elected officials. New York City Lutherans did not develop the extensive parochial school system of the American Catholic Church.[89]

German immigrants had more influence over New York City's religious landscape, reorienting American Lutheranism back toward the German language and more traditional German orthodoxy and founding dozens of German-language congregations within the American Baptist, Methodist, and Evangelical Reform Churches.[90]

In 1880, New York had seventy-five German-language churches, thirty-three of which were located in Kleindeutschland, with the others scattered around Manhattan.[91] Roman Catholics made up the largest religious group within the city's German community, but only four of the city's eleven German-language parishes were in Kleindeutschland in 1880. Yet these parishes were the spiritual foundation of German Catholics in New York City.[92]

Of the twenty German Lutheran churches in Manhattan, one of the more important was St. Mark's Evangelical Lutheran Church on East 6th Street. In 1880, the church welcomed a new assistant pastor, twenty-six-year old Philadelphia native George C. F. Haas, to assist the Rev. Hermann Raegener, whose health was beginning to fail.[93]

But despite the large number of German churches, several of these congregations were small, and many German immigrants did not attend church regularly to the dismay of German religious leaders.[94]

Of the major social welfare institutions that German immigrants founded in the city—including the German Hospital (now Lenox Hill Hospital), founded 1857, at Park Avenue and 77th Street; the German orphan asylum, Wartburg, in Mount Vernon; the German Legal Aid Society at 39 Nassau Street; and the Deutsche Sparbank (German Savings Bank) and the Germania Bank, both located on the Bowery—only the Deutsche Gegenseite Unterstützungsgesellschaft für Witwen und Waisen (German Support Society for the Widows and Orphans) was based at a church. The others were secular organizations.[95]

By 1880, three generations of German immigrants and their children and grandchildren had created a well-organized community full of businesses, social and cultural organizations, churches, and other institutions that maintained the German language and culture in the city. But this community was also in the process of geographic and socioeconomic transition as more prosperous and more upwardly mobile residents began moving out of the neighborhood in search of better housing in northern Manhattan, the Bronx, and Brooklyn. This dispersal was part of a larger trend within New York City society, as middle- and upper-class New Yorkers of all ethnic backgrounds moved out of Lower Manhattan to northern neighborhoods and other boroughs.

2

Climbing the Economic Ladder in Kleindeutschland in 1880

• •

This fresh-off-the-boat German immigrant in 1880 had probably left Germany out of a fear of downward mobility, particularly if he was a master craftsman, or with the hope of upward mobility and economic independence, especially if he was a journeyman. If he did not already have a job offer in hand, he would have had to find work very soon after arriving in the United States.[1]

German immigrants in New York City were primarily working-class skilled craftsmen, with nearly half of German men working in manufacturing as master craftsmen or journeymen, while another quarter worked in trade, as traders, clerks, and salesmen. The ground floors and rear yards of most residential buildings in Kleindeutschland were devoted to commercial and industrial activities, and the neighborhood had thousands of stores, workshops, and eating and drinking establishments.

There was, however, upward mobility for some German immigrants in New York City in the second half of the nineteenth century, as a small minority of artisans and business owners became successful and wealthy enough to move into the city's middle and then upper-middle classes. These German entrepreneurs moved out of Kleindeutschland and expanded their businesses into the larger, English-speaking American city and nation.

Yet as these men and their families moved up and out of the neighborhood, they retained their identities as German and remained active in promoting and maintaining German culture in New York City. The typical successful German entrepreneur was Lutheran, Republican, and a member of either the Liederkranz or Arion singing societies and at least one American industry lobbying group. If he was a Democrat, he was probably either involved in the liquor industry or politics (or both).[2] These men's sons followed in their father's footsteps, working for the family business, marrying German or German American women, and joining both German Vereine and American business organizations.

The degree to which German immigrant workers and entrepreneurs integrated or adapted to the American economic environment depended on the industry in which they worked. Workers in Kleindeutschland can be classified in three ways: those who provided goods and services to the immigrant community, such as bakers, butchers, grocers, brewers, and saloon keepers; those who provided goods and services both within and beyond the community, such as tailors, shoe and boot makers, carpenters, furniture makers, and cigar makers; and those who imported to and/or from Europe, such as wine importers, bankers, and commodities dealers and shippers. But these dividing lines were not rigid; most German men produced goods and services for people in and outside of Kleindeutschland, and most German men had to learn at least some English to deal with non-German-speaking customers.

Our newly arrived immigrant had many kinds of work from which to choose, and by 1880, the New York City economy had recovered from the Panic of 1873.[3] The industries that employed the most people in New York City in 1880 were trade (which included saloon keeping as well as retail and banking), domestic service, garment making and shoe making, carpentry and furniture making, and cigar making.[4]

German immigrants were well represented in these industries, with Germans accounting for 20 percent of the city's tailors, 42 percent of the city's boot and shoe makers, 34 percent of the city's carpenters and cabinetmakers, and 27 percent of the city's cigar makers. German men predominated in other industries, including 74 percent of the city's brewers, 54 percent of the city's bakers, and 46 percent of the city's saloon keepers.[5] When one considers that many boys worked with and for their fathers, the German dominance of these fields was probably even more pronounced. Outside of the stereotypical German brewer, there was no occupation clearly associated with Germans the way the jobs of maid and day laborer were associated with Irish immigrants.

These Germans' economic concentrations in New York City reflected national trends: Germans were highly concentrated in manufacturing (especially in brewing), butchering and sausage making, musical instrument making, and sugar and vinegar making. Germans also predominated in baking, tailoring, and cigar making.[6]

Table 2.1
German Occupations, 1880, New York City

Occupation	Number of Germans	Economic sector
Tailors	9,465	Manufacturing
Traders, dealers	9,303	Trade
Domestic servants	6,814	Professional, personal services
Retail clerks, salesmen, and store accountants	5,901	Trade
Cigar makers	3,555	Manufacturing
Saloon keepers and bartenders	3,235	Trade
Boot and shoemakers	3,220	Manufacturing
Butchers	3,102	Manufacturing
Laborers	2,955	Professional, personal services
Cabinetmakers and upholsterers	2,833	Manufacturing
Bakers	2,721	Manufacturing
Carpenters	2,507	Manufacturing
Hotel and restaurant keepers	2,122	Professional, personal services

SOURCE: U.S. Census, 1880, vol. 1, 892, table 36, "Persons in Selected Occupations in Fifty Principal Cities, Etc: 1880, New York, New York." 48,908 Germans worked in manufacturing in 1880. This figure would be even higher if the number of Americans with German-born parents were counted as German and not American.

The industry that employed the largest number of workers (both German and non-German) in New York City was garment making, with 43,540 people (9,465 of them German) working in nearly 1,300 establishments. Another 7,616 people (3,220 of them German) worked in 1,029 boot- and shoe-making businesses.[7] The New York City garment industry was viciously competitive, but some immigrant tailors were able to grow from being small shops to large factories and successful retail and wholesale businesses.

The Jewish immigrants and brothers-in-laws Marx Hornthal and Meyer Whitehead emigrated from Bavaria in the early 1840s and opened their tailoring business, Hornthal, Whitehead (later called Hornthal, Whitehead, Weissman & Co) in 1844. Moving their business from shop to shop in search of both space and cheaper rent, the partners were based at 296 Grand Street by 1852.[8] But while Hornthals and Whiteheads lived in Kleindeutschland, as a mark of their success, they did not live above their store.[9]

Like most businessmen, Hornthal and Whitehead were active in their industry's associations, especially the Clothing Manufacturers Association, and their sons were leaders in the general business group the Traders and Travelers' Union, organized in 1884. Despite the large numbers of German clothing makers, most of the members of this business association were Anglo American, not German or Jewish.[10]

The Hornthal and Whitehead families were involved in several Jewish charities, especially Mount Sinai Hospital, in which they took an active interest in the education and training of nurses.[11] Originally called The Jews Hospital, this institution had been founded in 1855 on West 28th Street and served poor Jewish immigrants. In 1864, it became nonsectarian, and in 1866, it changed its name to Mount Sinai Hospital. In 1872, the hospital moved to Lexington Avenue between 66th and 67th Streets. It is now located on Fifth Avenue between 98th and 103rd Streets and is the oldest and largest teaching hospital in the United States.[12]

Marx Hornthal's son, Lewis Marx Hornthal, married the daughter of Jewish immigrants from Bavaria and received a master's degree from the College of the City of New York. But instead of moving into a profession or starting his own business, Lewis Hornthal continued to work for Hornthal, Whitehead. He was also a leader in the Clothing Manufacturers Association.[13]

Hornthal, Whitehead Clothiers stayed in Keindeutschland, but the Hornthal and Whitehead families moved uptown in the mid-1870s. When he died in 1880, Marx Hornthal was living at 117 East 56th Street, while Meyer Whitehead lived at 192 East 70th Street.[14]

While Hornthal and Whitehead were able to build a successful wholesale business out of their tailoring, another tailor, Lucas Glockner, ultimately gave up sewing and moved into real estate. Here he joined thousands of entrepreneurs trying to take advantage of the city's rapid growth, as every year thousands of new immigrants, many from German-speaking states, settled in New York City.

Glockner emigrated from Baden in 1846, settling with his wife Caroline and two young sons at 118 Essex Street, a building that housed six other German tailors and their families.[15] In 1863, after nearly twenty years of tailoring, Glockner and two other German immigrant tailors bought the Second (Dutch) Reformed Presbyterian Church on Orchard Street, demolished it, and built three five-story tenement houses, each with twenty apartments. Glockner moved his family from their previous home at 119 St. Marks Place into his new building in 1864. When the Civil War ended a year later, immigration resumed and increased, bringing many potential new tenants to New York City and Kleindeutschland.

In the late 1860s and early 1870s, Glockner gave up tailoring completely and concentrated his energies on real estate development. He built at least two other tenement houses, 23 Allen Street and 25 Allen Street, behind his house on Orchard Street, and identified himself in the 1880 census as a "gentleman," meaning someone who did not work but who lived off of rents from his properties. But he stayed in Kleindeutschland, living in his building at 25 Allen Street.[16]

Piano making was an important subset within furniture manufacturing, and more than half of all piano makers were German. The most successful piano maker in New York City, and eventually in the United States, was Steinway & Sons, founded in 1853 by Heinrich Steinweg and his adult sons, Karl, Heinrich Jr., and Wilhelm. (The family's and company's names were anglicized to "Steinway" in 1864.)[17]

Starting with ten employees, Steinway & Sons quickly grew to have four hundred workers by 1863. The company opened its first Steinway Hall on East 14th Street in 1865, built a factory on Fourth (now Park) Avenue between 52nd and 53rd Streets, and then built a factory town in Astoria, Long Island City, Queens, in 1870. The company also sold pianos at 91 Mercer Street and 84 Varick Street.[18] Henry Steinway Sr. died in 1871, and his fourth son, William, assumed management of the business. In 1880, Steinway & Sons opened a factory in Hamburg, which was managed by the eldest son, C. F. Theodore, while William oversaw the American factories. Although the Steinway sons were trained in the woodworking skills needed to make a piano, by the 1870s, they were strictly management, with Henry Jr. and Theodore also devoting time to innovation in design.[19]

From the beginning, the Steinways rooted themselves in the German community while at the same time orienting their business toward the larger English-speaking community, especially the upwardly mobile middle class. Within a few years, Steinway & Sons was making more than one thousand pianos per year, a small number when compared to larger firms, such as Kimball and Cable, but Steinway's instruments were designed for the luxury market, and so sales and marketing were oriented toward middle- and upper-class Americans. By 1870, Steinway & Sons was selling twice as much as its main competitors in the luxury piano business, Chickering & Sons of Boston and Wm. Knabe & Co of Baltimore. Unlike many German craftsmen, the Steinway brothers had learned English in school in their home state of Braunschweig before they emigrated, and this enabled William Steinway to successfully network with wealthy English-speaking New Yorkers.[20]

Key to Steinway & Sons' success was its ability to link its sales and marketing to the promotion of German culture in the United States. The company was a major patron of classical music in New York City. The New York Philharmonic was based at Steinway Hall between 1865 and 1891, when it moved to the new Carnegie Hall. Steinway & Sons also sponsored American tours by famous pianists, such as Anton Rubenstein and Ignace Paderewski. Steinway and other German musicians and instrument makers used classical music as a way of bringing German speakers and English speakers together in a supposedly cosmopolitan culture that was in fact dominated by German classical music performed by German musicians.[21]

As their business became successful, the Steinway family moved out of Kleindeutschland to 84 Walker Street on the west side of Lower Manhattan by 1857. Eventually, in the 1870s, William Steinway moved to 26 Gramercy Park

South while his mother, Julia Steinway, lived at 121 East 52nd Street and his brother, Albert, lived next door at 125 East 52nd Street.[22]

Although Steinway & Sons became successful by reaching out to Anglo American customers, the company remained in many ways a German business. Most of the company's employees were Germans, and German was the official language of business in the factories; several managers came from Braunschweig.[23] At the Steinway Village factory town in Astoria (which was 81 percent German in 1880), the Steinway company paid for a bilingual teacher who taught English to the German children and German to the few English-speaking pupils at the company-funded public school.[24]

Despite this perceived paternalism, William Steinway embraced the ruthlessness of American-style industrial capitalism and repeatedly clashed with his workers over issues ranging from higher pay to an eight-hour workday. Steinway employees went on strike in 1872, 1878, 1879, 1880, 1882, and 1886 in protest of Steinway's management practices.[25] Workers who lived in Steinway Village also chafed at having their employer as their landlord, with all of its inherent problems of surveillance and control.

In some ways, the Steinways resembled other nouveau riche Anglo Americans: William Steinway built himself a thirty-eight-room "chateau" on Long Island and owned a yacht. Among his neighbors in exclusive Gramercy Park was New York governor and Democratic presidential candidate Samuel J. Tilden.

But the Steinways continued to see themselves as German and—as they became more successful—as cultural and social leaders of the German community. The Steinway brothers continued to associate mainly with other (upper-middle-class) Germans like themselves. Charles Steinway was a director of the charitable Deutsche Gesellschaft (German Society) in the early 1860s.[26] William Steinway was also active in the Deutsche Gesellschaft, as well as the German Press Club, the German Athenaeum Club, and especially the singing societies, the Liederkranz and Arion.[27]

As the Liederkranz came to be seen and used by non-German business and political elites as a venue for networking, William Steinway complained privately in his diary (ironically in English) about members speaking English or bad German.[28] At a celebration of the Liederkranz's twenty-fifth anniversary in 1872, he described the Verein as a special haven for Germans living in a predominantly English-speaking city, and he defined "American" as "English-speaking": "If one is surrounded the whole day by Americans—the evening here allows one not to forget the old homeland but brings it closer."[29] Yet since Steinway wrote his diary in English (he often used German words but did not write in German), it appears that his using English was a choice and a reflection of his education versus a sign of assimilation or abandonment of German culture.[30]

The Steinway family was somewhat unusual in that, of the six children to marry, only brother Charles married a woman from the same region of Lower Saxony as the Steinways. The other siblings married either immigrants from other parts of Europe (Dresden, Württemberg, Paris) or German Americans. But a commonality that Steinway spouses shared was either working for the family business or being musicians. Even more unusual (and certainly shocking and titillating to New Yorkers of all backgrounds) was William Steinway's divorce from his first wife, Regina, in 1876 for adultery. William and Regina's tumultuous fifteen-year marriage was a lesson to other upwardly mobile Germans that compatibility in background—as well as personality—was more important than passion. In 1880, Steinway remarried, this time to a German woman from Dresden, Elizabeth Ranft, whom he met in Germany.[31]

Fewer German immigrants worked in beer brewing than in garment or furniture making, but nearly 74 percent of the 1,680 New Yorkers working in brewing in 1880 were German. Nationally, the figure was more than 80 percent. Germans brought their brewing traditions with them, and German breweries in the United States reinforced German immigrant recreational traditions before eventually influencing other Americans' drinking and recreational habits.[32] Rather than adapting their product to meet English and Irish American drinking tastes, German brewers instead converted non-German Americans from being English-style ale drinkers to being German-style lager drinkers.

Brewers were essential to the German community and yet were often geographically removed from the neighborhood. This was because breweries occupied a lot of space: besides the actual brewing facilities, breweries had cooperages (keg making), ice houses, stables for deliveries, and usually beer gardens or saloons attached. The largest breweries were located in Yorkville, Harlem, the Bronx, and Murray Hill, all far from Kleindeutschland.

To the outsider, German brewers appeared to be very traditional in their business practices, but in fact, brewery owners were very modern. They embraced new technology and used scientific research to help them increase production, lower costs, expand distribution, and improve their product. They quickly allied themselves with American politicians who would either ignore or undermine the city's alcohol laws and engaged in lobbying and partisan politics. And the brewers maintained tight control over their workers while adopting American capitalistic ideas that said they had no obligation to their employees beyond a paycheck. In particular, brewers maintained and adapted a medieval German tradition of requiring their unmarried workers to live together in communal housing (the so-called *Herbergszwang*). In New York City, the *Brauerherberge* (brewer lodging house or hostel) made breweries similar to factory towns in which brewers were both employers and landlords.[33]

Brewery workers, for their part, routinely worked very long hours (typically fourteen to sixteen hours per weekday, six or more hours on Sundays) doing physically demanding labor: moving heavy barrels, carrying water and stirring boiling liquids in large vats, carrying blocks of ice, and so on. The continuous movement from cold icehouse, cool storage, warm mashing room, and hot brew house caused many brewery workers to regularly suffer from bronchial infections, tuberculosis, and rheumatism and made brewery work a young man's job. While there were skilled jobs involved in brewing, especially the brewmaster (*Vormann* in German), these positions were often reserved for owners' sons and so were becoming increasingly impossible for journeymen brewers to achieve by the 1880s, leading to a large economic and social divide between managers and workers in the brewing industry.[34]

The largest breweries in New York City in 1880 belonged to George Ehret, John Christian and Adolph Glaser Hupfel, and Jacob Ruppert. These men dominated the New York and American brewing industries for decades and created huge companies that survived for several generations. With few exceptions, these brewers came from Bavaria, intermarried, and maintained tight family control over their businesses. Most of these entrepreneurs lived in mansions built within their factory complexes in Yorkville, Harlem, and the Bronx, reflecting the expectation they had of their workers to live in company housing.

Like the Steinways, the brewers also straddled German and Anglo American culture, especially as they moved up socioeconomically. Most were active in one of the elite singing societies, usually either the Liederkranz or Arion, and supported various community charities, particularly the Deutsche Gesellschaft and the German Hospital.[35]

These men also dominated trade groups in their industry, particularly the United States Brewers' Association. German was the language of business of the Brewers' Association, although the organization did begin to use English in addition to German in the 1860s in an effort to reach out to English-speaking ale brewers.[36] Many German brewers were also members of the Democratic Party, especially Tammany Hall, because the Democrats opposed alcohol prohibition and often favored more relaxed laws regarding alcohol sales and drinking on Sundays.[37]

The largest brewer in the United States by 1880 was George Ehret. Ehret had immigrated in 1857 to join his father, a cooper who had emigrated five years earlier from their home of Hofweir in Baden. The younger Ehret initially worked for Romell & Co. and then the Anton Hüpfel Brewing Company, where he became a foreman and then brewmaster. Borrowing money from Anton Hüpfel's stepson, John Christian Glaser Hupfel, Ehret bought land in northeastern Manhattan, near Hell Gate in the East River, and built his Hell Gate Brewery there in 1867, making a Munich-style lager. Ehret expanded the factory in 1871 after a disastrous fire, and the new facility encompassed the entire block between 92nd and 93rd Streets and Second and Third Avenues.

By 1879, Ehret was the largest brewer in the country, making more than 180,000 barrels per year, or about 1.5 percent of the nation's beer.[38]

Ehret required his apprentice and journeymen brewers to live in company-owned boarding houses, but he also lived on-site: he; his wife, Anna; their nine children; his father, Anton; his sister, Julia; her husband, W. F. Herres, and their two daughters; Herres's sister; and six servants (including three nurses for the nearly dozen children) all lived in a large house located in his factory complex at 93rd Street and Park Avenue that was built in 1879.[39]

Ehret got his start working for Anton Hüpfel, an immigrant from Bavaria who arrived in New York City in 1836. Hüpfel initially worked as a wood turner before buying a brewery in 1863 in the Bronx on 161st Street, which he named A. Hüpfel Son's Brewing Company of Morrisania. In 1874, Hüpfel retired and left his business to his two stepsons, John Christian Glaser Hupfel and Adolph Glaser Hupfel. (Anton Americanized the name by removing the umlaut.)[40] By the late 1870s, A. Hupfel's Sons had two locations: the Morrisania factory and a brewery at 229 East 38th Street.[41]

The living arrangements of the Hupfel brothers were typical of New York City's German brewers. John Christian lived near the East 38th Street brewery with his wife, five children, and his sister-in-law, while Adolph lived with his wife, their five children, and two boarders (one a salesman of lager beer from Schleswig-Holstein and the other a bartender from Michigan) in a house at the Bronx brewery. With five children each, both families had two servants each to help with the housework. Besides Adolph Glaser Hupfel's family, five other families lived in buildings at the brewery, presumably all brewery workers. Next door to the Hupfels was the brewer Philip Ebling, who owned the Philip & William Ebling Brewery at St. Ann's Avenue and 156th Street and who also lived with a large extended family plus boarders.[42]

John Christian and Adolph Glaser Hupfel were also typical in their extensive club membership and their patronage of many charitable and social welfare organizations, both German and non-German. Both brothers were also members of German and Anglo American fraternal orders. Adolph Glaser Hupfel was active in several brewing trade organizations, as well as the non-German New York Produce Exchange and the North Side Board of Trade.[43] John Christian Glaser Hupfel was an active sportsman (common among upper-class men), engaging in yachting, bowling, and polo, and he was a member of the prestigious New York Athletic Club.[44] All of these club memberships and charity support were a signal to the rest of the German community that the Hupfels, like many other successful German immigrants, were paternalistic and benevolent capitalists, generously sharing their wealth with the less fortunate of their community and of the city at large.

For instance, like many brewers, John Christian Glaser Hupfel organized an Unterstützungsverein, the Original Brewers' and Coopers' Sick Benefit and

Mutual Aid Association, for his workers in 1867. He also organized and funded a military company, the Original Brewers' and Coopers' Guard, to parade for the entertainment of employees at the company's annual picnic, which was usually held at Jones's Wood, a picnic ground at what is now 66th Street to 75th Street between Third Avenue and the East River that was popular among German Vereine.[45]

But neither the Hupfels nor the Ehrets nor any of the other large brewers tolerated their workers organizing labor unions to negotiate for better pay and working conditions. Workers who tried found themselves blacklisted and evicted from company-owned housing.[46]

The Ruppert brewing family also reflected the German tendency toward intraindustry marriage and involvement in both German and Anglo American business, social, and political organizations. Jacob Ruppert was born in New York City to immigrant parents; his father, Franz Ruppert, had emigrated from Bavaria and owned the Turtle Bay Brewery. Jacob Ruppert opened first a restaurant and then his own brewery, Jacob Ruppert Brewing Co. He married Anna Gillig, the daughter of the brewer George Gillig, in 1864, and had six children. (His oldest son, Jacob Ruppert Jr., would later serve in Congress in the early 1900s and own the New York Yankees baseball team.) Ruppert was also connected to the Ehret brewing family through his sister Eliza's marriage to one of George Ehret's sons.[47]

German brewers were an extreme example of how dominance over an industry resulted in German immigrants significantly changing Anglo American culture to become more German. Within a generation, German-style lager beer had replaced English-style ale as the most popular form of beer drunk in the United States. Although immigrant brewers and their sons joined industry groups that included non-Germans, Germans quickly came to dominate these groups, German became the language of business of these organizations, and German business practices became common in the industry. Geographically removed from Kleindeutschland, German brewers lived in northern neighborhoods dominated by their breweries, which became important satellites of New York City's German community, with German stores, churches, and other institutions.

German immigrants also established lasting and successful businesses in the smaller but highly technical fields of chemicals, pharmaceuticals, and scientific instrument manufacturing, industries that were critical to the growth of the American industrial economy. Four men—Conrad Poppenhusen, Carl Pfizer, Wilhelm Keuffel, and Hermann Esser—established businesses that employed thousands of mostly German workers living in College Point, Williamsburg, and Hoboken, satellites of Kleindeutschland in Queens, Brooklyn, and New Jersey.

Conrad Poppenhusen emigrated with his wife, Bertha, from Hamburg in 1843, after a fire destroyed his textile business. They settled in the German neighborhood of Williamsburg, Brooklyn (across the East River from Klein-deutschland and connected by ferry), where Conrad started a business with the son of a family friend that made household items out of whalebone (particularly corset stays, the inflexible part of a corset that was traditionally made of whalebone).[48] Although the venture was successful, the profit margin was small and the industry competitive.

In 1852, Poppenhusen made the business connection that would finally earn him financial success: he loaned the chemical inventor Charles Goodyear money to improve his process of vulcanizing rubber and, in return, received the exclusive right to manufacture hard rubber for the next several years. Closing down his factory in Williamsburg, Poppenhusen bought land and built a large factory in College Point, manufacturing rubber combs and corset stays. By 1880, College Point was a factory town, with 1,000 men out of the community's 4,192 residents working for Poppenhusen's Enterprise Works.[49] So many of the residents were from Prussia that the neighborhood was sometimes called "Little Heidelberg" by English speakers. (Heidelberg was not part of Prussia but of the Palatinate; it is now part of the state of Baden-Württemberg.)[50]

A devout member of the Dutch Reform Church, Poppenhusen supported the establishment of the German Dutch Reformed Church and the St. Johannes German Evangelical Lutheran Church in College Point and was very active in providing paternalistic social welfare for his workers. He organized an Unter-stützungsverein for his employees and paid for employees and their families to attend the Centennial Exposition in Philadelphia in 1876. Poppenhusen also paid for German teachers to teach in the local public schools and created the Poppenhusen Institute in 1868 to provide vocational and manual arts training.[51] He served as treasurer of the Deutsche Gesellschaft from 1846 to 1848 and was a director of the Germania Life and Fire Insurance Companies and the German-American Fire Insurance Company.[52]

Unlike most German immigrants, Poppenhusen was a teetotaler, and he frowned upon drinking, even beer, although he loaned fellow immigrant Joseph Witzel money to open a hotel and beer garden on Point View Island in 1871. Poppenhusen's opposition to alcohol resulted in the social gatherings of College Point industrialists (held at the merchant Adolph Erbsloh's Conservatory on 8th Street) not to allow beer drinking.[53]

As the two largest employers in northern Queens, Poppenhusen and Steinway and their families socialized together, and Poppenhusen was, of course, a member of the Liederkranz.[54] The family also socialized with the family of the Prussian immigrant Hugo Funke, who owned a large silk mill in College Point and who was related to the owners of the Funke & Elbers steel company in Prussia. The Funkes owned a large estate next to the mansion belonging to Poppenhusen's partner, Frederick Koenig, on what would become 120th Street.[55]

Thus did German immigrant industrialists network with German industrialists in Germany.

As was traditional, Poppenhusen's three sons—Adolph, Herman, and Alfred—worked for the family business and assumed control of Enterprise Works in 1871 when their father retired. Adolph married a woman from Krefeld, Rhineland-Palatinate, while Herman and Alfred married German American women from New York.[56]

Herman Poppenhusen introduced the German tradition of shooting to Queens, and he sold the National Rifle Association (NRA) a seventy-acre farm next to the tracks he was building for the Central and North Side Railroad of Long Island, which he also owned. The NRA built a shooting range there called Creedmoor in 1874, and the railroad transported large crowds from Manhattan and Brooklyn out to Queens to watch shooting contests.[57]

Like other wealthy Anglo American businessmen, Conrad Poppenhusen also speculated in other businesses, particularly railroads. In 1876, he became president of the Long Island Railroad Company and began consolidating the numerous competing railroads on Long Island into a single company to be managed by his son, Herman. But by late 1877, Poppenhusen found himself $4 million in debt and had to declare bankruptcy. Court hearings revealed that of Poppenhusen's twenty-six railroad creditors, the largest were a bank in Hamburg, his son Adolph, the brokers Knoblauch & Lichtenstein of New York City, the Bremen merchant Hermann Wätjen, and Poppenhusen's original partner in Enterprise Works, Frederick Koenig. The financier J. P. Morgan's bank, Drexel, Morgan & Co. was the only non-German creditor of the group (although it was also the largest).[58]

Chastened by the failure of his railroad business, Poppenhusen and his second wife, Caroline, returned to Germany, where he opened another hard rubber manufacturing company. But he regularly returned to New York to visit his children, and he died at his son Alfred's home in College Point in 1883. He was buried, however, in his hometown of Hamburg.[59]

Steinway Village and College Point were German factory towns as much as they were German communities. Williamsburg in Brooklyn was another German neighborhood that emerged as a result of German industrialists building factories, in this case, the W. & F. C. Havemeyer Company's sugar refinery and especially the Pfizer chemical company.

Charles (born Karl) Pfizer grew up in a family of grocers and candy makers in Ludwigsburg, Kingdom of Württemberg, but he trained as an apothecary (pharmacist). He planned his move to the United States carefully, studying English and the history and laws of the United States before he emigrated in 1849 with his cousin Charles Erhart. That same year, Pfizer and Erhart opened Charles Pfizer & Company, Manufacturing Chemists, in Williamsburg.[60]

The cousins' first product was santonin, a drug used to eliminate intestinal worms. Since santonin tasted bitter and the standard treatment called for three doses per day for several days, Pfizer drew on his family background and developed a palatable way of administering the santonin in an almond toffee-flavored candy.

Although the sweetened santonin was successful, Pfizer did not make other drugs to be sold over the counter but instead focused on manufacturing pure chemicals for sale to wholesalers and retailers, particularly doctors and pharmacists. By 1860, Pfizer was producing iodine and iodine compounds, such as potassium iodide and iodoform; Mercury compounds, such as calomel (used to treat malaria, yellow fever, syphilis, and intestinal worms); and borax, boric acid, and refined camphor. Pfizer also began importing and refining tartaric acid and then citric acid as flavoring agents in beverages.[61]

Although German immigrants played an important role in the development of the American chemical and pharmaceutical industries, in 1880, most doctors and pharmacists in New York City and the United States were English-speaking Americans, so Pfizer and Erhart, like Poppenhusen, focused their business on the English-speaking American market.[62]

But Pfizer was still very much a German business. Most of the workers at the company were German, causing the factory to be called "the German Navy Yard," for another large industry in the area, the Brooklyn Navy Yard. Pfizer and Erhart traveled often to Europe to establish contacts with exporters of raw materials and to investigate new products.[63]

It was on one of these business trips to Germany that Pfizer met his future wife, Anna Hausch. The couple had seven children, and two of his sons, Charles Jr. and Emile, along with his nephew William H. Erhart, worked for the family business. The family lived in Brooklyn but in upscale Clinton Hill, not Williamsburg.[64]

By the time of his death in 1906, Pfizer had a vacation home in Newport, Rhode Island; two daughters married to European aristocrats; and sons who (unfortunately for Pfizer) spent much of their time fox hunting and playing polo. "Pfizer was virtually the prototype of a Gilded Age millionaire," according to his biographer William Stevenson.[65]

Although Charles Pfizer was a member of the Germania Club of Brooklyn, the Brooklyn Riding and Driving Club, and the Downtown Association of New York City, he was active only in the Manufacturing Chemists Association, which he helped organize in 1872. Unusually for a German immigrant businessman, Pfizer was not a member of the Liederkranz or Arion singing societies, but he was an opera lover and attended the Metropolitan Opera regularly. Upon his death in 1906, Pfizer left $10,000 (approximately $258,000 in 2011 dollars) to the German Hospital Society of Brooklyn.[66]

Unlike many (German) American business leaders, Pfizer had relatively progressive views on labor-management issues. The company had an emergency reserve fund for employees and their families in times of distress, and the company established a profit-sharing plan in 1906.[67]

The Bronx, Brooklyn, and Queens had several German neighborhoods, but Hoboken was probably the second most important German community in the New York City area, after Kleindeutschland itself. By 1880, Hoboken had 31,000 residents, 13,000 of them foreign born, and about half of these from German-speaking states. German immigrants and their American-born children composed 37 percent of the city's population in 1880.[68]

Of the hundreds of German businesses in Hoboken, the scientific instrument manufacturer Keuffel & Esser (K&E) was one of the largest. Wilhelm Johann Diedrich Keuffel and his partner, Hermann Esser, emigrated separately in 1866—Keuffel from Thuringia and Esser from North-Rhine-Westphalia—after meeting and working together at an engineering business in Hannover. Recognizing New York City's explosive physical development, the two men founded Keuffel & Esser in 1867 in New York City, selling imported drafting and surveying equipment to architects and builders. In 1880, they began selling the product that would be most firmly associated with K&E: the slide rule (a calculating device).

Initially working as door-to-door salesmen, Keuffel and Esser opened a retail store on Fulton Street in Lower Manhattan in 1870 and built a factory in Hoboken in 1874. But they continued to import materials from Germany and alternated traveling to Europe on extended buying trips and staying home to oversee sales and domestic manufacturing. Keuffel's third child, Ottilie, was born in Germany during one of her father's business trips.

Although New York City had several German immigrant architects (including Theodore W. E. De Lemos & August W. Cordes, who designed K&E's new store at 127 Fulton Street in 1892), Keuffel and Esser could not rely simply on German architects and builders as customers; they had to reach out to English speakers working in the architectural, design, engineering, and building industries. Keuffel and Esser regularly attended trade shows, scientific and technical conferences, fairs, and expositions to meet with customers and demonstrate their products. The partners were members of the New York Stationers Board of Trade; Keuffel also belonged to the Hoboken Board of Trade (equivalent to a chamber of commerce) and the Technical Society of New York.

Yet Keuffel and Esser remained closely tied to the German community even as they became economically successful. Both partners spent considerable time in Germany on business and so maintained their connections to German business practices and German culture. K&E hired German craftsmen, and German was the language of work and business at the company's factory.

Although Keuffel and Esser lived in an upper-middle-class neighborhood that was the least German area of Hoboken, the partners were active in mostly German civic, cultural, and educational organizations in both New Jersey and New York City. Both Keuffel and Esser were actively involved in two of the more important German institutions in Hoboken, the Hoboken Deutscher Club and the Hoboken Academy, a private German school. Keuffel also sat on the advisory board of the German Hospital in New York City. Both men were active members of the Liederkranz and owned vacation homes in the Liederkranz's exclusive Elka Park resort in Greene County, New York, in the Catskills.[69]

Keuffel's wife, Bertha Caroline Schneeberger, was born in St. Louis, Missouri, to parents from Hesse-Darmstadt and Schleswig-Holstein, while Esser's wife, Bertha Michelmann, was an immigrant from Hannover. The Keuffel and Esser children married either Germans or German Americans, and the sons and sons-in-laws all worked for K&E.[70]

Class divisions within the German community, which were already becoming apparent in the 1860s, hardened in the 1870s and 1880s. Of the hundreds of thousands of German immigrants, a small minority became economically successful, and these entrepreneurs established lasting family businesses in the garment, brewing, chemical, pharmaceutical, and instrument-making industries, in part because of the family networks they developed and were able to rely on for financial and human capital. Sons were groomed for leadership positions in the family business, which was almost always named for the family, and marriages were as much strategic alliances with business partners and competitors as they were emotional commitments. These children tended to marry people who were either from their parents' home state or who had parents from that German state. In many instances, these marriages were often within industries as much as between people of the same backgrounds. For German Jews, religion was more important than German state of origin. But for both German Jews and Christians, marriage within the German community was paramount and ensured that the American-born children of immigrants remained closely tied to the German community, whether they lived in Kleindeutschland or one of its many satellite communities.

German immigrant men were active in German Vereine for social reasons and American trade groups for business. Their sons tended to join American clubs, especially for sports and recreation, but still kept close ties to the German community through membership in increasingly elite organizations, such as the Liederkranz, Arion, and Deutsche Gesellschaft. Patronage of German-founded charities, like the German Hospital, was also common.

But this German elite was voluntarily highly segregated. According to David Hammack, "It is appropriate to speak of the ethnicity of particular firms, for few Germans and no Jews were to be found in the largest law firms, banks, and corporations headed by those of British origin. Instead most Germans and nearly all Jews formed their own firms, which in turn usually included no outsiders."[71]

In addition, when it came to social clubs, "only a few of the very wealthiest German-Americans gained membership in the higher of the social circles dominated by British-American Protestants; this was the great period of an independent and almost self-sufficient German world within New York."[72] New York City's famous *Social Register* included neither the Liederkranz nor Arion among the seventy-one clubs it listed in 1896, and although forty members of the Deutscher Verein were listed in the register, only sixteen of them were members of other elite, non-German clubs.[73] Germans and German Americans continued to prefer to socialize with people like themselves in what they considered to be a German style.

The late nineteenth and early twentieth centuries were a period of maturity and transition for German immigrants and their children. The German community became more visible in this period as Germans increasingly left Kleindeutschland for other neighborhoods, creating new communities in other parts of the city.

3

Decades of Change, 1880–1900

•••••••••••••••••••••

The 1880s and 1890s were a period of change, maturity, and movement for New York City's German community, although not obviously apparent to an immigrant newly arrived in the neighborhood. More established German immigrants and their American-born children and grandchildren began moving out of Kleindeutschland uptown and to the outer boroughs in search of better housing. But this geographic mobility did not necessarily mean residential integration with Anglo Americans or other groups. Instead, Germans moved their businesses, churches, and other social and cultural institutions with them, creating new German neighborhoods and rejuvenating and enlarging older ones in Brooklyn, Queens, and the Bronx.[1]

Germans also continued to self-segregate socially at all class levels, including the small but growing German/German American upper class. Although wealthy Germans lived similar lifestyles and sometimes in the same neighborhoods as the city's Anglo-Dutch elite, they continued to socialize with other Germans, withdrawing themselves from both poorer Germans and other non-German elites.[2]

But the old community divisions of class, religion, and politics persisted, as strikes, Verein conflicts, and election battles revealed. It was only at special events, like the visit of Prince Henry of Prussia to the United States in 1902, that German New Yorkers came together as a community.

Ironically, as Germans more clearly defined themselves as a distinct community, many German cultural practices began to make their way into Anglo

American culture. Non-Germans began eating German foods, such as the hot dog (*Frankfurter*) and drinking German lager beer, while such German holiday traditions as Santa Claus, the Christmas tree, and the Easter Bunny became mainstream among Christians of a variety of sects. German ideas about education and recreation were also adopted by Anglo Americans, as were approaches to labor organization.

Although many of these cultural transfers occurred in cities other than New York City, the size and visibility of Kleindeutschland meant that German New Yorkers' cultural practices were observed and adopted by large numbers of non-Germans and, due to New York City's concentration of media, disseminated around the country.

The 1880s was a period of a large increase in emigration from the German Empire, as more than 1.4 million people immigrated to the United States in that decade alone. Another nearly 580,000 Germans immigrated in the 1890s. The German population of New York City grew also, and by 1890, German immigrants and their children composed about 36 percent of the city's population.[3]

Table 3.1
German Immigrants, by County, plus Brooklyn, 1880

Total population of four counties	New York (Manhattan)	Kings	Brooklyn City	Queens	Richmond (Staten Island)	Total Germans, four counties	%
1,935,359	163,482	59,367	55,339	8,212	2,972	234,033	12

SOURCE: U.S. Census, Population, by Race, Sex, and Nativity, 521, table 14, "Native and Foreign-born Populations, by Counties, etc: 1880, New York"; U.S. Census, 1880, Population, by Race, Sex, and Nativity, 539, table 16, "Foreign-born Population of Fifty Principal Cities, distributed according to place of birth, among the various foreign countries: 1880, New York."

Table 3.2
German Immigrants, by County, plus Brooklyn 1890

Total population of four counties	New York (Manhattan)	Kings	Brooklyn City	Queens	Richmond (Staten Island)	Total Germans, four counties	%
2,533,570	210,723	97,648	94,798	14,520	4,883	327,774	13

SOURCE: U.S. Census, 1890, Statistics of Population, Country of Birth, 645–646, table 33, "Foreign born population, distributed according to country of birth, by counties: 1890, New York"; U.S. Census, 1890, Statistics of Population, Country of Birth, 671, table 34, "Foreign-born population distributed according to country of birth, for cities having 25,000 inhabitants or more: 1890, New York"; Statistics of Population, 247–248 and 250, table 5, "Population of States and Territories by Minor Civil Divisions: 1880 and 1890—continued."

Table 3.3
German Immigrants in New York City, 1900

New York City total, five boroughs	NY (Manhattan)	Kings	Brooklyn City	Queens	Richmond (Staten Island)	Total Germans in New York City	%
3,437,202	189,729	106,654	n/a	20,380	5,580	322,343	9

SOURCE: U.S. Census, 1900, Statistics of Population, Country of Birth, 772, table 34, "Foreign born population, distributed according to country of birth, by counties: 1900, cont., New York," and 801, table 35, "Foreign born population, distributed according to country of birth, for cities having 25, 000 inhabitants or more: 1900, continued"; Statistics of Population, 31–32, table 4, "Population of States and Territories by counties, at each census: 1790 to 1900, New York," and 465, table 8, "Population of Incorporated cities, towns, villages, and boroughs in 1900, with population for 1890, New York."

When one factored in grandchildren and German communities outside of Manhattan, the community was even larger.

Germans and German Americans also increasingly lived outside of Kleindeutschland. By 1890, only the Eleventh and Seventeenth Wards had sizable numbers of German residents, and there German immigrants composed 23 percent of the wards' populations, down from a high of 32 percent in 1875.[4] German immigrants and their children and grandchildren increasingly lived on the Upper East Side, especially in the Nineteenth Ward in Yorkville, between 86th and 100th Streets. There was also a large concentration of Germans on the Upper West Side and in the western part of Midtown near what would become Times Square.[5] Other German neighborhoods, such as Williamsburg, Astoria, and Hoboken, continued to be dominated by Germans in terms of population and in social, cultural, religious, and economic institutions. But Germans lived almost everywhere in the city (with the exception of the heavily Irish neighborhoods in Midtown between Sixth and Park Avenues).[6]

From the outside perspective of English-speaking New Yorkers, Germans were a homogeneous, unified group. Yet Kleindeutschland as a community had always been divided, especially in the areas of state of origin and religion and increasingly by socio-economic class.

Jews composed about 10 percent or more of the German community, and while they were fully integrated into German immigrant neighborhoods and societies, they also maintained a degree of separation, having their own Vereine and, of course, synagogues.[7] But the question of whether Jewish Germans were full members of the German community arose just at the time when anti-Semitism was becoming more visible in American society at large.

On June 19, 1877, the German Jewish banker and Bavarian-born immigrant Joseph Seligman traveled with his family to the upstate resort town of Saratoga Springs, where they had long vacationed for the summer at the luxury

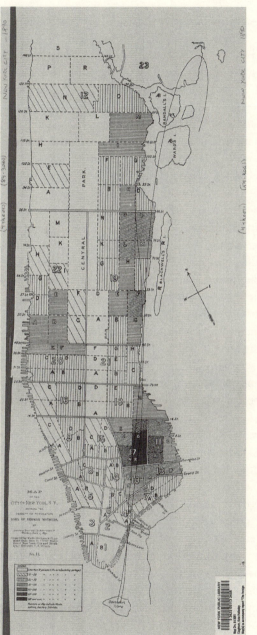

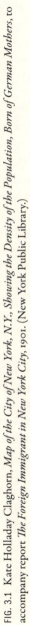

FIG. 3.1 Kate Holladay Claghorn, *Map of the City of New York, N.Y., Showing the Density of the Population, Born of German Mothers*, to accompany report *The Foreign Immigrant in New York City*, 1901. (New York Public Library.)

Grand Union Hotel. But upon arrival this time, the Seligmans were denied entry, with the reason given that the hotel would no longer accommodate Jews. The outcry—from both Jews and non-Jews—was immediate, and the ensuing boycott of A. T. Stewart's department store, which owned the hotel, caused Stewart's to go bankrupt and be sold.[8]

Seligman died on April 25, 1880, in New Orleans, where he had retired after the Grand Union Hotel controversy. His funeral on May 4 at his New York City home at 26 West 34th Street was presided over by the philosopher Felix Adler and attended by many members of the city's German Jewish banking community, as well as several politicians. Perhaps in reference to the Grand Union Hotel affair, Adler stressed Seligman's commitment and pride in his Jewishness, both ethnically and religiously, insisting that Seligman was "never a traitor to the race from which he sprang."[9]

But despite the apparent conclusion of the Grand Union Hotel affair, social and economic discrimination against Jews, especially those less wealthy and socially and politically connected, continued.[10] The city's old money families increasingly refused to socialize with Jews, regardless of how rich, and the *Social Register* that wealthy New Yorkers used to define themselves as elite (and which was established by Louis Keller, the son of French immigrants, in 1886), did not include any Jewish clubs, not even the Gesellschaft Harmonie, the second oldest men's club in New York City.[11]

This anti-Semitism was not limited to Anglo American New Yorkers. In the spring of 1881, the Liederkranz president William Steinway recorded in his diary that there was "strong anti-Jewish sentiment springing up in the Society."[12] By this time, membership in the Liederkranz had become prestigious, and more and more upwardly mobile non-Germans began seeking to join to take advantage of the many networking opportunities membership afforded.

After several months of negotiation and lobbying against the exclusion of Jews, Steinway achieved a compromise: one Jewish applicant would be admitted, but several other applicants would withdraw their names. To placate Jewish members who were unhappy about the anti-Semitic policy, Steinway arranged for the Liederkranz to perform at the funeral of the liberal Jewish Prussian politician Eduard Lasker, who had died suddenly on January 5, 1884, while visiting New York City. Lasker's funeral was attended by many prominent non-Jewish German Americans, including the former Missouri senator and Grant cabinet member Carl Schurz. Steinway also later ensured the successful membership application of the German Jewish banker, Jacob H. Schiff, an immigrant from Frankfurt.[13] But Jewish Germans who were not at the same financial or social level of Schiff had to content themselves with membership in the Arion and in the predominantly Jewish Orpheus Sängerverein.[14]

Wealthy German Jews also withdrew more into their own Vereine, especially the Gesellschaft Harmonie. Yet even here, Germanness persisted: it was not until 1889 that English was allowed to be used in debates by the club's debating society, and English became the official language of the club only in 1893.[15]

As uncomfortable as the debate about the membership status of Jewish Germans was, the problem of non-Germans or English-only-speaking German Americans was even more difficult, because it raised the essential question of what it meant to be German in the United States. German businessmen who spent the day speaking English with English-speaking clients and customers wanted to be able to speak German away from work and were unhappy to encounter non-German speakers at supposedly German social events. When someone as prominent as the former New York City mayor C. Godfrey Gunther (the son of German immigrants) could not speak German well, it reflected poorly on the community's ability to preserve its language, the supposed foundation of its identity and structure.[16]

But by the 1880s, fewer Americans of German heritage spoke German (or spoke it well), and New York elites who were not German, such as Theodore Roosevelt or Col. William E. Van Wyck—both descendants of New York Knickerbocker Dutch families—were allowed to join the Liederkranz.[17] German Americans' adoption of English as their primary language continued as the end of the century approached.[18]

The Liederkranz debates about membership and language occurred among Kleindeutschland's tiny elite. But the 1881 brewery strike affected many more people and exposed increasingly deep class divisions within the German community.

By 1881, brewery workers had had enough of brewers' dictatorial control of working conditions and went on strike. The main issues in the strike—which began in early June and affected most of the breweries in Manhattan, as well as Brooklyn, the Bronx, Staten Island, Jersey City, Newark, and Union and Guttenberg, New Jersey—were long hours (often eighteen hours per day) and working on Sunday. Although fourteen smaller breweries agreed to the demands of the Union der Brauer Gehülfen (Union of Journeymen Brewers), the larger brewers—including George Ehret, Jacob Ruppert, Henry Clausen, David G. Yuengling, and Peter Doelger—refused, and so more than twelve hundred men walked out. Strikers also organized a boycott of saloons that served beer from the breweries being struck and were able to gain the support of a small but important minority of saloon keepers, many of whom had exclusive contracts with breweries.[19] Sustaining the boycott was especially challenging, given that union leaders were asking people to not drink beer during the summer.

By July, the strike had ended, with both sides claiming victory. But brewery workers had suffered during the monthlong strike: union members were blacklisted, and workers who lived in company housing were evicted. Brewers also persuaded New York City police to arrest picketers for disorderly conduct.

Brewers had agreed during the strike to reduce hours to "only" twelve hours per weekday and two hours on Sundays, but by the fall of 1881, fourteen- to sixteen-hour weekdays and six hours on Sundays were normal working hours in the breweries.[20]

The brewery strike was just one of dozens of major strikes to happen in New York City in the 1880s and 1890s. It has been estimated that between 1881 and 1900 more than five thousand strikes involving more than 33,000 factories and 962,470 workers occurred in the city, and more than 45 percent of these strikes were successful.[21]

Workers struck for the right to organize into labor unions and negotiate collectively with management about working conditions, for higher pay, and for shorter hours. German workers were more likely than other immigrant workers, especially Irish, to be skilled and to work in trades that had traditions of organization. The Verein tradition also encouraged German workers to organize themselves for mutual support and protection.

But a key question for German workers was whether to join with English speakers in labor or political organizations. The Union der Brauer Gehülfen was an all-German organization; the few English and Irish brewery workers were not members; nor did they join in the German brewery strike. The question of organizing on the basis of occupation versus ethnicity was not simply a logistical one of what language to use in meetings but also reflected cultural expectations of what a labor union was supposed to do for a worker. At the same time, Marxist and other socialist theories emphasized class versus ethnic/national unity, so German workers faced conflicting pressures.[22]

Most of the writings of Karl Marx, Friedrich Engels, Ferdinand Lassalle, and other radical European political theorists were not translated into English until the late nineteenth century, so many socialists and labor activists influenced by theories of class struggle in the United States were German immigrants. An important group of German socialists were active with the few English-speaking socialists in the increasingly powerful Central Labor Union (CLU).

The CLU was an umbrella organization of craft labor unions and Knights of Labor assemblies that had been established in 1882 by members of the Irish Land League. It quickly grew in strength and popularity, and by 1886, it had about 150,000 members drawn from more than two hundred unions in the city. But the CLU differed from the Knights of Labor and many other labor unions in that it believed that engaging in electoral politics was a central tool in defending workers' rights. Despite—or perhaps because of—its socialist and Marxist orientation, the CLU comprised many factions: socialists (both German and English speaking), Marxists, anarchists, and apolitical trade unionists. It was also divided ethnically, although Irish and Irish American workers predominated. German socialists made up a small but influential element in the organization.[23]

The presence of German socialists and labor union members in the CLU ensured that German workers would participate in large numbers in the nation's first Labor Day parade, which was organized by the CLU and held on Tuesday, September 5, 1882, in New York City. About 10,000 men marched in this first Labor Day parade, not a huge number, especially when compared to the number of workers who participated in demonstrations for the eight-hour day. But the turnout was respectable. Workers who participated included clothing cutters, dress and cloak makers, cigar makers, printers, jewelers, shoemakers, framers and cabinetmakers, and bricklayers, all trades in which Germans either predominated or composed a large minority of workers.[24]

German socialist participation in the CLU was unusual. More often, German-speaking and English-speaking socialists and labor activists established parallel organizations and then (occasionally) attempted to coordinate policy and activity with each other.[25] Unwilling or uninterested in working with English-speaking workers, a dozen German craft unions created the United German Trades in 1885. This organization ultimately represented fifty different unions and functioned as a type of central labor council that sought to shape labor policy and politics for the city's working class at large.[26]

In 1884, brewery workers organized a new union, this time as part of the Knights of Labor, but the union remained a German-speaking organization. After the brewer Peter Doelger fired several workers for their labor organizing, the new union called for a boycott of Doelger's, and surprisingly, Doelger backed down and even paid $1,000 (or $26,338 in 2020 dollars) to reimburse the union for some of the costs of the boycott.[27] Even more surprising was the apparent conversion experience of several of the city's largest brewers to the advantages of having an organized workforce. Brewers pressured their workers to join the union, and by 1886, 90 percent of the city's brewery workers were union members. This union was thoroughly German: German was the language of business at meetings, and non-Germans and unskilled workers were not included. The union secretary and organizer Louis Herbrandt spoke limited English.[28]

But the new brewery workers' union had none of the militancy of the previous Union der Brauer Gehülfen. Although most employers opposed their workers organizing into unions that could challenge their power and control over their businesses, the brewery owners found that supporting unionization mitigated the socialist leanings of many German workers, and the union was content to leave social welfare benefits, particularly sickness and death insurance and unemployment benefits, to the owners, thus making workers more dependent on management. The brewery workers' union quickly became more conservative, limiting membership to only skilled workers, requiring nomination by an existing member, and charging high initiation fees (twenty dollars and then fifty dollars).[29]

In all of these efforts to organize unions, the central question of whether German immigrants were Germans or workers first continually arose. Even in industries in which Germans predominated, as in brewing, non-Germans also worked (although rarely at the same company), and the logistical challenges of what language to use in union meetings was continually present.

The biggest effort to unify New York's ethnically and religiously divided working class came in the mayoral campaign of Henry George in 1886. In the spring of 1886, the CLU was actively involved in supporting a boycott of one of the largest beer gardens in the city, Theiss's on 14th Street, where the German waiters' union and a German musicians' union, the Carl Sahm Verein, were seeking a union shop. Although the owner, George Theiss, gave in and agreed to pay the boycotters one thousand dollars as part of the settlement, he turned around and sued the union for extortion and won. On July 2, 1886, a judge sentenced five of the leaders of the waiters' union to six to eighteen months in prison.[30] Although the Theiss boycott was an issue mainly in Kleindeutschland, Theiss's successful extortion suit was immediately recognized as a serious threat to all labor unions in the city and mobilized the CLU to political action. In August 1886, the Central Labor Union created the United Labor Party (ULP) and nominated the author Henry George to be its candidate for the mayor's race to be held that November 2.[31]

Henry George was neither Irish nor German but American born to lower-middle-class English American parents, and by the late 1870s, he was one of the most famous intellectuals in the United States. In 1879, George had published his best known work, *Progress and Poverty*, which argued that the concentration of wealth, and particularly the monopoly ownership of land, was the single greatest problem confronting the United States. He advocated a large tax on land that would force property owners to sell their holdings, thus allowing more people to own their own farms, businesses, and homes. In a city like New York—where the majority of residents rented their homes—the idea of a tax on landlords was very popular. George was also enormously popular in Ireland, where the two major issues of independence from Great Britain and tenants' rights were closely linked. Since many leaders and members of the Knights of Labor were Irish, and the CLU was dominated by Irish Knights, George was an obvious candidate for the union's new political party.

As a third-party candidate, George could not rely on the mainstream political parties to get his supporters to the polls, so he and the CLU/ULP sought to create an alternative political structure in the city. Here, German socialist labor unions were especially helpful in organizing Henry George clubs in German neighborhoods, where they registered voters, many of them new citizens. German socialists and labor activists also held rallies, meetings, and parades to drum up support for George. George's popularity among Germans was such that German socialists persuaded the Socialist Labor Party, a fringe party dominated by Germans, to not run its own candidate and to instead endorse George.[32]

By 1886, German immigrants made up more than 25 percent of the city's population, and those Germans who were citizens tended to support the Democratic Party, because of that party's opposition to temperance legislation and general laissez faire philosophy toward government-enforced morality. But Germans were often unhappy with New York's Democratic machine, Tammany Hall, because of its favoritism toward Irish and Irish Americans in handing out patronage jobs. German small businessmen, especially saloon keepers, grocers, and other store owners, also resented the machine's extortionist "taxes" and the predominantly Irish police force used to collect them.[33] When the local Republican Party toned down its antialcohol rhetoric and/or ran German American candidates, German Americans were more likely to vote Republican or else support reform Democrats who opposed Tammany Hall.[34] But a minority of German workers were socialists and supported alternative candidates, such as George.[35]

As George became more popular among working-class Germans, the German newspaper the *New Yorker Staats-Zeitung*, edited by the conservative Democrat Oswald Ottendorfer, began lobbying for the Tammany Hall candidate, Abram Hewitt. Although Ottendorfer had long despised Tammany, Hewitt was enough of a reformer that Ottendorfer could endorse him. William Steinway and the leading German American politician Carl Schurz also supported Hewitt.[36] The Republicans nominated another reformer, Theodore Roosevelt. In the end, Hewitt won the mayoralty, but George came in second, and while most Irish Americans remained loyal to Tammany Hall, German American voters were among George's strongest supporters, especially among those who had traditionally voted Republican.[37]

The Henry George campaign was the last significant challenge to Tammany Hall, although reform candidates would still occasionally be elected in the early twentieth century. But George's popularity was enough to cause Tammany to gradually incorporate other ethnic groups besides Irish into the machine, and more and more German American politicians began winning political office, mostly as Democrats but also as Republicans. There had been German American politicians elected to prominent office before—most notably New York City mayors William F. Havemeyer (1845–1846, 1848–1849, and 1873–1874), Daniel F. Tiemann (1858–1860), and C. Godfrey Gunther (1864–1866)—but these men all came from wealthy families and had tenuous connections to Kleindeutschland.

German American support for George also reflected the growing disconnect of elite German Americans, such as Ottendorfer, Steinway, and Schurz, from the political values of the larger German American community. Ordinary German American voters were often more concerned about the effects of social

Table 3.4
Political Districts in German Neighborhoods, 1880s, 1890s

LES Ward 10	LES Ward 13	LES Ward 17	LES Ward 11	Yorkville Ward 19 (East 40th St–86th St)	Yorkville Ward 12 (East 86th St north–East 96th St)
Assembly District 8	AD 6	AD 10, 14	AD 12	AD 20	AD 21
Senate District 6	SD 6	SD 6	SD 6	SD 8	SD 8
Congressional District 5	CD 5	CD 7	CD 7	CD 9	CD 9

policies, such as Prohibition, than the broader philosophical questions of what constituted "good government." Upper-class German Americans sought to make themselves kingmakers in the rough world of New York City politics, with varying degrees of success.

In general, German immigrants and German Americans were less active in city and state government as elected officials than other immigrant groups, particularly Irish Americans. In the 1880s and 1890s, there were usually one or two German Americans elected to the New York City Council (then alternately called the Municipal Assembly and the Board of Aldermen) each year, not surprisingly from Kleindeutschland districts. Reflecting the prevalence of saloon keeping among Germans and the importance of bars to urban politics, many German politicians were in the liquor business. But Irish Americans often represented Kleindeutschland districts because party leaders, not residents, chose the candidates.[38]

In the 1880s, Irish Americans almost always represented Assembly District (AD) 6 and 8. A naturalized German immigrant or German American would occasionally be chosen by Tammany Hall to represent predominantly German neighborhoods, particularly AD 10, 14, and 17. But these would-be politicians would be replaced by Irish Americans in the next election cycle, ensuring no opportunity for German Americans to develop power bases. In the 1890s, more German Americans began to be elected to those seats, although not consistently.[39] AD 10, which covered the heavily German Seventeenth Ward, was often represented by German Americans in the 1880s and 1890s, while AD 12 was designated by city leaders as "Jewish" and had several German Jewish representatives. AD 14 sent mainly Irish Americans to the Board of Aldermen in the 1880s and 1890s. The Yorkville districts, AD 20 and 21, were represented mainly by Anglo Americans and Knickerbocker elites, such as Theodore Roosevelt, who represented AD 21 from 1882 to 1884.[40]

A 1904 profile of a group of Lower East Side politicians described the Seventeenth Ward (AD 10 and 14) as "overwhelmingly German. Avenue A was its chief thoroughfare. It was generally known among politicians as Dutchtown, and it was the starting place of nearly all the Germans who attained celebrity in public life."[41]

AD 10 was represented by such characters as George F. Roesch and William Sohmer, and where the future congressman and governor William Sulzer began his career. Both Roman Catholic, Roesch was born in New York City to immigrant parents, while Sohmer immigrated as a child with his parents from Württemberg; his family owned the Sohmer piano making company that rivaled Steinway & Sons. Roesch represented AD 10 as a Tammany Democrat in 1883, 1885, 1888, and 1889 and then represented the Seventh Senate District from 1890–1893. He was also a Tammany leader of the Seventh District in the early 1890s. In the Lexow Committe investigation of police corruption in 1894, Roesch was accused of bribery and paying off police to protect brothels. "The greater part of his 'law business' consisted of acting as a mediator between houses of prostitution, their 'girls,' and the police," reformers alleged.[42]

The German-born saloon keeper Philip "Foul-Mouthed Phil" Wissig represented AD 8 in 1888, 1890, and 1892. His saloon at 74 Stanton Street was called "one of the lowest groggeries on the east side" by reformers. But Wissig respected and advocated on behalf of his working-class constituents. Of his legislative record it was said: "Whenever a strike came up he favored it; when the lobby wanted a worker he was always on hand. A saloon-keeper himself, he was naturally active in protecting their interests."[43] Wissig also wrote legislation that regulated the type of manufacturing that could be done in tenement houses, a progressive law generally opposed by Tammany Hall.[44]

Another saloon keeper, Jacob Kunzenman, was elected to represent the AD 14 in 1885 as an anti-Tammany Democrat Kunzenman, who was known as "Jakey Biff," "maintained a saloon on First avenue for many years, and it was a headquarters for his Seventeenth Ward followers. He was accustomed, when he ran for an office, and he ran nearly every year, to 'make his campaign on a shoestring,' as it is called."[45]

Kunzenman's method of campaigning was described as the following:

He would leave his saloon at 7 o'clock in the evening, taking with him whatever money there was in the cash drawer, and would start out to see his constituents. About 8 o'clock he would return and denude the cash drawer of whatever had been taken in during his absence, and would continue this process, at intervals, until midnight.

At 1 o'clock, the hour of closing, he would count what remained, which was usually the receipts between 12 and 1, and on one occasion was heard to remark:

"This saloon business is not what it is cracked up to be. Forty-five cents for a day's business! I could make more money pushing a handcart."[46]

In the 1880s, a German neighborhood developed on the west side in Chelsea, where the Prussian immigrant John P. Windolph had his Utah House Hotel at 28th Street and Eighth Avenue. A Civil War Union Army veteran, Windolph was active in local Republican Party politics and was first elected to the Board of Aldermen in 1885 and 1886 to represent AD 13 and then in 1893 to represent AD 15. He also served as vice president of the Board of Aldermen in 1894.[47]

Roesch, Wissig, and Kunzenman came from and represented Kleindeutschland's working class, but upper-class Germans also served in city and state government. The German Jewish lawyer Randolph Guggenheimer entered politics in the 1890s and served as the president of the city's Board of Aldermen from 1898 to 1901. He also served as school commissioner for three terms.[48] Another German Jewish immigrant, the Palatinate-born Isidor Straus—who, with his brother Nathan, owned Macy's department store—was elected as a reform Democrat to Congress in 1894 and represented AD 15, which encompassed the south Bronx. After a two-year interval, the seat was held by the brewer Jacob Ruppert Jr., who was elected as a Tammany Democrat. German immigrants also held a variety of high and low offices in Brooklyn, including Frederick A. Schroeder, a German cigar maker from Trier who was the Republican mayor of Brooklyn from 1876 to 1877 and who sat in the state senate in 1880.

Several German immigrants held appointed federal office in the 1880s, especially during the Grover Cleveland administrations. Cleveland was personally and politically close to the *New Yorker Staats-Zeitung* publisher Oswald Ottendorfer and piano manufacturer William Steinway, who had hired Cleveland as a young attorney to handle his mother-in-law's estate after she died in 1869. Cleveland, in turn, appointed the Bavarian-born Democrat and future New York State Supreme Court judge Leonard A. Giegerich internal revenue collector for New York in 1887 and the Republican Edward Grosse to the same position in 1894. The Republican Ferdinand Eidman, a Civil War veteran from Hesse, was appointed internal revenue collector by President Benjamin Harrison and then reappointed by William McKinley in 1897.[49] Anton (or Anthony) Eickhoff was another German-born (in Lippstadt, North Rhine-Westphalia) politician who was elected and appointed to a wide variety of positions, ranging from congressman, U.S. Treasury auditor, and New York City fire commissioner and was active in conservative, anti–Tammany Hall reform politics.[50]

In the early 1890s, middle- to upper-middle-class German American anti-Tammany Democrats and Republicans organized the German American Reform Union (GARU), which, by 1894, had more than 25,000 members and organizations in twenty assembly districts, mostly German, but also in those parts of the Lower East Side that were becoming predominantly eastern European Jewish. Key leaders of the union were Carl Schurz, Oswald Ottendorfer, the banker Louis Windmüller, the banker James Speyer, and the shipping agent Gustav H. Schwab; Ottendorfer became the group's president in 1894. Through the GARU, these upper-middle-class German American men became power brokers in both the Democratic and Republican Parties due to their willingness to form coalitions with whichever factions appeared more likely to defeat Tammany Hall candidates.[51]

Yet the union was plagued and divided by partisan politics, with many members, such as Ottendorfer, being longtime Democrats, while only a few leaders, such as Schurz and Schwab, were Republicans. By the fall of 1894, the GARU had split into Ottendorfer and Schwab factions. To avoid being "captured" by Republican Party machine politicians, Democratic members insisted that the organization focus only on municipal politics, and the Union was particularly active in the city election of November 1894, when reformers of all ethnicities were particularly mobilized by the findings of the antipolice corruption Lexow Committee, which was headed by New York State Senator Clarence Lexow, the son of the immigrant journalist and 1848 revolutionary Rudolph Lexow. But even here, Democratic members were disappointed when the Republican William L. Strong was chosen to be the "reform" candidate over the Germans' preferred candidate, the Lexow Committee chief counsel John W. Goff, an Irish-born anti-Tammany Democrat. An outraged Ottendorfer called Strong a "nonentity" in reform circles and declared in the *New Yorker Staats-Zeitung* that "to place Strong at the head of a reform ticket is, we repeat, ridiculous, if it is not infamous." In retaliation, Schwab threatened to quit the GARU, and Strong declared he would quit the race without the Germans' support.[52]

In a desperate attempt to keep German Democratic support, Tammany Hall nominated Macy's owner Nathan Straus to be its candidate for mayor, but Straus withdrew, after his friends threatened to socially shun him. Tammany turned to the former mayor Hugh J. Grant, who had served as mayor from 1889 to 1892.[53] Ultimately, Strong was elected by a large margin and appointed several reformers to important city offices, including Theodore Roosevelt, who was made police commissioner in 1895.[54] After the November 1894 election, a small number of upper-middle-class German American activists tried to maintain a cross-ethnic coalition with Anglo American reformers in the mid- to late 1890s, especially around the issue of police reform, but failed to draw the interest or support of the larger German community, which was much more concerned about Prohibition.[55]

German American politicians held a wide variety of positions on political questions, but the one issue that united Tammany members and reformers was alcohol control: Germans were uniformly against the city's laws against alcohol sales on Sundays, regardless of socioeconomic class status or occupational background. One example of this was the Austrian-born reform Democrat and German Free School principal Otto Kempner, who was elected to represent the Greenwich Village AD 7 in 1893 on a "liberal Sunday" platform. It was said, "He is known among the Germans of New York city as a thoughtful and impressive speaker, and was selected by them last year to appear before the excise committee of the assembly to plead for a liberal excise law."[56] In the mid-1890s Kempner organized the United Societies for Liberal Sunday Laws when New York City officials began cracking down on Sunday drinking.[57]

Joseph Koch, one of the few Germans (or Jews) to be elected to the New York State Senate, represented the Tenth Senate District as first an anti-Tammany Democrat and then a member of Tammany Hall. "As he had a considerable German following," the Tammany mayor Grant appointed him an excise commissioner in 1889 and then a police justice in 1893, where Koch allegedly "voted for the licensing of saloons near schools and churches and in purely residential neighborhoods, without regard to the protests of school trustees, clergymen, and property owners."[58] In May 1890, while he was excise commissioner, Koch was indicted by a grand jury for "willful neglect of duty" for refusing to revoke the license of a German saloon keeper named Scheuplein who had violated the election law by selling alcohol on Election Day. After several legal battles, Koch was found guilty but convinced the Tammany leader State Senator George Plunkitt to push through a law that amended the excise law and saved Koch from punishment.[59]

Germans New Yorkers overcame their traditional political divisions in 1895 when newly appointed police commissioner Theodore Roosevelt decided to enforce the excise laws regarding alcohol sales on Sundays. Roosevelt declared, "My position is a simple one. There is an excise law on the statute books and I am going to see that the police enforce it. It makes no difference what public sentiment may be. I am not dealing with sentiment, but with the laws as they stand."[60]

Germans—who saw nothing immoral in spending time in a beer garden on a Sunday with family and friends and wanted city leaders to focus on police corruption—were offended. Even New York County sheriff Edward Tamsen, a Hamburg native and book publisher, opposed Roosevelt's new strictness, declaring at a meeting of the GARU in September 1895: "You cannot argue with a Dutchman when it comes to his beer. They must have it." Edward Grosse, a German newspaper publisher and internal revenue collector for the Cleveland administration, wrote a resolution adopted by the GARU demanding "a change in a law that is puritanical, that is a mockery of personal freedom, and is degrading the metropolis of the United States to the level of a bigoted New-England hamlet."[61]

FIG. 3.2 Charles Jay Taylor, *A Rational Law, or—Tammany*, *Puck* 37, no. 956 (July 3, 1895): cover.

Mayor Strong attempted to straddle the political divide by saying that he personally favored allowing the sale of beer on Sundays, but the law had to be enforced as it was written. Although the mayor praised the "morality" of the "quiet German beer garden," he insisted that the solution was a new law, not laxer enforcement.[62] Germans, especially Tammany opponents, felt betrayed.[63]

Although Roosevelt and his police did keep most of the saloons closed on Sundays in the summer of 1895, German Americans were serious about their intention to elect politicians who would change the excise law to allow for a "local option," meaning that each community could decide what the laws regarding alcohol should be. The United Societies for Liberal Sunday Laws organized a parade on September 25, 1895, in which about 30,000 people marched in protest of the excise law and the stricter enforcement of it; Roosevelt observed the parade from a stand across from the Aschenbroedel Verein building on East 86th Street.[64] That November, German American voters angered by Roosevelt's closing of the saloons voted for Tammany Democratic candidates in large numbers, whereas the year before, they had supported Strong and anti-Tammany candidates.[65] A small number of wealthy German American Protestants and Jews active in charity organizations helped create the political reform lobby group, the Citizens' Union in 1896, but the organization failed to attract the support of most German American voters because of its support for alcohol prohibition.[66]

Despite repeated attempts, Germans and German Americans did not achieve their main political goal, which was local control over alcohol laws. Instead, the state legislature passed the Raines Law in January 1896, which kept the prohibition of the sale of alcohol on Sundays but exempted hotels serving guests as part of a meal. New York saloons had long provided free food to customers who bought drinks, and so under the Raines Law, saloon keepers began converting storage space into bedrooms, applying for a hotel license, and renting the rooms to prostitutes.[67] Germans, who had long objected to Anglo Americans' puritanism about men and women drinking together, were outraged at the presence of prostitution in bars. The family-friendly atmosphere of the Lokal (and the beer garden) was seriously threatened by "Raines hotels."

By 1897, German American Reform Union leaders fretted that ordinary voters had been alienated from political reform movements by Roosevelt's perceived puritanism. GARU secretary Carl. A. Lewenstein declared: "I will say candidly that our people are disgusted with reform. They hate the very word. They feel, exactly as Mr. Ottendorfer says, that government by the reformers has been a fiasco. Several times there has been an effort within the organization to cut the word reform out of our title, because the leaders say the Germans are so sick of reform they won't join us on account of the name."[68]

This frustration with reformers' support for temperance or alcohol prohibition caused many Germans to vote for the Tammany Hall candidate, New York chief justice Robert Anderson Van Wyck, over the Citizens' Union reform candidate, Brooklyn reform mayor and Columbia University president Seth Low, in the November 1897 mayoral race.[69]

During Van Wyck's mayoralty, New York City consolidated with Brooklyn, Queens, and Staten Island in 1898 to form the existing five boroughs of New York City. Mayor Van Wyck also rolled back several of the reforms initiated during Strong's term before it was revealed that the mayor owned shares in an ice company for which he had not paid. The GARU joined again with several anti-Tammany reform groups to elect Seth Low as mayor in 1902. This time, Low received widespread German American support, despite initial anxieties that he would engage in what Germans had begun to call "Rooseveltism" (meaning Anglo American morality regarding alcohol, although Roosevelt was of Dutch heritage).[70]

The GARU reflected the political organization and maturity of the German American community by the end of the nineteenth century. Solidly middle- and upper-class GARU members saw themselves as both distinct within and central to New York City partisan politics. German Americans expected the

FIG. 3.3 Louis Dalrymple, *How Will Our German-American Vote? Puck* 48, no. 1223 (August 15, 1900): cover. (Library of Congress.)

various factions of the two main political parties to court them and appeal to their interests, which were increasingly limited to opposition to prohibition and defense of the German language in the public schools.[71] German Americans were fully integrated into the American and New York political systems by nature of their being citizens, but they did not control that system or regularly vote as a bloc, something the GARU was designed to change. In addition, while the GARU was more than willing to work with English-speaking groups and frequently held joint meetings, members at GARU meetings still demanded that German be the language of discussion and debate and only reluctantly tolerated English.[72]

Despite the Henry George campaign and the rare labor collaboration, Germans and German Americans tended to stand apart from other groups in New York City, and nothing emphasized Germans' distinctiveness as their Volksfeste. These festivals celebrated the various regional cultures in the German Empire and became huge events attended by hundreds of thousands of people in the late nineteenth and early twentieth centuries. Some of the festivals were held annually, such as the Volksfeste, the *Sängerfeste* (singing festivals), and the Turnfeste (gymnastics competitions), while others were organized to commemorate special events or anniversaries.

FIG. 3.4 Friedrich Graetz, *A Family Party—the 200th Birthday of the Healthiest of Uncle Sam's Adopted Children*, *Puck* 14, no. 343 (October 3, 1883): Centerfold.

But Germans also began holding festivals to celebrate and/or observe American holidays or individuals. So while Germans held festivals to celebrate the composers Beethoven, Wagner, and Schubert; the poets Goethe, Schiller, and Heine; and Kaiser Wilhelm I's ninetieth birthday, they also organized festivals to observe the one hundredth anniversary of the British evacuation of Manhattan (on November 26, 1883), the twentieth anniversary of the death of Abraham Lincoln (on April 15, 1885), and the victory of the United States in the Spanish American War (on August 20, 1898).[73]

In 1891, German New Yorkers finally began transcending their regional identities and organized a Deutscher Tag (German Day) to celebrate and observe the two hundredth anniversary of the founding of the Germantown settlement in what is now Philadelphia on November 9, 1683. (Pennsylvania Germans had held the first Deutscher Tag in 1883.)[74] But it would not be until 1902 that Deutscher Tag became a regular event in the New York City German social calendar.[75]

By the turn of the twentieth century, Germans and German Americans in New York were well organized and highly visible, with German organizations found at all levels of society. But these organizations became increasingly highly structured and hierarchical, as federations of Vereine were established. In 1901, the largest of these federations, the National German-American Alliance, was established. The NGAA had its headquarters in Philadelphia, although the

New York chapter had 148 organizations with a total membership of 30,000 people. Ultimately, 300 New York Vereine would join the alliance.[76]

The mission of the NGAA was "to awaken and strengthen the sense of unity among the people of German origin in America with a view to promote the useful and healthy development of the power inherent in them as a unity body for the mutual energetic promotion of such legitimate desires and interests not inconsistent with the common good of the country, and the rights and duties of good citizens; to check nativistic encroachments; to maintain and safeguard the good friendly relations existing between America and the old German fatherland."[77] Besides lobbying against alcohol prohibition, immigration restriction, and perceived threats to the German language, primarily in public schools, the alliance encouraged German immigrants to naturalize and be politically and socially active in their communities.

The NGAA also supported an academic journal, the *German American Annals*, in which German American scholars published research of varying quality about German American history. Some of the more important and most active in publishing in the German Historical Society were the Cornell University professor Albert Faust and University of Pennsylvania professor Marion Dexter Learned, the journal's editor.[78] Deeply concerned about the noticeable assimilation of German Americans, especially in the area of English-language use, these German American intellectuals and community activists began arguing for a pluralistic understanding of American society in which the preservation of the ethnic group and its language, culture, and institutional structure was defined as a societal benefit and thus should be promoted.[79]

But the NGAA did not mean that all ethnic groups and their cultures and traditions should be preserved; only German immigrants had made important enough contributions to American history and society to justify their preservation of Germanness rather than being absorbed into Anglo-American culture. And this contribution was not simply in the manual labor for building the nation's infrastructure or as military service but in the areas where materialistic Anglo Americans were seen (by Germans) as being the most lacking: in music, literature, and the arts—in effect, culture (or *Kultur*).[80] As Carl Wilhelm Schlegel wrote in the introduction of his three-volume genealogy of whom he considered to be the most important German Americans in the 1910s: "From the first to the present day, German-Americans have held a foremost position, and have, by their example in whatever line of endeavor, contributed greatly to the advancement and civilization of the various communities wherein they have established their homes, giving pre-eminence to commerce, to industry, to the arts and sciences, to education and religion—to all that is comprised in the highest civilization of the present day."[81] What went unspoken (because it was obvious to people such as Schlegel) was that other immigrant groups, especially the Irish, could not make such historical claims.

Alliance president Charles J. Hexamer, a Philadelphia engineer, emphasized this belief in the uniqueness and specialness of the contributions of German immigrants in his lobbying Congress in 1910 for the establishment of a monument in Philadelphia to the Germantown settlers of 1683: "To read the history of German immigration is to be convinced how much it has contributed to the advancement of the spiritual and economic development of this country, and to realize what it is still destined to contribute, and how the German immigrant has at all times stood by his adopted country in weal or in woe."[82] But Hexamer could also not resist a dig against English Americans' heritage, adding: "While Puritan New Englanders maltreated unfortunate Quakers who fell into their hands, and 'killed witches,' the first successful German colony, at Germantown (now the twenty-second ward of Philadelphia), in 1688 drew up a remonstrance against slavery—the first of all such protests," before he continued to iterate a long list of German contributions and successes. Sounding more petulant than proud, Hexamer insisted that Germans "deserves (sic) as much respect as the 'Pilgrim fathers.'"[83]

Since the beginning of mass emigration from German states to the United States, Kleindeutschland had been home to a small but very vocal group of writers, publishers, and artists who were highly conscious of their community's status and relationship to that of the larger, English-speaking majority and who saw themselves as leaders in promoting and defending German culture in the United States. These writers created a genre of literature written by Germans for Germans about Germans.[84] German immigrant artists, such as Joseph Keppler, Friedrich Graetz, and George Friedrich Keller, began depicting American society as pluralistic but "with one relevant and specifically German ethnic twist: Within such images the *German* immigrant was always visually marked as superior to his ethnic cousins."[85]

This cultural chauvinism of German Americans in the late nineteenth century was particularly pronounced in the German-language press and other organizations devoted to maintaining the German language. As the *New Yorker Herald* pronounced: "The German immigrants bring far more than any other people with them, excellent qualities in our country: health, good manners, common sense and besides that, much property."[86]

The GARU and the NGAA were middle-class German American organizations and reflected the successful socioeconomic mobility of the German community. As Hammack has noted, "By 1900 the region's bankers, wholesalers, and professional men were still predominantly of native American and British background, with a large minority of German origin. But those who followed semiprofessional, managerial, and clerical pursuits were as likely to be German as native American."[87]

FIG. 3.5 Joseph Keppler Jr., *Our Beloved German-American*, *Puck* 47, no. 1209 (May 9, 1900): cover . (Library of Congress.)

Nearly one-third of New York City entrepreneurs (including manufacturers, shopkeepers, and restaurant and saloon keepers) were of German heritage. A study of living standards among several different immigrant groups in the city in 1909 found that the median income for German families was the highest, at $950 per year, $100 higher than the median income of white native-born Americans.[88] These German Americans made up the bulk of the GARU and NGAA memberships.

Despite the loud insistence of NGAA members of the superior value of German immigrants to American society, most of the cultural contributions of Germans were more prosaic and reflected the working-class and peasant traditions of most German immigrants. In the early nineteenth century, common snack foods sold and eaten on New York City streets were hot corn, clams, and oysters, but by the late nineteenth century, hamburgers (initially called Hamburg steak), hot dogs (Frankfurters), pretzels (*Bretzeln*), pickles, honey-roasted nuts, and sugar-coated popcorn (later called Cracker Jack and invented by either Charles Frederick Gunther or Frederick William Rueckheim) were commonly sold from street carts as well as open-air markets, grocery stores, and delicatessens (from the German word for "fine food"). Beginning in 1867, the German baker Charles Feltman began selling "dachshunds" (hot dogs) in a roll from a food cart on Brighton Beach.[89] Frankfurters, now called hot dogs, appeared as the concession food of choice at baseball parks in the 1890s, when the Prussian immigrant and St. Louis Browns owner Chris von de Ahe began selling them, and other baseball owners, including the New York Yankees owner and brewer Jacob Ruppert Jr., quickly followed suit.

German influences on American religious cultural traditions, especially regarding Christmas and Easter, came from both high and low culture. English-speaking Americans in the eighteenth and early nineteenth centuries observed Christmas with church attendance and Bible reading, when they observed it at all; Christmas was viewed as a Catholic holiday by many American Puritans. But in the 1850s, Anglo American Protestants began to adopt the German Protestant tradition of a decorated tree at Christmas, influenced by both the British royal family's custom of having a tree and German immigrants' practice.[90] The first printed image of a Christmas tree appeared in the German immigrant and Harvard professor Hermann Bokum's Christmas gift book, *The Stranger's Gift*, in 1836.[91] The character of Santa Claus, a blending of the British Father Christmas and the Dutch Sinterklaas, was first drawn as a cheerful round person by the German immigrant illustrator Thomas Nast in 1863. This was during the same period that Nast was developing other iconic images for American culture: the donkey and elephant as symbols for the Democratic and Republican Parties, the tiger as the symbol of Tammany Hall, and "Columbia" and "Uncle Sam."[92] By the late nineteenth century, celebrating Christmas with such traditions as a decorated tree, images and stories about Santa Claus, hanging stockings, and gift giving had become nearly universal among American Christians, regardless of their ethnic background.

The traditions of the Easter Bunny (Osterhase) and of decorating and hiding eggs were also brought to the United States by German immigrants. Again, as with Christmas, English-speaking Puritan traditions of church attendance and Bible reading gave way to German and Central European traditions.[93] These were both popularized and often commercialized by German immigrant entrepreneurs, especially in the candy and printing industries.

And despite the persistence of Sunday blue laws, the general trend, especially in cities, was to violate rather than observe prohibitions on alcohol consumption, theater attendance, and other forms of recreation with friends and family on the Sabbath.[94] Between 1902 and 1919, baseball (and other sport playing and watching) on Sundays was legalized in Chicago, St. Louis, Cincinnati (all cities with large German communities), and finally New York City in 1919.[95] Some German American cultural leaders might have considered baseball "low class" and thus an "American" form of culture, but German immigrants and German Americans had been eager participants and attendees of the game since the beginnings of baseball before the Civil War.[96]

14853. Crowds awaiting Prince Henry at the pier, New York.

FIG. 3.6 *Crowds Awaiting Prince Henry at the Pier, New York,*
B. W. Kilburn Co. (Littleton, N.H.), February 22, 1902. (Library
of Congress.)

By the late nineteenth century, German ideas about education, including
early childhood education, differentiated grades, the high school, and physical
and vocational education, had also all been adopted in the New York City
schools.[97]

In late February–March 1902, the United States hosted the visit of Prince
Henry of Prussia, the younger brother of Kaiser Wilhelm II. The media and
public attention paid to the visit reflected German Americans' status as a fully
"arrived" immigrant group in American society. But the visit also revealed German Americans' position in New York City society, which was still a minority
one. Although German Americans were actively involved in planning the visit,
they still had to share time with the prince with New York's Anglo-Dutch elite,
and non-German socialites predominated as attendees at events featuring the
prince.

Those Germans and German Americans chosen to help organize the visit
were the clear leaders of the community and recognized as such by both Germans and non-Germans: Carl Schurz, the former Republican senator from
Missouri; Gustav H. Schwab and Hermann Oelrichs, chief ticket agents for
the North German Lloyd steamship company; Emil L. Boas, chief ticket agent

for the Hamburg-America steamship company; Herman Ridder, now the publisher of the *New Yorker Staats-Zeitung*; and Oscar S. Straus, Macy's department store owner. These German business leaders, along with others in New York City government and the chamber of commerce, divided themselves into several committees responsible for organizing aspects of the visit, overseen by a special Prince Henry General Committee, run out of Mayor Low's office.[98]

During his time in New York City, Henry attended a couple of events that highlighted the high status and socioeconomic success of the city's German community. The most important was a banquet hosted by the Deutsche Gesellschaft at the Waldorf-Astoria Hotel on March 8 in honor of Carl Schurz (located on the site of the German immigrant and millionaire John Jacob Astor's mansion and owned by the Astor family). Unlike other social functions at which Anglo Americans predominated or were the hosts, at this banquet, most of the attendees were German or German American, and the prince spoke in German, knowing that most of the more than fifteen hundred attendees would understand him. (Several other speeches were given in English.) The few non-German Americans in attendance included Mayor Low, Columbia University president Nicholas Murray Butler, American admiral Robley D. Evans, and Assistant Secretary of State David J. Hill.[99]

Another important event that highlighted Germans' cultural contributions to the city and the country was the night at the opera on February 25. Although the Metropolitan Opera had long abandoned performing opera only in German (as it had in the early 1880s), opera and classical music in general were seen as an important gift of German culture to the United States, and German New Yorkers had long seen themselves as being at the forefront of promoting high European (especially German) culture in the United States. At the time of the visit, the principal conductor of the opera was Walter Damrosch, the son of the famous immigrant conductor Leopold Damrosch, and several of the principal singers were also German. In the spirit of ecumenicalism, Damrosch shared the baton with two other conductors, and the program included Italian and French opera as well as German opera (*die Lohengrin, Carmen, Aida, Tannhauser, La Traviata*, and *Le Cid*).[100]

The next evening, February 26, the prince was serenaded by a torchlight parade of members of 320 German Vereine outside of the Arion clubhouse and then attended a banquet for 1,100 journalists hosted by the *New Yorker Staats-Zeitung* at the Waldorf-Astoria. The occasion of the prince's visit was deemed important enough for Roman Catholic archbishop Michael A. Corrigan to give a special dispensation to Catholics attending the editors' dinner to eat meat on what was a Lenten fast day. Yet an Episcopal church bishop, Henry C. Potter, not a Lutheran minister, said the grace for the dinner.[101] The prince was also given "the freedom of the city," a New York City honor that not even Edward, Prince of Wales, received on his visit in 1860.[102]

Although Germans took the lead in organizing many of the events, they were careful to assert their dual national identities, not simply their German one. When the parade grand marshall, Kriegerbund president Richard Muel-ler, announced that only German songs were to be played by the marching bands, the Austrian immigrant and former immigration commissioner Joseph H. Senner protested, demanding that American songs, such as "Yan-kee Doodle," also be played. A compromise was made in which both Ameri-can and German songs were performed.[103]

But the visit also emphasized the fact that as successful as German immi-grants had been, they were still not members of the city's social elite. Again and again, the Vanderbilts, the Morgans, and other wealthy Anglo Americans or Dutch Americans dominated events attended by the prince. Although New York was home to several successful and prominent German businessmen, the few of these immigrant entrepreneurs who met with the prince at a special lun-cheon on February 26 at the upscale restaurant Sherry's were outnumbered by the many American "captains of industry." Rather, the primary guests of the meal were the bankers J. P. Morgan, George F. Baker, James Stillman, and Alex-ander E. Orr; the railroad magnates William J. Vanderbilt, E. H. Harriman, and Edward D. Adams; the wholesale dry goods store owner John Claflin; the steel magnates E. H. Gary and Charles M. Schwab; the oil magnates John D. and William Rockefeller; and the tobacco magnate James B. Duke. The inven-tors Alexander Graham Bell, Thomas A. Edison, and Nikola Tesla also attended. Henry O. Havemeyer, Gustav W. Tietjens, Emil Boas, Gustav H. Schwab, Adolphus Busch, Frederick Pabst, W. A. Roebling, and Friedrich Weynhäuser were the few Germans in attendance.[104]

A dinner hosted by Mrs. Cornelius (Grace Graham Wilson) Vanderbilt Jr. on March 9 was described as an opportunity for the prince to be "entertained at dinner by some representative American family."[105] Although Vanderbilt had met the prince prior to her marriage (while yachting with Mr. and Mrs. Rob-ert Goetlet), the description of the Vanderbilts as a "representative American family" was comical, and the other guests were also members of the city's Knick-erbocker elite. The only Germans in attendance were members of the prince's retinue and the German ambassador to the United States, Theodore von Hol-leben. There were several wealthy German Americans, children or grandchil-dren of German immigrants, who could have been described as "American" (most notably the Astors), but instead that honor was given to a family of Dutch heritage.

But despite these snubs, Prince Henry's visit helped stimulate more outward displays of German American patriotism. New York City's Deutscher Tag cele-brations in October 1902 were much larger than in previous years. The newly organized National German-American Alliance organized a huge event at Madison Square Garden at which the German American scholar and booster

Rudolf Cronau and NGAA president Charles J. Hexamer spoke (in English) and emphasized the contributions of Germans to American history: the revolution and the Civil War, the fight against slavery, cultural contributions like Christmas and Easter, and scientific and educational contributions.[106]

By 1902, German immigrants and German Americans in New York City had moved out of the Lower East Side and had created new German neighborhoods in Yorkville, Brooklyn, and Queens, making German culture and the city's German community even more visible to non-German New Yorkers. German New Yorkers were active, albeit usually divided, in city politics, except when the question of alcohol control was raised, when the community came together. Class and religious divisions also continued to exist and strengthened as more German Americans became middle-class, while German Jews sought to define themselves as both Jewish Americans and German Americans in contrast to the growing number of eastern European Jews. During the celebrations held for Prince Henry's visit, Germans showed themselves to be both fully American and comfortably German. Whether German Americans could convince other Americans to embrace dual ethnic identities and a pluralistic understanding of American society remained unclear in the early twentieth century.

4

Disappearing
and Remembering

● ●

The June 15, 1904,
General Slocum disaster

On June 15, 1904, New York City suffered its greatest loss of life until September 11, 2001, when 1,021 people died when the *General Slocum* steamboat caught fire and sank in the East River near Hell Gate. When the disaster happened, city attention zeroed in on Kleindeutschland, because most of the victims were German immigrants living in the neighborhood.

But within a decade, New Yorkers' memories of the accident began to fade, replaced by a myth: the *General Slocum* disaster had "destroyed" Kleindeutschland and caused Germans to leave the neighborhood, quietly disappearing in their collective grief. By 1934, it was possible for a popular Hollywood film, *Manhattan Melodrama*, which starred Clark Gable and William Powell as two men who survived the *General Slocum* accident as boys, to completely deny the German heritage of the victims.[1]

When the *General Slocum* burned, New York City's German community had long been defined more by its institutions than its geographic location, and German New Yorkers had recreated Kleindeutschland all over the city. What was distinctive about the victims and survivors of the *General Slocum* accident was that they were more often German-born than second- or third-generation German American, and they were more likely to remain in Kleindeutschland despite the neighborhood's demographic changes. As devastating as the *General Slocum* disaster was for the families of its victims, that devastation did not apply to New York City's German community as a whole.

The St. Mark's Evangelical Lutheran Church annual picnic to celebrate the end of the Sunday school year was scheduled for June 15, a Wednesday, and was to be held at Locust Grove near Oyster Bay on Long Island. In the 1840s–1880s, the most popular place for Germans to hold such a picnic was at the Elysian Fields in Hoboken or Jones's Wood on the Upper East Side. But by 1904, both of these open spaces had been developed, so German New Yorkers sought new spaces farther afield. When it first instituted its Sunday school picnic in 1887, St. Mark's chose Locust Grove. To get to and from Long Island, the church rented a steam-powered paddleboat, the *General Slocum*, and the river journey was expected to be half of the fun of the outing, a chance to get out on the river and see a different view of the city.

The *General Slocum* was a steam-powered paddlewheel boat, built in 1891, with the capacity to carry 2,500 people on its three decks—the main, promenade, and hurricane. The boat had a kitchen, a bar, 10,000 square feet of open space on its upper hurricane deck, and extensive, comfortable seating in two "saloons," lounge spaces located on the middle promenade and lower main decks. The veteran sailor William Van Schaick had been the captain since the *General Slocum*'s first voyage.

Going to a picnic such as the St. Mark's Sunday school excursion or any other large Verein event was not a casual, drop-in affair; one needed to buy tickets, in this case, for 50 cents each, just as one would to go to the theater or a baseball game. Although St. Mark's congregation numbered in the hundreds, ticket sales would not be enough to pay for the charter (which cost $350) plus a band to play music during the voyage and at the picnic.

As was common among German churches and Vereine seeking to raise money for events, the excursion committee chair, thirty-four-year-old Mary Abendschein, produced a souvenir program of the picnic and sold advertising and tickets to local businesses. The program provided useful information about the church and the event (prices for hot dogs, potato salad, sandwiches, ice cream, milk, coffee, and cake noted on the first page) along with a music program, song lyrics, jokes, and witty anecdotes, printed in both German and English. Donors and advertisers were acknowledged prominently. More than one hundred businesses bought advertising to show support for the church and to remind picnic goers that while many German businesses had left the area, some were still in the old neighborhood.[2] Among the advertisers were Adickes Fine Confectionary and Ice Cream Saloon at 49 Avenue A between 3rd and 4th Streets. The Adickes family—German-born Ernst; his wife, Annie; and their five children—lived above the store with his wife's mother, Margaret Stüve, and were members of the church.[3]

Attending such an event as the St. Mark's annual picnic also meant dressing up. Although the phrase "summer picnic" now implies casual dress, in the nineteenth and early twentieth centuries, attending a church event in anything other than one's Sunday best was seen as disrespectful. The few men who went wore suits and ties, while women and girls wore their Sunday dresses and brought out treasured pieces of jewelry; boys wore junior suits as well. Many baths had been taken on the Tuesday evening before the big day, and several haircuts had no doubt also been secured.

According to the program, the "commodious steamer, General Slocum," would leave the East Third Street Pier at 8:45 A.M., but in actuality, the boat did not depart until about 9:40 A.M., because the Rev. George C. F. Haas kept delaying the sailing to allow latecomers to catch the boat. As the head of the church, Haas stood at the gangplank to personally welcome each guest on board. His wife, Anna; thirteen-year-old daughter, Gertrude; thirty-five-year-old sister, Emma; his mother-in-law, Emma Hansen; his wife's sister, Sophia Tetamore, and her three-year-old son, Herbert, were also on board. His nineteen-year-old son, George Jr., stayed at home.

Since the excursion was a church event, most of the St. Mark's leadership was in attendance: the superintendents of both the German and English Sunday schools, most of the church elders, members of the board of trustees, and nearly all of the Sunday school teachers. The Sunday school treasurer and church elder William Pullman had a check ready for $350 to the Knickerbocker Steamboat Company, the owner of the *General Slocum*.

As a major church event, many families attended and invited extended relatives and neighbors and friends to join them on the excursion. A total of 622 families were on board the *General Slocum* that Wednesday. In addition, the picnic was an opportunity for people who had left the old neighborhood for Yorkville, Harlem, Brooklyn, or the Bronx to return to see old neighbors and friends.

The bartender Paul Liebenow was able to get off from work at the Pabst brewery's restaurant, Pabst Harlem, on West 125th Street, to attend with his wife, Anna, and their three daughters, six-year-old Helen, three-year-old Anna, and six-month-old Adella. The Liebenows were joined by Paul Liebenow's unmarried sister, Martha Liebenow; sister and brother-in-law Anne and Frank Weber; and their two children, eleven-year-old Emma and seven-year-old Frank Jr., who lived at 404 East 5th Street, around the corner from St. Mark's.

For the eighteen members of the Kassebaum, Torniport, and Schnude families, who lived next door to one another on Guernsey Avenue in Greenpoint, Brooklyn, the picnic was an opportunity to see friends from the church. Although the Schnude family had moved to Brooklyn, they were still very active in the church: Henry Schnude was head deacon and a Sunday school superintendent and was responsible for collecting tickets and selling lemonade at the picnic. The Schnudes invited their widowed neighbor, Clara Roberts, and her thirteen-year-old daughter, Blanche, to join them.

The desire to see former neighbors was the same for John and Catherine Muth, who lived with their four children on 146th Street in the Bronx around the corner from Catherine's mother, Wilhelmina Hessel, and Catherine's sister and brother-in-law Christina and Edward Schnitzler and their five-year-old daughter, Catherine. The six Muths, Hessel, Christina and Catherine Schnitzler, and former neighbors Caroline and Edward Ochse, twelve-year-old Minnie Christ, and two other children made up a party of fourteen who went on the excursion.[4]

In many cases, only mothers and children were able to go, because Wednesday was a weekday and most men could not get off from work. The Hungarian cabinetmaker Joseph Justh could not go but sent his wife, Emilia, their four daughters, and one son. The tailor Magnus Hartung also could not go, but his wife, Louisa, and their five children could. The German-born waiter Joseph Vollmer sent his wife, Mary, and three children, sixteen-year-old Joseph, nine-year-old Auguste, and six-year-old Marie, without him.[5]

A few families were prosperous enough to have servants to help them with their children. The saloon keeper Peter Fickbohm's wife, Maria, brought their serving girl, Kate Cibijsky, with them to help with the Fickbohm's three children, as did Frances Iden, who brought her Czech-born servant, Mary Zabilansky, to help with her five children. Emma Fischer brought her Hungarian-born servant, Barbara Hegyi, to help with the Fischer's two daughters, six-year-old Edna and four-year-old Lillie.[6]

But most young mothers did what Johanna Horway did: she asked her mother, Christina Beck, to come along to help Johanna with her two young children, five-year-old Della and one-year-old Carl. Caroline Gettler, who lived next door to her daughter and son-in-law Mollie and Valentine Braun and their three children at 233 5th Street, came to help with Mollie's children.

Catherine Diamond could not go on the trip, so her mother, the Irish-born Katherine Birmingham, who lived with Diamond and her family in Flushing, escorted seven-year-old May and three-year-old Francis.

Emelia Richter, a widow with seven children, ages eight to twenty-one, who lived at 404 6th Street, had to manage without servants or parental help. She bought tickets for herself and six of her children; her oldest son, fifteen-year-old William, went to work as a clerk at a commission house.

There were also several groups of young friends on the *General Slocum*, teenagers making up a party, and older siblings escorting younger ones because their parents had to work. Sixteen-year-old Lillie Stiel accompanied her three brothers, fourteen-year-old George, twelve-year-old Emil, and six-year-old Frederick, from their home on First Avenue, while her widower father went to work as a butcher. Fifteen-year-old Matilda Merseles, sixteen-year-old Ellen

Breden, and seventeen-year-old Gustav Lutz went together, Ellen and Matilda coming from Brooklyn. Thirteen-year-old Leone Goetz and her ten-year-old friend and neighbor Wanda von Rekowski went together without a parental escort.

Because of the nature of the event, almost everyone on the *General Slocum* was a member of St. Mark's Lutheran Church, but not all. The DeLuccia and Galewski families—Italian-born Lena DeLuccia and her four children and Russian-born Flora Galewski and her two children—lived behind the church at 54 7th Street and so, of course, had heard about the picnic. Through the generosity of Mary Abendschein, the two families were able to get tickets. Another neighbor in the building, twenty-two year old Romanian-born Sophia Siegel, also came along. The Gallagher family—Veronica and her three children, eleven-year-old Catherine, nine-year-old Walter, and baby Agnes—were Catholic but had been given tickets by a grocer who was a member of the church. At least four children of Russian Jewish immigrants who lived in the neighborhood also went on the excursion.

Mary Abendschein had hired George Maurer's band to play during the outing, and Maurer, who lived a few blocks from the church at 421 East 9th Street, brought his wife, Margaret, and their two children, fourteen-year-old Matilda and twelve-year-old Clara, along. The band members August Schneider and Julius Woll also brought their wives and daughters with them. To help the adults maintain a degree of order and decorum, the church had hired New York Police Department officers Albert T. Van Tassel and Charles Kelk of the River and Harbor Division.

At 9:40 A.M., on a beautiful sunny morning, the *General Slocum* finally set sail. People chatted with friends and neighbors and listened to Maurer's band, which started playing a popular Lutheran hymn, "Ein Feste Burg Ist Unser Gott" ("A Mighty Fortress Is Our God"). Parents watched over more than sixty-five babies and toddlers, while children explored the boat before hurrying to the lower deck for ice cream and sodas. The boat sailed past Blackwell's (now Roosevelt) Island across from 86th Street and was heading toward Randalls and Wards Islands and Hell Gate, where it would go past Rikers Island, College Point and Throgs Neck, Kings Point and Sands Point, and Hempstead Bay before sailing up to Oyster Bay.

By 9:56 A.M., twelve-year-old Frank Prawdzicky noticed smoke and flames coming from the stairwell leading from the lamp room below the main deck. He notified the captain. But Van Schaick, suspecting a prank, ordered the boy to "get the hell out of here and mind your own business!"[7]

After finally confirming that the ship was indeed on fire, Van Schaick made the fatal decision to sail the *General Slocum* toward North Brother Island, one mile upriver near the Bronx versus running the boat aground on Sunken Meadow Island beyond Hell Gate or on the Bronx or Queens waterfronts. The decision to keep sailing into the wind caused the flames to spread further, fueled by the *General Slocum*'s dry, lacquered wood. The twenty-two-member crew, which had never performed a fire drill in the thirteen-year history of the boat, alternately abandoned ship or futilely fought the flames with rotted hoses that could not handle the water pressure.

The alarm of "Fire!" created a stampede among the passengers trying to escape the flames and find life jackets, 2,500 of which were suspended from the boat's ceilings, more than eight feet from the floor. Once people pulled down clusters of jackets, they discovered that the cork inside the life preservers had disintegrated, and the canvas covering ripped like paper. The six lifeboats and four life rafts on the Hurricane deck had long been wired into place and could not be released. The best efforts of Rev. Haas and the policemen to calm people were ineffective. Panicked passengers, most of whom could not swim, confronted the choice of jumping overboard or being burned alive. People trapped on the lower decks were not given a choice.[8]

As the burning ship sailed up the East River, the rescue effort began, with tugboats and other small craft rushing toward the *General Slocum* to get close enough to allow passengers to jump onto their decks but not so close as to catch fire themselves. Several police officers on both the Manhattan and Bronx sides of the East River saw the fire, called the fire department, and commandeered boats to try to save people. Doctors, nurses, and other staff on North Brother Island, where the city had its contagious ward hospital ("Typhoid Mary" was its most famous patient), ran to the shore, swam out, and began dragging people out of the water and performing resuscitation efforts. Those who could not swim formed a human chain into the river to pass passengers to the shore. Nurse Nellie O'Donnell could not swim but nonetheless dog-paddled into the river, ultimately rescuing ten people. The patient Mary McCann, a seventeen-year-old immigrant from Ireland who had been sent from Ellis Island to North Brother Island to recover from scarlet fever, saved five people, despite being weak from her illness. Some passengers even rescued other people once they had reached shore. After finding the drowned bodies of his mother and grandmother on the beach of North Brother Island, eighteen-year-old Charles Schwartz joined the rescue effort and was credited with saving twenty-two people by swimming out to drowning people and pulling them into a small boat manned by another rescuer.

The *General Slocum* finally ran aground on North Brother Island around 10:25 A.M. and proceeded to burn down to the waterline, barely thirty minutes after the fire had first been discovered. By noon, the remains of the *General Slocum* sank about 250 feet from shore and burned out, allowing rescuers to begin to search the wreckage for survivors and bodies.

New York City mayor George B. McClellan Jr.; the police, fire, and health commissioners; and the coroners Gustav Scholer of Manhattan and William

FIG. 4.1 *The Mass of Burned Timbers and Ruined Metal, Showing Broken Paddle Wheels S[h]a[f]t. General Slocum Disaster, New York Harbor, June 15, 1904*, H. C. White Co. (North Bennington, VT), August 13, 1904. (Library of Congress.)

O'Gorman of the Bronx were notified, as were medical personnel from the city's hospitals. Journalists began converging on the uptown piers to find boats to get to North Brother Island.

Within an hour of the *General Slocum* sinking, the first newspaper special editions were out, and word of the fire quickly spread to Kleindeutschland. People converged on St. Mark's Church, where only George Haas Jr. was at home at the rectory next door. When thirteen-year-old Edward Matzerath of 330 East 6th Street arrived home with bruises and burned clothing, he confirmed the rumors that had begun to spread through the neighborhood. Hundreds of men abandoned their stores and workshops to go uptown to search northern Manhattan and Bronx hospitals and police stations for loved ones.

By late afternoon, several thousand people were crowding in front of the Alexander Avenue police station in the Bronx, as well as on the piers near

138th Street, where bodies were being brought to Manhattan morgues for identification. By seven P.M., the city had established a temporary morgue downtown on a city-owned pier shed at the end of East 26th Street, and thousands of people converged there to search for relatives. A huge crowd also gathered at the East 8th Street elevated train station, where anyone coming downtown from the Bronx would disembark to go to the Lower East Side, as well as at St. Mark's, where church members began keeping records of victims and survivors. For the rest of that night and the week, ambulances brought injured people released from hospitals to their homes, and hearses transported identified bodies to funeral homes and then to their families' homes for funerals. Rev. Haas, who suffered severe burns to his hands and face, was released from Lincoln Hospital and sent home around six P.M. Wednesday evening. After sleeping for about three hours, Haas was told that his wife was dead and his daughter, mother-in-law, sister-in-law, and nephew were all missing. (All had died.) Only his sister, Emma, had survived (with injuries).

In the following days, it would be discovered that the death toll, thought to be a shocking one hundred persons or more, was actually more than one thousand people. As the city coroners struggled to get bodies recovered and identified, New York police inspector Max Schmittberger sent one hundred German-speaking officers to Kleindeutschland to do a house-to-house canvass of the neighborhood to sort out survivors from victims.[9] The *New York Times* did its own survey of the neighborhood and uncovered dozens more names of victims.[10] But even today, it is not known exactly how many people were on the *General Slocum* on June 15.

Over the course of the next several days, the bodies of dozens of young children wearing life preservers were recovered from the East River. The rotted cork inside had become like wet earth inside the fabric and had dragged the wearers down. Other life preservers were found to have iron bars inside, added to ensure that the vests were of a required weight.[11] New York—nor any other American city—had never suffered such a loss of life from what was increasingly starting to look like a preventable accident.

Beginning on Friday, June 17, and continuing for more than a week, funerals were held in hundreds of homes in New York City. This was both in accordance with Victorian funeral rituals as well as the practical realization that churches, funeral homes, and meeting halls could not accommodate the high demand. The Lutheran church was so overwhelmed by the demand for pastoral care that more than one hundred ministers, priests, and rabbis from the city's other faiths stepped in to perform funeral services.[12]

Since nearly all of the victims were Lutheran, Christian burial according to that faith was important to family members, but not often possible; the same went for German- versus English-language services. Whichever minister or priest was available performed the funeral. The comfort of having a minister who was known to the family and who had known the deceased was denied to many families. The sheer number of dead needing burial also meant that these funeral rites were abbreviated, running for about fifteen minutes and with no eulogy. Ministers performed dozens of such services in a day, going from tenement house to tenement house in the neighborhood.[13] The death of Rev. Edward Frederick Moldehnke of St. Peter's Lutheran Church on 46th Street and Lexington Avenue, who died a week after the accident, was attributed to the emotional strain of such activity.[14]

On that first Friday after the accident, two hundred funerals were performed. A mass burial of twenty-nine unidentified victims was held on Saturday, June 18, the same day as the funerals for Rev. Haas's wife and other family members. Mass burials continued for the next few days.[15] The Lutheran Cemetery in Middle Village, Queens, received the bulk of the remains, but Lutheran, as well as Episcopal, Catholic, and Jewish, cemeteries all over New York City and northern New Jersey received *General Slocum* victims. A large public memorial service was also held at Cooper Union on June 30 to honor all of the dead.[16] An observer wrote: "From almost every house, not alone the crape on the door told of grief, but black-draped American and German flags and long streamers of black and purple and white swung from windows. In the windows of shops were black bordered cards bearing in German and English the legend: 'We mourn the loss of our beloved,' or 'We mourn of loss . . .' In accordance with German custom, many of the funeral parties adjourned to nearby hotels and partook of food and refreshment."[17]

While most of the victims were members of St. Mark's, attendees of several other churches also went on the excursion. About seventy members of the Second Avenue Collegiate Church were on the *General Slocum*, with nearly thirty of them dying. Funerals were also held at St. Mark's Protestant Episcopal Church at East 10th Street and Second Avenue for victims.[18]

Immediately after the disaster, Mayor McClellan established a relief fund to raise money from the public to aid survivors and families with medical and funeral bills, as well as the longer-term care of orphans. Within ten hours, more than $9,000 had been donated, most of it in small donations made by ordinary New Yorkers horrified by the disaster. Ultimately, the relief fund would collect more than $107,000 and be managed by a committee of eighteen prominent businessmen, most of them German or German American, appointed by McClellan. The *New Yorker Staats-Zeitung* publisher Herman Ridder was the chairman.[19]

In addition to the mayor's relief fund committee, other political leaders stepped up to provide help. The Tammany Hall leader and German American politician Julius Harburger, who had represented Assembly District 10 in the late 1890s, mobilized Tammany Hall to raise money for the families of victims, passing the money along to the mayor's relief committee.[20] The German

American politician William Sulzer, who had also represented the neighborhood in state government and was now in Congress, promoted a bill to provide financial assistance to victims' families, which ultimately failed.[21]

Yet it would take persuasion to convince surviving family members to accept financial assistance. St. Mark's committee of elders eventually had to promise people that it would burn the list of recipients, so no one would know who had had to accept charity to help pay for funerals and medical bills.

Later, some survivors who suffered from disabilities caused by the accident sought more financial help. The waiter Albin Boenhardt—who lost his children, Otto and Ella, and was blinded in his left eye by a burning piece of timber—sued St. Mark's charity fund in 1907, seeking more funds to help pay for ongoing doctor's bills, but the case was dismissed in 1908.[22] Nearly 440 families applied for aid, with 161 families seeking funds to pay for funerals.[23]

The fund also became a major source of conflict within the St. Mark's congregation. Survivors organized the Organization of General Slocum Survivors and, within a few weeks of the accident, had already held a rally at Schuetzen Hall to protest how the Relief Committee was allocating funds. Although the committee had spent the majority of the fund (more than $81,000) on funeral expenses, survivors alleged, falsely, that money was being spent on consultants.[24]

In actuality, the controversy was about the Relief Committee's refusal to pay for expensive funerals, as well as its decisions in some cases to deny financial assistance to families the committee believed could support themselves, either through savings or with the help of extended family and friends. The biggest source of conflict was the committee's decision to allocate the last $20,000 in the fund to the church. Rev. Haas argued that with the loss of so many parishioners, especially prosperous ones, St. Mark's faced bankruptcy and possible closure. Haas wanted the money to pay the church's bills and to continue its charitable work. Some members of the Organization of General Slocum Survivors became upset, and a permanent schism in the congregation developed.[25] Churches had long suffered from internal conflict over control of church funds and other resources, but the fight over the relief funds was particularly bitter and hurt St. Mark's at a time when the continued survival of the congregation was in question.

After an investigation led by the coroner's office, Captain Van Schaick, Captain John A. Pease, First Mate Edward Flanagan, the Knickerbocker Steamboat Company executives Frank A. Barnaby and James K. Atkinson, five other company directors, and U.S. Steamboat Inspection Service inspector Henry Lundberg—who had attested to the seaworthiness and safety of the *General Slocum* only six weeks earlier on May 5—were charged with criminal negligence.[26]

There would be a series of investigations, hearings, and trials over the next two years, but ultimately, only Van Schaick would be held responsible for the disaster. After a lengthy delay, he was tried and found guilty of criminal neglect and manslaughter in 1906 (for failing to make sure that the crew was properly trained in emergency procedures and that the *General Slocum* had adequate safety equipment). He was sentenced to ten years in prison but served only three years in Sing Sing before he was pardoned by President William Howard Taft in 1912 on account of his age. (He was sixty-seven in 1904.)[27]

Unwilling to wait for the courts to provide justice for their loved ones, some *General Slocum* family members sued the Knickerbocker Steamboat Company for damages. The brewer Adolph Molitor, who lost eight family members, including his wife and three children, sued the Knickerbocker for $800,000.[28] The barber Henry Wiedemann, who lost his wife, Caroline, and thirty-year-old daughter, Caroline, sued for $50,000 worth of damages, while his twenty-three-year-old daughter, Eleanor Reichenbach, and her husband, Herman, sued for $5,000 for the loss of their two-year-old son, Herman. Eleanor Reichenbach had watched her son drown and had been the only one in her party to survive, only because she had removed the life preserver she was wearing when it had caught fire.[29] But these suits were unsuccessful.

In fact, the Knickerbocker Steamboat Company paid nothing to survivors or victims' families and, in fact, successfully limited its liability to the value of the *General Slocum* after the fire, which was about $5,000 (or less than $5 per fatality and injured).[30]

Other family members battled with insurance companies. Life insurance had been a foundation of American life, especially for the immigrant working class, and Germans especially were strong believers in insurance. Some of the earliest insurance companies in the United States had originated out of German Unterstützungsvereine. But making claims was harder for some than for others. An insurance trade journal reported:

A baffling tangle of claims arising from the General Slocum disaster has just been settled by the New Amsterdam Casualty Company. Mary Hagenbucher, of Yonkers, and Fanny Irwin and Julia Dunn, of New York city, each took out an accident policy for $1,000 in the New Amsterdam, naming one another as beneficiaries. All three sailed on the General Slocum on that fatal day, and none came back. The claims were legally impossible of settlement, as no one knows which of the girls died first. Mary Hagenbucher was the beneficiary of the policy of Julia Dunn, and in case the beneficiary died before the insured, the heirs of the beneficiary were to receive the insurance. The brother of Mary Hagenbucher made a claim, and was allowed by the surrogate to settle with the company for $1,000, the full amount which his sister would have received had she survived the death of Julia Dunn. The claims of the other heirs have been rejected by the company under the conditions of the policy, as no notice of death was given within six weeks of her death.[31]

In German fashion, survivors organized themselves into a Verein, the Organization of the General Slocum Survivors, initially headed by Charles Dersch, whose wife and daughter had died. The organization held annual memorials on June 15 and raised funds for the building of a memorial fountain in Tompkins Square Park, as well as a monument to the unidentified victims erected at All Faiths Lutheran Cemetery, Middle Village, Queens. The Tompkins Square Park foundation was built by the Hoboken-born sculptor Bruno Louis Zimm, and the dedication and acknowledgment text (of the "Sympathy Society of German Ladies") was written in English. The All Faiths monument was designed by Joseph Bermel, a future Queens borough president and stonemason; the side statues were sculpted by the father-and-son team Adam and Paul Bock.

In their struggles for justice and to keep public attention on the tragedy, the members of the Organization of General Slocum Survivors positioned themselves as Americans first and Germans second. At a meeting of survivors in late September 1904, organized in reaction to the local steamboat inspectors' investigation of the accident, the organization declared: "While most are of German birth of descent, we are here to demand our rights as American citizens; we are not 'easy marks.' We have accepted the fate that has come to us, but we will fight not be trifled with. We are here to fight for the memories of our dear dead, and we warn the authorities who are the superiors of the inspectors who are whitewashed themselves that we will demand recognition of our rights and the adequate punishment of those who are to blame."[32]

How New Yorkers could forget the *General Slocum* disaster so quickly and how the remaining memories could be so wrong has its roots in some creative writing at the time, as well as the later misinterpretation of facts.[33]

On June 26, eleven days after the accident, the *New York Times* wrote of the impact of the disaster: "Nor will the church be the only sufferer. What has been such a dire blow to its life will be a blow to the neighborhood of which it was the centre, 'Little Germany,' as it is called affectionately by the people who live in it." The *Times* predicted that

> the exodus of the dead to the Lutheran Cemetery will be followed by an exodus of the living to other parts of the city and new surroundings, where they can forget the dark days and the tragic scenes enacted during the last weeks in a quarter they were wont to treasure as the nearest reproduction to "die alte Heimath" on American soil.
>
> With them the festive song and story of the 'Liedertafel' and the pomp of the 'Schuetzenbund' will disappear also, and the district which has maintained

its characteristics for over half a century, longer than any other part of the city, will have lost its identity and be given over to the overflow from the lower east side.

"I will bury my dear ones that are dead from their old home," said a business man who had lost his wife and children on the excursion, "then I will take a last look at the church, bid good-bye to good Pastor Haas, and turn my back on this part of the town forever."[34]

The *Times'* romantic nostalgia for a community it had never really understood made for good copy, but the story was complete speculation. More realistically, the newspaper noted that the "exodus" of Germans from the Lower East Side had begun "in recent years" (actually in the 1880s) and that St. Mark's only had about six hundred regular attendees from a high of thirteen hundred parishioners in the 1870s.[35] Another source of the claim that Germans were abandoning the neighborhood came from the city's Department of Public Charities, which observed that 170 (28 percent) of the 622 families known to have been on the *General Slocum* had moved out of the area by 1905.[36]

There was certainly a lot of movement among survivors after the accident, both within Kleindeutschland and outside of the neighborhood: orphaned children moved in with relatives; married men now widowed and sometimes with no children became boarders with other family members or strangers. The three surviving sons of Bernard Mueller, for instance, moved from 95 Second Avenue to East 87th Street when they moved in with their grandmother, Johanna Hager, after their parents died on the *General Slocum*. After his mother, Anna, and eleven-year-old sister, Martha, died, eight-year-old William Hotz lived with his maternal grandparents on Sutton Place on the Upper East Side until 1918, when he moved in with his father and his father's second wife on East 90th Street.[37]

The tailor Christian Schoett, who lost his wife and three children, was only one of many Germans who were already buying real estate uptown at the turn of the century. Schoett bought property on 159th Street in 1904, and he continued to buy land in the Bronx after he remarried in 1905.[38]

Remarriage—not grief—was the main predictor as to whether an adult *General Slocum* survivor moved, and even then, several men who remarried in 1905 stayed in the homes they had lived in with their previous wives and children.[39] The trend of moving to the outer boroughs between 1905 and 1915 was part of the larger movement out of Manhattan and was not specific to either German New Yorkers or *General Slocum* survivors.

One move, however, helped give the false impression that *General Slocum* survivors were leaving Kleindeutschland: by 1910, Rev. Haas and his second wife, Clara Holthusen, had moved uptown, to 254 West 136th Street, which was in Strivers' Row, in Harlem.[40] But Haas remained the pastor of St. Mark's, retiring only in 1921, when he moved to Staten Island and became a faculty member of Wagner College. His move was probably prompted more by his marriage in 1906 than by the supposed ghosts haunting Kleindeutschland.

There were several distinctive aspects about St. Mark's Evangelical Lutheran Church as compared to the city's larger German community. By 1904, most New Yorkers of German heritage were the grandchildren or even great-grandchildren of immigrants, who had arrived in the first large wave of German immigration in the 1850s. Others were the children or grandchildren of the third large wave in the 1880s. These people might still identify themselves as "German" and consider themselves part of the city's German community, but they were themselves far removed from the immigrant experience. But many members of St. Mark's congregation were either immigrants or the minor children of immigrants and had immigrated in the 1890s, a period of declining German immigration. There were even some very recent immigrants: the Stockermann family of 225 5th Street—Lizetta Augusta, son Herman, and daughters Anna, Hulda, Augusta, and Louisa—had only arrived in the United States in February 1903 to join their father, Gustave, who had immigrated earlier.[41] Only seven-year-old Herman survived the fire, along with Gustave, who had not been on the boat. Fifty-seven-year-old Bertha Jonck had emigrated from Berlin two months before the *General Slocum* accident, arriving in New York on April 23 to live with her daughter Alice Fischler and her family.[42] Bertha Jonck died along with her two granddaughters, seven-year-old Hertha and six-year-old Antonia Fischler.

The other distinctive thing about the members of St. Mark's was their willingness to live in an immigrant neighborhood dominated by other ethnic and religious groups. By 1900, the Lower East Side was a predominantly eastern European Jewish neighborhood, with a large Italian immigrant minority. Germans only lived in large numbers and in high concentrations in the Seventeenth Ward.[43]

The fact that the disaster affected what was normally derided as a poor immigrant neighborhood posed a conundrum for some mainstream English-language papers in their postdisaster coverage. The *New York Times* attempted to correct the popular belief that "the district devastated by the disaster to the General Slocum was the abode of sordid poverty, and of the evils that sordid poverty entails." Instead, the neighborhood, while "not a fashionable quarter," was home to "a sturdy, thrifty, and self-respecting population, of the middle class in respect to fortune, of the very best class as respects the essentials of citizenship. It has always been a German district. While a great part of the population it had twenty years ago has migrated to the northward, carrying its institutions with it, those who remain are of the same kind and character as those who removed," the *Times* insisted.[44]

Table 4.1
Place of Residence of 1,331 Passengers

Residence of passengers	Number
Manhattan	1,146
Brooklyn	99
Queens	2
The Bronx	52
Other New York	11
Hoboken, NJ	11
Jersey City, NJ	5
Bayonne, NJ	3
Other New Jersey	2

SOURCE: "'General Slocum' Disaster, June 15, 1904," *Annual Report of the Department of Public Charities of the City of New York for 1904* (New York: Martin B. Brown, 1905), 134, "Percentage Table 'C,' Location of Residences of 1,331 Persons Who Were on the 'General Slocum' at the Time of the Fire."

A rush-to-print history of the disaster observed: "This is a concentrated tragedy. Ninty per cent. [*sic*] of the dead and injured live in a territory embracing less than a square mile on the East Side. It is a quiet, clean neighborhood, in which the predominating language is German."[45] Yet the same author recognized the congregation for what it was: "a German Protestant colony in the midst of a huge population of Roman Catholics and Jews."[46]

An analysis of the addresses of 1,296 passengers (excluding crew members and an unnamed family that refused to give its address) shows that a large majority (935, or 72 percent) lived on the Lower East Side. Another 56 passengers lived on the border of Kleindeutschland between East 15th and 18th Streets.

What was unusual about St. Mark's members and *General Slocum* passengers was how few of those who lived outside of the Lower East Side lived in Yorkville, the largest German neighborhood in New York City in 1904. Of nearly 1,300 passengers, only 24 people lived in Yorkville. More passengers lived around Union Square (38) than lived in the new Kleindeutschland uptown. More popular among passengers was north of Yorkville in the Bronx, Harlem, and the Upper East Side (90 passengers).[47]

Rather than abandoning Kleindeutschland, the large majority of *General Slocum* survivors and their families stayed in the old neighborhood, sometimes as late as the 1930s, and it is their persistence in the face of demographic change that is remarkable. Ernest Rueffer, who lived at 109 First Avenue with his wife, Annie, and son, Arthur, was a prominent music store owner and publisher and

Table 4.2
Country of Origin of Passengers of 863 Dead

Country of Origin	Number
Austria	8
Bohemia	1
England	2
Hungary	4
Ireland	2
Romania	2
Russia	1
Germany	172
United States (nearly all born to German-born parents)	450

SOURCE: "'General Slocum' Disaster, June 15, 1904," Annual Report of the Department of Public Charities of the City of New York for 1904 (New York: Martin B. Brown, 1905), 132, "Percentage Table 'B,' 924 Lives Lost on the 'General Slocum,' as to Sex, 863 Identified Dead."

composer of popular music for the German theater; he specialized in zithers, selling, repairing, and writing music for the instrument. Rueffer's was on First Avenue for decades into the 1920s.[48] The importer clerk Joseph Schaefer and his wife, Augusta, both survived the fire but lost their only child, six-year-old Kate. The Schaefers had no other children and remained on the Lower East Side into the 1930s, only moving from 142 Second Street to East 18th Street in the late 1910s.[49] Mary Illig, who was injured on the *General Slocum* and lost two of her four children, stayed at 433 East 5th Street as late as 1940 and possibly until her death in 1946 at the age of eighty-four. Her husband Conrad died in 1907.[50] The cigar maker Charles Schumacher, who lost his two children, fourteen-year-old Katherine and ten-year-old Edward, was already a widower by 1900 and stayed in his family home at 434 East 6th Street until the 1930s.[51]

In 1880, twenty-four German churches were located on the Lower East Side (and seven others were in Lower Manhattan); twenty-three were located between 14th Street and Central Park, equally distributed between the east and west sides.[52] By 1900, there were fewer than ten German churches: St. Mark's in the Bowery Episcopal Church at Second Avenue and East 10th Street; the Second German Evangelical Reformed Church at Madison and Montgomery Streets; First German Methodist at St. Mark's and Second Avenue; the First German Baptist at East 14th Street near First Avenue; and Most Holy Redeemer Roman Catholic Church at Third Street near Avenue A. Besides St. Mark's Lutheran Church, there was also Trinity Lutheran at Avenue B and East 9th Street.[53] Most German congregations had long moved uptown or had shuttered their doors as their congregations moved or died.

For their congregants, and the other German immigrants who remained in Kleindeutschland, St. Mark's and the few other German churches were seen as a rock in a rapidly changing society. But there was much about St. Mark's that reflected the changes in New York City's German community. St. Mark's minister, George Haas, had not been born in Germany but in Philadelphia, to immigrant parents who were successful enough to send their two sons to university to train to become ministers. The Rev. Haas married a Dutch American woman, Anna Hansen, showing a willingness to marry outside of the ethnic group that few other Germans possessed. The church also began offering English services on Sunday evenings in 1893 and had both a German and an English Sunday school. The German language was important to both German immigrants and German Lutherans, but clearly, St. Mark's was adapting and adjusting to the needs and desires of its congregation in the early 1900s.[54]

To keep the memory of the victims of the *General Slocum* disaster alive, it is worth reflecting on the experiences of the passengers and their families.

Of an estimated 1,358 passengers on board the *General Slocum* that Wednesday, only 407 people survived, 267 of these were injured, and only 140 were uninjured. The total official death toll was 1,021 persons. Children suffered especially badly, with nearly 500 people (or 57 percent) of the dead being between the ages of infancy and twenty. Three times the number of women and girls died than men and boys, probably because men and boys had more opportunities to learn how to swim and were also not burdened with the heavier weight of skirts and petticoats. There were also four times the number of girls and women as boys and men on the *General Slocum*, which also contributed to the higher female death toll.[55]

General Slocum survivors and family members can be classified in several ways: survivors of the accident, both injured and uninjured; children orphaned; children who found themselves only children; parents, either on the boat or not, who lost one or more children; adults (mostly men) who were widowed; and those who remarried and had new families versus those who did not.

What is immediately obvious is how many families with members on the *General Slocum* suffered some kind of loss. Fewer than five families in which all members were on the *General Slocum* survived the accident: Fred and Emma Ferneisen of 40 East 7th Street and their two sons; Ferdinand and Meta Frese of 509 East Houston and their fifteen-year-old daughter, Anne; plus a family of four that refused to give their names after being treated for injuries. There were also a few groups of siblings whose parents were not on the *General Slocum* who survived: twelve-year-old Charles and ten-year-old August Lemp of 108 Second Avenue, and fourteen-year-old Francis, thirteen-year-old Julia, and ten-year-old Louisa Schmidt of 69 First Avenue.[56]

In at least five cases, entire families—both parents and all children—died on the *General Slocum*, as was the case with Otto and Eliza Gress and their four children; Rudolph and Dorothea Schultz and their three children, fourteen-year-old Rudolph, eleven-year-old Henry, and seven-year-old Dorothea; Peter and Christina Fettig and their two-year old daughter, Elsa; and Henry and Anna Schnude and their two children, four-year-old Grace and one-year-old Mildred. The Schnudes had been part of a party of eighteen, along with the Torniports and the Kassebaums, of which only three in the group survived. The entire Kohler family was lost with the deaths of Henry, Mary, and twelve-year-old Henry Jr., and twenty-six other extended family members also died.

There were several widows with their children on board, so the deaths of Fredericka Weaver and her four daughters; Frances Stenger and her ten-year-old daughter, Rosina; Emma Gruben and her thirteen-year-old daughter, Carrie; and Clara Roberts and her thirteen-year-old daughter, Blanche, meant the end of their families. Emma Gruben's sister, Mary Beneke, also died on board the *General Slocum*.

The saloon keeper Richard Gerstenberger, who owned Central Hall at 147 West 32nd Street, and his wife, Annie, had had no children. Their deaths were mourned by thousands of representatives of more than one hundred labor unions that used to meet regularly at Gerstenberger's establishment, where the couple's funeral was held.[57]

Twenty-seven children were orphaned completely by the disaster, including ten-year-old Frances Richter, who was the only one of her family of eight on the *General Slocum* to survive the fire. She and her fifteen-year-old brother William, who was not on the boat, were taken in by their maternal grandmother, Elizabeth Hennig, who lived next door on East 6th Street, and their aunt and uncle, Henry and Alice Richter, who lived on Seventh Avenue between West 25th and 26th Streets. The three surviving sons of the Tammany Hall leader Bernard Mueller and his wife, Valesca—thirteen-year-old Grover, ten-year-old Walter, and six-year-old Arthur—moved in with their grandmother Johanna Hager on East 87th Street. When St. Mark's deacon and butcher Herman Pottebaum and his wife, Eliza, and youngest son, nine-year-old William, died on the *General Slocum*, their surviving children—twenty-one-year-old Henry, nineteen-year-old Charles, and seventeen-year-old George—left St. Marks Place and became boarders with a family in Brooklyn.

As a prosperous ethnic group, German immigrants had had relatively large families compared to other groups (eight children was not uncommon for German families), and most of the children on board the *General Slocum* had at least two siblings, usually more. After the accident, several survivors found themselves only children. Twelve-year-old Henry Oellrich, whose family had lived in Brooklyn, was the only one of his four brothers and sisters to survive; his mother, Anna, died as well. His father, William, a grocery store owner, had not gone on the excursion because he had jury duty that day. Twelve-year-old Kate Finkenagel was the only one of the four Finkenagel children to survive;

her mother, Kate, also died. When eleven-year-old Catherine Gallagher's mother, Veronica, and nine-year-old brother, Walter, and baby sister, Agnes, died on the *General Slocum*, her stepfather, John Gallagher, a clerk, found himself unable to care for his remaining child, so Catherine was sent to live with her grandparents and then an aunt and uncle.[58]

According to the Charity Organization Society, which investigated the social aftermath of the accident, "the excursionists were mainly women and children, only nine male heads of families having been known to be lost, and in comparison with the appalling loss of life there was comparatively little loss of property." The society's 1904 report continued:

> One hundred and twenty men lost their entire family by the disaster. Of these twenty-nine lost wife only; thirtynine (*sic*) lost wife and one child; thirty-two wife and two children; ten, wife and three children; three, wife and four children; and one, wife and five children; two widowers lost each two children, and one widower four children, while the remaining three of the 120 men left alone as the result of the disaster lost other relatives with whom they were living. Twenty-one men, whose wives and one or more children were lost, were left with one child under fourteen, and eleven others were left with more than one small child, having lost wife and one or more children.[59]

These surviving parents, mainly men, adjusted to life after the *General Slocum* disaster in several different ways. Some men, if their wives survived or else were not on the boat, had additional children after 1904, but this was only an option for younger couples. Twenty-four-year-old May Klenen lost her baby daughter, Ethel, and was badly burned in the fire. She and her husband, Frederick, a bookkeeper in the Bronx, had another daughter in 1905, whom they named for Frederick's mother, Meta Klenen, who also died on the *General Slocum*. The twenty-seven-year-old upholsterer Peter Edward Kiesel and his twenty-five-year-old wife, Annie, were among the few couples to both survive, along with their three-year-old son, Edward, but their five-year-old daughter, Lillian, did not. Peter and Annie had another child, Grace, in 1906.[60] Thirty-year-old Mary Schumann lost two of her three children, but she and her husband, Arthur, a butcher from Saxony, had two more children between 1904 and 1910.[61] Thirty-two-year-old Louisa Bock, who had married her husband, Charles, in St. Mark's and who had regularly attended the church picnic even after she and her husband had moved to Brooklyn, had already lost two children by 1900 and then watched her two surviving children, seven-year-old May and five-year-old Grace, drown. She and Charles moved to Queens after the accident and had a son, Charles Jr., in 1906.[62] After four of their six children died, thirty-two-year-old Katie Mettler and her husband, Robert, an embroider who was not on the boat, had two more children after 1904.[63]

But in most cases, surviving couples did not have more children. The average age of both men and women on the *General Slocum* was thirty-seven, so for many of these mothers, their childbearing years were behind them. Henrietta Gassmann and Sophia Zipse were both forty-one years old in 1904. The Gassmanns' three children and five of the Zipses' six children died on the *General Slocum*; neither couple had any more children after 1904.

In several instances, men who lost their wives and several or all of their children remarried relatively quickly, often within the first year or two. Modern-day sensibilities might see these sudden remarriages as insensitive, but early twentieth-century men lived in a society in which sacrifice for the family was central to masculine identity. For these widowers, the *General Slocum* accident had destroyed their reason to live, so remarriage was a way of renewing their purpose in life. In some instances, it was also to find help in raising children. Nearly eighty remarriages of men connected to the *General Slocum* accident have been identified, but only twenty-five of these new marriages produced additional children.

The most notable of these remarriages was the Rev. Haas, who married Clara Holthusen, the daughter of the church's sexton, John Holthusen, in 1906.[64] Clara Holthusen, her stepsister Wilhelmina Hayden, and her father had all been on the *General Slocum* but were among the few families to survive without a death or serious injury. Haas's wife's brother-in-law William Tetamore—whose wife, Sophia, and three-year-old son, Herbert, died—also remarried in 1906, this time to George Haas's sister, Emma, who was injured in the accident.

The Lutheran Emigrant Home superintendent Rev. George Doering, whose wife, Ida, and two of their three children died, remarried as well in July 1906. He and his second wife, Irma, had five children, in addition to his surviving daughter, six-year-old Edna.[65]

The Hungarian-born carpenter and cabinetmaker Mathias Bretz and his wife, Mary, had already lost their three oldest girls to disease in February 1904; then Mary and their two youngest daughters, three-year-old Edith and seven-month-old Elsie, died on the *General Slocum*. Mathias Bretz remarried in November 1904 and moved to East 64th Street. He and his second wife, Annie, had three children, one of whom had died by 1910.[66]

The Brooklyn grocer William Oellrich, who lost his wife, Anna, and four of their five children (only twelve-year-old Henry survived), remarried in February 1905 and had five more children with his second wife, Marie.[67]

The brewery foreman Adolph Molitor lost his wife, Margaret, and three children, nine-year-old Eva, four-year-old Carl, and six-month-old Joseph. He remarried in April 1905 and had three other children with his second wife, Emma, a recent immigrant from Austria.[68]

The baker Henry Fischer lost his entire family—wife, Emma, and two young daughters—but remarried in August 1905 and had one son, Henry, with his second wife, Theresa. Fischer and his second family stayed on First Avenue before finally moving to the Bronx in the 1920s.[69]

The Prussian-born cloth cutter John Muth, who survived the *General Slocum* along with two of his sons but lost his wife, Catherine, and their three daughters, as well as several other relatives, remarried and had a child by his second marriage. His brother-in-law, the policeman Edward Schnitzler, who was not on the *General Slocum* and whose wife, Christina, and daughter Catherine died, also remarried by 1910 and had a second family.[70]

The musical instrument manufacturer Edward Müller lost his wife, Hermine, and all four of their children. He remarried in 1906, and he and his second wife, Anna, had five children, possibly because the second Mrs. Müller was only twenty-three when they married.[71]

In most instances, though, men remarried but did not have any more children, although in several cases, their second wives were much younger than their husbands. Perhaps the pain of losing children was too great, and they did not want to risk suffering more. In other cases, their second wives were possibly too old to have children or already had children from previous marriages.

The German-born woodworker Frederick Baumler and his wife, Margaretha, had already suffered the death of two children before the *General Slocum* accident, a baby who died after four months and another who died at the age of two. Margaretha and three of their four children, fifteen-year-old Amelia, eleven-year-old Annie, and ten-year-old Charles, died on the *General Slocum*, leaving Frederick Sr. only one child, eleven-year-old Frederick Jr., who was uninjured. Baumler remarried in 1906, but he and his second wife, fellow *General Slocum* survivor Catherine Zausch (who lost her mother and a sister in the fire), had no children, although Catherine was twenty-six at the time of their marriage.[72]

The bedding salesman Philip Borger, whose wife, Pauline, nine-year-old son, Philip Jr., and five-year-old daughter, Pauline, all died on the *General Slocum*, remarried and moved to Brooklyn by 1910. But he and his second wife, Florence, did not have any children, despite Florence being twenty-three in 1904, fifteen years younger than Philip.[73]

The thirty-seven-year-old grocer Henry Siegwart had just become a widower in May 1904, and then he lost his two daughters, nine-year-old Caroline and six-year-old Phoebe, in the accident. Henry remarried in August 1905 but had no children with his second wife, Louisa, who was twenty-five when they married.[74]

The lithographer Louis Geissler, who lost his entire family (wife, Minnie, and three children), remarried in 1906, but he and his second wife, Louisa, did not have any children, possibly because Louisa was thirty-seven at the time of their marriage.[75]

The German-born butcher Charles Timm remarried in 1905 after the death of his wife, Marie, and all three of their children but did not have any more children with his wife, Agnes, who was thirty-one when they married.[76]

The tailor Christian Schoett lost his wife, Josephine, and their three children on the *General Slocum*. In January 1905, he remarried a widow with a five-year-old daughter, but Schoett and his second wife, Elizabeth, did not have any children themselves.[77]

Not all men remarried. Henry Frech, already a widower by 1904, lost his fourteen-year-old son, Charles, on the *General Slocum* but had three other sons. He moved the family to Carlstadt, New Jersey, by 1910 but did not remarry. Neither did the painter Henry Foelsing, who lost his wife and three of his four children; he moved to the Bronx by 1910 and died in 1913. The provisions dealer Henry Gruning lost his wife, Helena, and their three children but did not remarry. The grocer George Dittrich, who became the first president of the Organization of General Slocum Survivors, lost his entire family—wife, Ardelinde, and four children—but did not remarry. Instead, he moved in with his sister-in-law and niece and stayed on the Lower East Side until the early 1920s.

A few people survived the disaster but ultimately died within a few years due to their injuries. Anne Weber, who had been on board with her family and her sister's family, the Liebenows, received severe burns to her back, which ultimately affected her lungs; she died in 1905. Seventy-five-year-old Margaret Herbolt also suffered burns and died of her injuries within the next few years.[78]

Many people, either survivors or family members, suffered extreme trauma in the days and weeks following the disaster. Newspaper reporters reported seeing people break down in hysterics or fainting upon discovering the bodies of their loved ones. A man who had overcome a stutter found that his speech impediment had returned, and he had to write to communicate; another man was so upset that he reportedly forgot his wife's name. The strong reactions of men, for whom emotional control was seen as a virtue, were often noted in the press as a way of emphasizing the extremeness of the situation.[79] Twelve-year-old Henry Heinz, who was injured, was so traumatized by his experience that he was unable to speak for three days after the accident. His case drew the attention of a journal devoted to deaf mutes.[80]

Many survivors and family members suffered what is now called post-traumatic stress disorder (PTSD) years after the accident, and this emotional trauma in some cases led to their early deaths. Men were particularly vulnerable to this emotional stress. Others were reported to have literally died of grief within the next few years.

The policeman Jacob Schrumpf lost his wife, Elizabeth, and their two sons, John and William; he and Elizabeth had already lost four children before 1900. He retired from the police force and lived alone in his family's home at 208 Avenue B. In July 1908, he was persuaded by his sister to go to Germany with the

Brooklyn Arion Society, with which he had become active after the loss of his family. But on the second day at sea on board the SS *Barbarossa*, Schrumpf became "mentally deranged" and was confined to the ship's hospital. He died in a Bremen hospital a few days after his arrival in Germany, and his body was returned to the United States to be buried with his wife and children in the Lutheran Cemetery. Schrumpf was fifty-two.[81]

In late January 1912, the barber George Wunner began suffering from gastric pains but then quickly exhibited signs of mental stress, "bewailing the loss of his wife and daughter, who perished in the General Slocum disaster." Wunner—who was vice president and secretary of the Organization of General Slocum Survivors—was admitted to Bellevue Hospital, where he underwent psychological evaluations after he "became delirious, calling again and again for his wife and daughter, and complaining of Capt. Van Schaick." Wunner died in early February 1912 at the age of fifty-four.[82]

When the oyster house owner Henry Heinz died in November 1916 at the age of seventy-six, the *Brooklyn Eagle* reported that Heinz had been in declining health "ever since his triple bereavement" of his wife and two daughters, "which almost unsettled his reason then and for some time after."[83]

Charles Scheele, who lost all three of his children, fifteen-year-old Anna, ten-year-old Lawina, and seven-year-old Clara, died in November 1904 at the age of forty-two, leaving his wife, Minna, a widow. Charles and Minna had not been on the *General Slocum* because Charles Scheele had been feeling ill that week. The German-born music publisher Herman Strickrodt, who lost his wife, Annie, and three of his four children, died in February 1905 at the age of forty-two, leaving only his seventeen-year old-son, Henry, as the sole surviving member of the family. The tailor Stephen Thoma lost his wife, Christine, and two children, eight-year-old Joseph and five-year-old Lydia; he died in February 1906 at the age of thirty-nine. The German-born bartender George Heilshorn, who lost his wife, Margaret, and three-year-old son, George, remarried in 1905 but died a year later at the age of forty-seven.

The waiter Paul Liebenow—who survived with his wife, Anna, and six-month-old baby, Adella, but lost his two older daughters and his sister, Martha—died in 1910 at the age of thirty-eight. His hands had been badly burned in the fire, and he also contracted pneumonia. Liebenow never fully recovered from the fire and suffered from poor health until his death, although he continued to work. That same year, the bank clerk Adolph Torniport also died at the age of thirty-eight. His wife, Fredericka, and two young children had died on the *General Slocum*, as well as his wife's parents, the Kassebaums, and all of his wife's sister's family, the Schnudes.[84]

For some parents, the grief was too much, and they turned to suicide. Upon finding the bodies of her two daughters and her mother, Catherine Diamond attempted to kill herself by jumping off the pier where the bodies were being brought. The newspapers reported of other suicide attempts by men reacting to the news of the deaths of loved ones.[85] At least four men committed suicide after losing most or all of their families in the accident.

The forty-four-year-old German-born butcher Andrew (Andreas) Stiel committed suicide soon after the death of his children, sixteen-year-old Lillie, fourteen-year-old George, twelve-year-old Emil, and six-year-old Frederick. He had been a widower at the time of the accident and suddenly found himself totally alone and unable to continue.[86]

For the next few years, around the anniversary of the fire, there were suicides of family members. The German-born waiter Joseph Vollmer killed himself on June 17, 1905, a few days after the first anniversary of the accident. The *New York Times* reported: "With the breaking up of his home by the loss of his wife and children, Vollmer went to live with his sister, Mrs. Katie Lutz. He did odd jobs that were offered, but brooded constantly. When Mrs. Lutz went out to market last night Vollmer turned on the gas and shot himself."[87]

Vollmer's brother, Fred Vollmer, killed himself in August 1906 in his saloon at 42 Avenue A (the former Germania Assembly Rooms, built in 1859). He left a note saying he was tired of living and wanted to join his brother.[88]

The saloon keeper George Feldhusen killed himself on the eleventh anniversary of the accident in his saloon on West 8th Street. Feldhusen's wife, Margaret, and twelve-year-old son, Nicholas, had died in the accident. He had remarried twice but was unable to rebuild his life.[89]

Children—often thought to be more flexible and adaptable in the face of tragedy—especially suffered without the kinds of emotional support and mental care that today is considered essential.

Public School 25 (PS 25) on East 5th Street near First Avenue had at least one hundred students on the *General Slocum* (fifty-one died), and the school suffered so many losses among its graduating class that annual commencement exercises were not held that June because most of the students who had been expected to graduate had died. Instead, a memorial service was held on June 22 in the girls' section, and the following week another service was held in the boys' section. (Public schools were often segregated by sex in this period.)[90] The *New York Times* said of the school: "The heaviest sufferer was Public School 25, at First Avenue and Fifth Street. Scores are missing there and the pupils yesterday were still in a state of grief which made all effort to keep up with the ordinary routine impossible. Whenever a funeral procession passed the structure dozens of children buried their heads in their hands and sobbed hysterically."[91]

Several other schools also suffered losses: twenty-one students from PS 122 on East 9th Street; nineteen from PS 129 on East 19th Street; fourteen from PS 40 on East 16th Street.[92] At least six boys were classmates at PS 19 on

334 East 14th Street; sixteen-year-old William Masterson of 62 Third Avenue was the only one to survive.

School Superintendent William H. Maxwell instructed teachers and principals to use the *General Slocum* disaster as a "teaching moment," to "admonish their pupils to remain cool and collected in the presence of sudden danger, which is always imminent in a great city; not to risk their lives unnecessarily; to learn to swim; and to always be ready to lend a helping hand to those weaker than themselves."[93]

Scholarship on the impact of violent events on communities shows that tragedy and trauma can bring people in a community closer together, as survivors connect to others through their shared experiences and through the experience of building and preserving memory.[94] This is what happened with the Organization of General Slocum Survivors and its efforts to keep alive the memory of the disaster and to honor their dead. The ultimate failure of this memory preservation effort was due to both the rapid death rate of survivors—by 1954 only twelve survivors were still alive—and by the refusal of the larger New York City population to recognize the pain of survivors after 1915. During World War I, English-language newspapers in the city refused to cover the June 15 observations of the accident and then were slow to resume their coverage after the war.[95] In 1934, when *Manhattan Melodrama* was playing in New York City's theaters, the city's German community was deeply divided by Nazism and the rise of the German American Bund, but there were still forty-seven survivors still alive and insisting that the city recognize their loss and honor their dead.[96]

The impact of the *General Slocum* disaster on St. Mark's Evangelical Lutheran Church was obviously devastating: about 1,000 members or former members had died, and the leadership of the church had been almost totally wiped out. The secretary, treasurer, chairman of the Poor Committee, the choir leader, the superintendents of the German and English Sunday schools, the Sunday school secretary, and 42 of 58 Sunday school teachers all died, as well as seven members of the church's board of trustees and three members of the board of elders. At least 23 members of the Women's Guild and about 375 out of 500 Sunday school students died.[97]

The fight between Rev. Haas and the leaders of the Organization of General Slocum Survivors over the relief fund money only weakened the church further, as people who otherwise would have become leaders of the congregation instead left. The fact that St. Mark's continued to survive as a Lutheran parish was a testament to the leadership of Rev. Haas.

The accident did not encourage either assimilation or the movement of Germans out of the Lower East Side. Rather, the schism that developed within St. Mark's fractured that community. Even as congregants had moved to

Yorkville, the Bronx, or Brooklyn, many of them commuted regularly, spending time and money, to return to the old neighborhood each Sunday. The fighting within the congregation about what to do about the relief fund caused more people to leave than the burning of the *General Slocum*.

By 1940, St Mark's had dwindled to only fifty members, who decided to close the church and merge with another bilingual -German-English congregation, the Zion Evangelical Lutheran Church. The church is now called Zion St. Mark's Evangelical Lutheran Church and is located in Yorkville at East 84th Street, where Zion had originally been founded in 1892. The church still holds a German-language service.[98] The old St. Mark's building was sold to a Jewish synagogue in 1940 and has been a historic landmark since 2003.

5

A False Sense of Security, 1904–1914

●●●●●●●●●●●●●●●●●●●●●●

In the immediate aftermath of the *General Slocum* disaster, German New Yorkers began a campaign to lobby for assistance for survivors and victims' families, but they did so as Americans, not Germans. German American New Yorkers rarely voted as an ethnic bloc anymore, and the German American Reform Union ceased to be active in the early twentieth century. Fewer immigrants from Germany arrived in the 1900s and 1910s, and those who did were just as likely to live in Yorkville or the Bronx as they were to settle in the Seventeenth Ward. Vereine, churches, and businesses moved out of the Lower East Side, as Kleindeutschland was now called, and these institutions increasingly looked and behaved like English-speaking American ones, as German and Anglo American culture in the city came to resemble one another more and more. At the same time during all of these changes, the National German-American Alliance continued to promote the idea that Germanness and Americanness were synonymous and that German Americans were the best example of a harmonious pluralism.

The *General Slocum* restitution campaign reflected both the Americanness and Germanness of the survivors. Longtime Tammany Democrat William Sulzer, now in Congress representing the Tenth Congressional District, pushed hard to have the federal government's Court of Claims consider granting monetary damages to *General Slocum* survivors and victims' families. He also lobbied to change the law to allow family members to seek damages from the

FIG. 5.1 Carl Hassmann, *One Year After, Puck* 57, no. 1476 (June 14, 1905): cover. (Library of Congress.)

Knickerbocker Steamboat Company. (Under federal law, the owners of vessels sailing on rivers had no personal liability.) Sulzer and *General Slocum* survivors argued that the federal government was responsible for the accident because of the failure of the federal Steamboat Inspection Service to enforce the safety laws, thus allowing the *General Slocum* to sail with defective safety equipment. But despite heavy lobbying by Sulzer, German American community leaders, and New York City newspapers, the bill failed to get out of committee, although Sulzer was able finally to obtain a hearing before the House Committee on Claims in 1910. Sulzer also sought a direct appropriation from Congress to grant pensions or a one-time payment to survivors, but this effort also died in committee.[1]

The lobbying effort of *General Slocum* survivors revealed the extent to which surviving family members had suffered financially and emotionally from the disaster. In hundreds of affidavits submitted to Congress, family members described the loss of wages from spouses and teenage children old enough to work and of the hardships endured by survivors suffering from lingering injuries that required ongoing medical treatment and prevented them from working. In addition, many survivors reported suffering from post-traumatic stress that sometimes manifested itself in physical symptoms that disabled the individual.[2]

The teacher Jacob Hartmann swore that his sister, Marie, formerly a teacher earning six hundred dollars per year in 1904, had become "insane" as a result of the disaster and was now in an asylum. The carpenter Henry Mahlstedt reported that his thirty-one-year-old daughter, Anna, had been "hysterical ever since" the accident. The tailor Magnus Hartung swore that his now thirty-year-old daughter, Minnie, had formerly earned twenty dollars per month doing housework but could no longer work due to the burns she had suffered. Hartung also noted that the family had lost the earnings of his wife, Louisa, who had worked as a "tailoress," earning seven dollars per week, and his daughter, eighteen-year-old Francis, who had earned twelve dollars per week as a piano teacher. The tinsmith Herman Heuer swore that his son, Adolph, now nineteen, had been "nervous ever since," which caused his earnings, also as a tinsmith, to be "trifling." Lulu Engel, now twenty-seven and married, reported that she had worked as a "saleslady" earning five dollars per week before the accident, but due to injuries to her spine, hip, and nervous system, she could no longer work and so was "at home" (a nineteenth- and early twentieth-century euphemism for not being formally employed). Anton Schwartz, now twenty-two and working as a lithographer's apprentice, had had his left leg amputated at the hip and suffered from "abscesses which form from friction of the artificial strap and limb. This naturally interferes with his business very much." The grocer John Vassmer stated that his wife, Wilhlemine, who had not been on the boat, had "died of nervous prostration and broken heart three years after" their eleven-year-old daughter and her sister-in-law, both named Johanna, had died and their son, William, now twenty-three, had been injured in the disaster.[3]

The affidavits were also a testimony to the parental aspirations that had died with their children. Gottlieb Klein, whose wife, Emma, and daughter, Amelia, both died, described ten-year-old Amelia as a "scholar." John H. Klatthaar described his dead fourteen-year-old son, George, as a "college" student. Barbara Doerrhoefer, who survived the disaster with injuries, noted that her daughter, Mamie, now fifteen, had been attending school before the accident but now was "at home unable to work" because of burns all over her body. Henry Cordes noted that his fifteen-year-old brother, Frederick, was a "graduate" before he was killed in the disaster. Butcher Fred Hauff also said his fourteen-year-old daughter, Mathilde, "went to high school," at a time when few children in New York City or State did.[4]

The affidavits were also a way that *General Slocum* survivors asserted their Germanness, correcting city officials and journalists who had misspelled or Americanized names on death certificates or in newspaper articles. Umlauts were added, an extra *n* was added to many names ending in *-man*, and formal

German first names were noted versus Americanized nicknames.[5] Yet at the same time, *General Slocum* survivors' lobbying of Congress reflected their Americanness, as they exercised their rights as American citizens.

The immediate years following the *General Slocum* disaster were also a period of transition in which the old guard of community leaders began to die off, raising the question of who among the younger generations would replace them.

The most important German American political leader to die in this period was Carl Schurz, who died in New York City on May 14, 1906, at the age of seventy-seven. Schurz embodied everything that German immigrants and German Americans liked to think made their community distinct and special: 1848 revolutionary hero, Civil War Union general, U.S. senator, cabinet member and adviser to presidents, journalist, lawyer, proud German, and proud American. Schurz represented for many Americans of German birth or heritage the ability to comfortably straddle the two cultures, borrowing the best from each. Proudly American, Schurz was also a leader of the German community and understood himself as such.[6] He was active in several German societies and regularly socialized with prominent German immigrants, such as William Steinway, Oswald Ottendorfer, and Gustav H. Schwab. Schurz had also been the keynote speaker at the Deutsche Gesellschaft's banquet for Prince Henry of Prussia in 1902, in acknowledgment of his de facto role as leader of the city's and the country's German community.[7]

Although Schurz's funeral and internment were private, German Americans in New York City (as well as in San Francisco and Milwaukee) still observed his death collectively as a community, with a public memorial service held in November. Within a few years, several permanent memorials to Schurz were dedicated in New York City and in his first American home, Wisconsin. Carl Schurz Park in Yorkville—where the mayor's official residence, Gracie Mansion, is located—was dedicated in 1910, and Carl Bitter's monument to Schurz at Morningside Drive and West 116th Street was erected in 1913.[8]

Although Schurz's death was the most prominent, several other important mid-nineteenth-century community leaders also died in the early twentieth century.[9] A new generation of community leaders was emerging, some immigrants but most sons or grandsons of immigrants, who understood themselves as Americans first and members of a particular ethnic group second, if at all. These younger politicians—who had grown up watching the great power struggles between an Irish Catholic–dominated Tammany Hall and anti-Tammany factions of Democrats and Republicans—understood that politics in New York City was about coalitions of various ethnoreligious groups, but a successful political leader could not represent only his particular group; instead, he had to represent all of his constituents.[10]

Two of the most important German American political leaders in the pre–World War I period were William Sulzer and Robert F. Wagner Sr.

Sulzer was not a typical New York City politician, German or otherwise. He had been born in rural Elizabeth, New Jersey, to a German father and an Irish mother, and was first elected to the state assembly as a Tammany Hall Democrat in 1890, where he earned the nickname "Plain Bill." He advanced quickly within the Tammany machine, and in 1893, Tammany boss Richard Croker made Sulzer Speaker of the assembly. A year later, Sulzer was elected to Congress, representing the Tenth District, which encompassed the northern part of Kleindeutschland (the Seventeenth Ward) and the streets just south of Yorkville. He served in Congress until 1912, when he successfully ran for governor of New York as a reform Democrat. But as governor, Sulzer quickly ran into trouble with his old allies in Tammany Hall, who objected to his aggressive reform agenda, especially regarding holding open primaries for party nominations and investigating political corruption. In retaliation, Tammany leaders moved to impeach Sulzer, accusing him misusing campaign funds to buy stock and lying under oath about it. With Tammany Hall loyalists controlling the state legislature, Sulzer was impeached in August 1913 and removed from office a month later.[11] But Sulzer was able to recover somewhat politically and was elected to the assembly from the Sixth District as a Progressive in 1914.[12]

While Sulzer was in Congress, Wagner was just beginning his political career. The future senatorial architect of the New Deal had been born in Hesse-Nassau and came to the United States in 1885 at the age of eight with his immigrant parents. He grew up in Yorkville—not Kleindeutschland—in the 1880s and 1890s in a Lutheran family. After attending public schools, City College, and New York Law School, Wagner was first elected as a Democrat to the state assembly for the Thirtieth District in 1905, when the aftermath of the *General Slocum* accident was still an important political issue. Wagner rose quickly within the Democratic Party and Tammany Hall, and after serving two more terms in the assembly (representing the Twenty-Second District [Yorkville]), he was elected to the state senate for the Sixteenth District in 1909. Within two years, he was president pro tempore of the Senate and then acting lieutenant governor beginning in 1913. Wagner would serve in the state senate until 1918, sit on the New York Supreme Court, and then be elected to the U.S. Senate in 1926.[13]

Wagner witnessed Sulzer's ultimately unsuccessful struggles in Congress on behalf of *General Slocum* survivors and maneuvered himself to be in the right place at the right time in Albany when the Triangle Shirtwaist Factory fire broke out on March 25, 1911, killing 146 garment workers, nearly all of them Russian Jewish and Italian immigrant women. As president pro tempore of the state senate, Wagner placed himself as chair of the state's Factory

Investigating Commission, along with fellow Democrat and assembly majority leader Alfred E. Smith, the future New York governor and 1928 Democratic Party presidential candidate. Advised by the progressive activist Frances Perkins (the future secretary of labor under Franklin D. Roosevelt), Wagner and Smith held widely publicized hearings around the state, interviewed more than 220 witnesses, and ultimately pushed through thirty-eight new laws regulating labor conditions in New York. Just as Sulzer had lobbied for *General Slocum* victims because they were his constituents, so did Wagner fight for the victims of the Triangle Shirtwaist Factory fire, regardless of their ethnicities.

But Wagner was also a loyal member of Tammany Hall, as was Smith, and both leaders followed Tammany boss Charles Murphy's orders to undermine Sulzer as governor in 1913.

In the early 1900s, New York City had more and more career politicians with German heritage, men such as the longtime Bronx president Louis F. Haffen (son of a Bavarian immigrant brewer) and the aldermen Frederick Richter (AD 15), Philip Harnischfeger (AD 39, Bronx), Max Greifenhagen (AD 25), John Dietmer (AD 50), and Joseph Schloss (AD 21). As with earlier generations of politicians, these men were a mix of Democrats and Republicans, for and against Tammany Hall, reflecting German Americans' ongoing political divisions.[14] Among the longest serving German American politician in New York City was John J. Dietz, the son of German immigrants. Dietz was first elected in 1901, served as Tammany's leader in AD 18 from 1905 to 1935, and held a wide variety of municipal offices.[15]

But by 1917, there were fewer clearly German names in the lists of aldermen.[16] This was in part because of the shrinking number of German immigrants in the city who could command the attention of local politicians representing traditionally German districts. Only 502,949 German immigrants entered the United States between 1900 and 1919, most of them arriving before 1915.[17] Fewer German immigrants settled in New York City, and those who did tended to live outside of Manhattan and Kleindeutschland.[18]

In 1900, New York City had 322,343 German-born residents (9 percent of the city's 3,437,202 residents); nearly 190,000 of these (59 percent) lived in Manhattan (New York County).[19] With another 600,000 New Yorkers with German-born parents, one could still say: "New York in 1900 was a city in which household heads of Irish or German parentage predominated."[20] But by 1910, mass immigration from other countries reduced the percentage of Germans in the city, and German American New Yorkers' move out of Kleindeutschland was largely complete. More than 278,000 German immigrants lived in New York City in 1910 (less than 6 percent of the city's 4,766,883 residents), with 117,990 of these living in Manhattan (42 percent of Germans). Another 328,000 New Yorkers had German-born parents, and two-thirds of these people lived outside of Manhattan, most of them in Brooklyn.[21] Always divided politically and now even more geographically dispersed, Germans became less relevant to the political decisions of local representatives in the pre-war years.

In 1910, New York's five boroughs had a total of 4,766,883 residents; in 1920, 5,620,048 residents. Of the 4.7 million people in New York in 1910, three-quarters (3,747,844 persons) were either foreign born or the native-born children of foreign-born parents. The largest ethnic groups in New York in 1910 were from Russia, mostly Jews (733,924, or 19.6 percent); Germany (724,704, or 19.3 percent of the foreign-born population, 15 percent of the city's popula-tion); Ireland (676,420, or 18 percent); and Italy (544,449, or 14.5 percent). New York also had 299,020 Austrian-born and Austrian American residents (8 percent of the city's foreign-born population).[22]

The largest German neighborhood in Manhattan was Yorkville, in AD 22, which was bounded by the East River at 82nd Street to 88th Street and then west and north to Lexington Avenue at 92nd Street. Here 9,800 German-born residents lived with 9,686 Americans born of German-born parents, for a total of 19,486 Germans and German Americans, out of a total of 54,135 residents (36 percent). Immediately south of AD 22 was the AD 20, which had 11,392 Germans and German Americans living between the East River and Lexing-ton Avenue between 82nd Street and 73rd Street.

Besides the large German population, many other immigrants from Cen-tral Europe settled in Yorkville, as previous generations had settled in Klein-deutschland. A large concentration of Hungarians lived on 79th Street east of Third Avenue, and 72nd Street east of Third Avenue was known as Bohemian Boulevard, for the large number of Czech-speaking residents. Austrians, Slavs from the Austro-Hungarian Empire, and many German Jews also lived in Yorkville.

Germans also settled in large numbers on the Upper West Side and in the Bronx. The next largest German district after AD 22 was AD 23, which was in upper western Manhattan, beginning at West 136th Street to Seventh Avenue, north to West 141st Street and Lenox Avenue, and then north again to the Spuyten Duyvil Creek at the Harlem River. Here 16,946 Germans and Ger-man Americans lived in rural suburbia bordering the Bronx.

AD 19 had 11,871 Germans and German Americans and was located between West 101st and 133rd Streets and the Hudson River and Central Park. Sand-wiched between AD 19 and 23 was AD 21, with 9,727 Germans and their German-born children. While this was less than the nearly 17,000 Germans in AD 23 and the 11,871 Germans and German Americans in AD 19, the com-bination of the three northwestern districts between 101st Street and the Bronx made for a large German settlement on the Upper West Side.

Germans and German Americans composed an even larger percentage of the residents of the Bronx and were that borough's largest ethnic group. Out

Table 5.1
Germans and German Americans by Assembly District (1910)

AD	German	German American	Total	Percentage
1	1,697	1,380	4,077	.05
2	711	425	1,136	.01
3	3,055	1,478	4,533	.05
4	499	593	1,092	.01
5	2,125	2,262	4,387	.07
6	965	980	1,945	.02
7	2,188	2,367	4,555	.08
8	729	359	1,088	.01
9	3,221	3,526	6,747	.12
10	5,062	4,197	9,259	.09
11	3,409	4,538	7,947	.15
12	4,226	4,055	8,281	.1
13	2,092	2,440	4,532	.08
14	3,476	2,876	6,352	.1
15	4,409	4,384	8,793	.12
16	5,462	4,825	10,287	.16
17	4,831	5,056	9,887	.15
18	4,917	4,081	8,998	.13
19	5,678	6,193	11,871	.14
20	6,283	5,109	11,392	.17
21	4,384	5,343	9,727	.13
22	9,800	9,686	19,486	.36
23	7,535	9,411	16,946	.14
24	4,315	4,375	8,690	.1
25	2,705	2,352	5,057	.09
26	3,405	3,274	6,679	.08
27	2,302	1,816	4,118	.07
28	3,068	2,952	6,020	.06
29	5,712	4,892	10,604	.16
30	5,006	5,064	10,070	.11
30 Bronx	1,977	2,409	4,386	.177
31	4,634	5,384	10,018	.155
32 (Bronx)	10,727	13,230	23,957	.18
33 (Bronx)	8,756	10,272	19,028	.23
34 (Bronx)	9,181	10,819	20,000	.19
35 (Bronx)	5,951	7,725	13,676	.15

NOTE: In Manhattan, assembly districts are not numerically contiguous; odd-numbered districts went up the west side of the island, while even-numbered districts marked the east side.
SOURCE: Thirteenth Census of the United States, 1910, vol. 3, Population Reports by States, Nebraska–Wyoming: New York (Washington, DC: Government Printing Office, 1913), section 2, chapter 1, 253–256, table 5, "Composition and Characteristics of the Population for Wards (or Assembly Districts) of Cities of 50,000 or more—continued."

of 430,980 residents, 36,592 were German born and 44,455 were American born to German-born parents (81,047, or 19 percent of the total population).[23]

In Brooklyn, German immigrants and their children lived in the northwest—Jackson Heights, and College Point—but also Greenpoint, Williamsburg, and Bushwick.[24]

In Queens, Germans composed 25 percent of the borough's population and were the largest immigrant group in the area: 30,252 German-born residents and 42,597 German Americans (72,849 total). Half of all Germans and German Americans in Queens lived in Flushing in AD 3, which had 15,548 Germans and 21,987 German Americans (37,535 total).[25] Other popular German neighborhoods in Queens were Astoria and Ridgewood.

By 1910, many institutions, especially Vereine—long central to German American identity and community in New York City—had moved to Yorkville. The Germania Music Verein was at 214 East 86th Street, the Aschenbroedel Verein was at 114 East 86th Street, the Freundschaft (Friendship) Verein was at 100 East 72nd Street, and the German Club had moved to 112 Central Park South.[26] The Gesangverein Schillerbund and the New York Turnverein moved to Yorkville in 1896 and 1897, respectively.[27]

But the Verein move north was not complete or universal. The shooting societies could be found all over the city: the Schuetzen Bund was at 620 Ninth Avenue by West 43rd Street, but the New York Gun Verein was at 427 Second Avenue by East 24th Street, and Zettler Rifles was at 159 West 23rd Street.[28]

The German Society, which had been based downtown at 13 Broadway in the 1880s, had moved to 147 Fourth Avenue near 14th Street (on the border of Kleindeutschland) by 1910.[29] The Vereinigte Deutsche Gesellschaften (United German Societies), organized to coordinate the visit of Prince Henry of Prussia, was based out of its secretary's home at 635 St. Ann's Avenue in the Bronx by 1910.[30]

Other fraternal organizations—such as the German Masonic Temple Association (at 220 East 15th Street), the German Odd Fellows Home Association (at 69 St. Mark's Place), and the German-American League (25 Third Avenue and St. Mark's Place)—remained downtown but in the Union Square area.[31]

The German Dispensary (later called the German Hospital and then Lenox Hill Hospital) had moved from 132 Canal Street to 8 East 3rd Street in 1862 and then to 137 Second Avenue at East 8th Street by 1884, to a new building paid for by Oswald and Anna Ottendorfer, the publishers of the *New Yorker Staats-Zeitung*. The hospital began moving some functions to a small building on Park Avenue at East 77th Street in the late 1880s and moved completely to the site in 1905.[32]

Social welfare organizations that served poorer, often recent immigrant clientele—such as the German Legal Aid Society (39 Nassau Street), the Teutonia Benevolent Society (295 Broadway between Duane and Reade) and the

German Mission House Association (25 Park Place)—stayed downtown where clients could more easily find them.[33] The immigrant aid societies—the Lutheran Emigrant Home Association and the St. Raphael-Verein for the Protection of German Catholic Immigrants—were also in Lower Manhattan, near the Battery, at 4 State Street and 6 State Street, respectively.[34] The Deutscher Press Club also remained downtown, at 21 City Hall Place, along with most of the city's other newspapers.[35]

Churches tended to follow their congregations and then faced the problem of what to do with real estate, unless they owned valuable real estate worth keeping. Often, branch churches were created in new neighborhoods. Roman Catholic and Lutheran churches faced the additional issue of the inflexibility and immobility of the parish model and the need for bishops to give permission to create a new parish. Thus, St. Nicholas (1833 Second Street), Most Holy Redeemer (1344 Third Street), and St. Mary Magdalen's (529 East 17th Street) remained downtown, while Immaculate Conception (East 151st Street near Third Avenue), St. Joseph's (408 East 87th Street), and another St. Joseph's (West 125th Street at Ninth Avenue) opened uptown.[36] St. Matthew's Lutheran at Broome and Elizabeth Streets opened a branch at Convent Avenue at 145th Street in the Bronx in 1906 and then finally closed the Broome Street church in 1913. St. James Lutheran Church moved from East 15th Street and Second Avenue to East 73rd Street and Lexington Avenue in 1890. St. Peter Lutheran—which had opened in 1871 on East 46th Street and Lexington Avenue—moved a few blocks north to East 54th Street and Lexington Avenue in 1910. New Lutheran churches opened uptown as well, such as Immanuel Lutheran, which opened its doors at 215 East 83rd Street in 1912.[37]

Other Protestant churches also opened new congregations, as people moved. The First Baptist Church remained at 336 East 14th Street, while First German Baptist of Harlem opened at 220 East 118th Street in 1888. The Second German Baptist Church (founded in 1878) moved to 407 West 43rd Street in 1892, while the Third German Baptist was at 1127 Fulton Avenue and East 166th Street in the Bronx starting in 1889 (this closed in 1912), and Eagle Avenue Baptist was at 921 Eagle Avenue in the Bronx. Immanuel Baptist moved to 411 East 75th Street in 1907.[38]

Of the Methodists, the First German Methodist Episcopal Church was at 48 St. Mark's Place, but the Second German Methodist was at 346 West 40th Street, and St. Paul's was at 308 East 55th Street. Other German Methodist churches were in the Bronx (German Methodist, Elton Avenue and East 158th Street; St. John's, Richard Avenue at Wakefield; Tremont Methodist, Bathgate Avenue by East 176th Street).[39]

Zion Presbyterian Church moved from East 40th Street and Lexington to East 45th Street and Lexington in 1902 before moving to the Bronx in 1910 and then merging with Zion Reformed Church on Stebbins Road in the Bronx in 1911.[40]

Other uptown Protestant churches included St. Paul's Evangelical Reformed Church at 608 East 141st Street and two Seventh Day Adventist churches, one at 356 East 72nd Street and the other at 2796 Third Avenue in the Bronx.[41] By 1910, none of the city's five German Evangelical churches were on the Lower East Side but rather were between Midtown and Harlem.[42] The German Moravian Church had congregations on West 34th Street (Beth-Tphillah), Wilkins Avenue and Jennings (Second Moravian), West 63rd Street (Third Moravian), and an English-language congregation on Lexington Avenue and East 30th Street.[43]

Among the important synagogues, Ansche Chesed moved to East 63rd Street and Lexington Avenue and then, in 1908, headed farther north to Harlem, where the congregation built a pillared, neoclassical structure at 114th Street and Seventh Avenue (now Adam Clayton Boulevard).[44]

German-language theater began to diversify in the early 1900s, in response to competition from vaudeville, an emerging Yiddish theater scene, and, after about 1910, silent films. The main German theaters were located around Union Square. (Times Square would not become such until 1905 and would not become a theater district until the 1920s.) The Thalia Theater was at East 15th Street and Union Square, while the Irving Place Theater was at 11 Irving Place near Union Square and East 14th Street, on the old Amberg's German Theater site. The actor-turned-producer Adolph Philipp owned both the Germania Theater on Broadway and Astor Place in the old neighborhood, and the Wintergarten zum Schwarzen Adler Theater on East 86th Street in Yorkville.[45]

These theaters offered a wide variety of German-language entertainment: classical plays, works by contemporary German playwrights, and American-style vaudeville in German. At Philipp's theaters, in particular, audiences enjoyed "Dutch Act" comedies that spoofed German American culture using stereotypes. These plays and light musicals reflected the modern urban life that German New Yorkers experienced every day—the Irish cop, the German butcher, the Italian ditch digger, and so—and reflected how Americanized Germans had become: "Whereas once they might have delighted in the familiarity of seeing themselves satirized as they were, they now delighted in seeing themselves satirized as they once were but no longer considered themselves to be."[46]

But even as German theater was offering more and different types of German culture, German-language theaters struggled as the number of German speakers in the city shrank and longtime audiences moved farther away. The Atlantic Garden (a longtime beer garden that also offered music and theater) became a Yiddish-language theater in 1910. The *New York Times* announced the change: "Dwellers of the Bowery paused and rubbed their eyes yesterday when they passed Atlantic Garden, for the front of the famous old resort, which has stood almost unchanged on its site just below Canal Street since before the civil war, was plastered over with billboards in Yiddish announcing a Hebrew variety programme."

As the former owner William Kramer Jr. explained: "The German and Irish population that formerly supported us has moved far away from the Bowery, and we must adapt ourselves to the changed conditions."[47] Kramer had already changed the original Thalia Theater—which was next door to the Atlantic Garden and which he also owned—into a Yiddish theater as early as 1879.

German theater producers also faced competition from film. Film (at least in the silent era) posed an economic threat to all kinds of live entertainment but especially stage theater, because film transcended language and thus allowed film entrepreneurs to pursue a potentially much larger market of customers, irrespective of what language they spoke.[48] But again, many of the pioneers of this new entertainment medium were German immigrants, men such as Carl Laemmle and Eberhard Schneider, who opened dozens of nickelodeons and then movie theaters in the 1910s.[49]

Vereine, the foundation of German American life in New York, became increasingly brittle and inflexible as they matured. Several prominent Vereine, including the Turnverein and the Deutsche Gesellschaft, celebrated their fiftieth, sixtieth, or even one hundredth anniversaries in the 1900s.[50] These organizations, along with the larger Sängervereine and Schützenvereine, were no longer intimate clubs organized by and for immigrants but were now mass membership organizations that often required nominations and fees to join and that were highly structured.

The ultimate example of this was the activities of the Deutsch-Amerikanischer Nationalbund (National German-American Alliance [NGAA]) in the prewar years.[51] The growth and activities of the NGAA reflected German Americans' increased self-consciousness about themselves as an ethnic group and language preservation at a moment when, for many German Americans, Germanness was becoming more optional as an individual identity versus central to community survival.

NGAA leaders were particularly concerned about language preservation and promotion. Recognizing that German immigrants had been mixing English words in with their spoken and written German since the 1870s, community leaders began to advocate for at least bilingualism, recognizing that they could not convince German Americans to give up using English. These bilingualism advocates also made the important concession that English was the de facto national language of the United States.[52] The German book publisher and seller Ernst Steiger observed:

It is sometimes expected of our fellow tribesmen in America that they should not learn English alone, but should also let the old mother tongue go completely. Those who do this to us are misunderstood people. Nobody will deny that the German-American should learn English. He owes it to his new fatherland and he owes it to himself. But the fact that he should therefore reject the German language is more than folly. As American citizens, we should Americanize ourselves. Certainly we should. I have always advocated sensible Americanization. But that does not mean complete de-Germanization. It means that we take the best traits of the American being and merge them with the best traits of the German being. This is how we make the most valuable contribution to the American national character and American civilization. And so we as Americans should acquire the English language and not lose our mother tongue in German.[53]

Other German American community leaders blamed parents for not doing more to maintain German as the primary language in the home: "Unfortunately, our first German clubs seem to be becoming more and more American and especially the German-Americans and their offspring seem to be the grave-diggers of the German language in America. Many parents are too comfortable to speak German with their own children. That is why the English language is gaining the upper hand."[54]

NGAA leaders began to argue that despite many aspects of assimilation occurring—English adoption, intermarriage, Anglicization of names, residential integration, and so on—German Americans could continue to exist as a distinct group, different from both Germans in Germany and other non-German Americans. But how this was to happen was left undefined by the NGAA or other German American intellectuals:

The future of the German element is therefore safe in America! The Germans will remain Germans there, but will be Germans of a different kind. They will differ from their brothers in Europe in their ideas for the state, in their views on civil rights, in the measures taken by the community, in the valuation of man power, in political freedom and worldly unrestrictedness. They will weigh all these goods of their part of the world against the lesser extent of them on this side of the ocean; but nonetheless those who fraternally embrace the sympathetic bonds of the two great tribes.[55]

But changes took a different course: "By 1900 the vast majority of German-Americans were assimilated into American society. Many had English-speaking neighbors and lived in predominantly English-speaking parts of the nation's cities. Their children attended public schools where English was the primary language of instruction, and the majority of the books in use had a decided Anglo American focus in terms of literature, culture and history. Within this community, however, were those who viewed themselves as American but who also sought to maintain Old World institutions and ties with the fatherland."[56]

In New York City, the German American community no longer had the elements that had helped it maintain linguistic and cultural autonomy in the mid-nineteenth century: geographic isolation and residential stability. It had never had religious or ideological homogeneity; political differences and divisions were the norm. By the 1900s, Germans and German Americans lived in all parts of the city, although more often in some neighborhoods than others, and regularly interacted with other ethnic groups. English—not German—had become the lingua franca of German New York.[57]

As the community continued to evolve into its fourth and fifth generations, community leaders began making self-conscious efforts to preserve the city's Deutschtum by asserting Germans' supposed uniqueness in highly visible ways. The United German Societies' annual Deutscher Tag (German Day) celebrations became more and more elaborate. In late September through early October 1909, German Americans held their German Day fest as part of the city's larger Hudson-Fulton Festival, which commemorated the three hundredth anniversary of Henry Hudson's exploration of New York Harbor and the one hundredth anniversary of Robert Fulton's establishment of steamboat service on the Hudson River.[58] In 1913, the one hundredth anniversary of the birth of the German composer Richard Wagner was observed at the Hippodrome with a mass concert featuring one thousand singers.[59]

German American intellectuals and activists also began publishing national magazines designed to bring German Americans together as a self-conscious community.[60] But these publications had small circulations and were generally unsuccessful, especially when compared to *Puck* and some of the older German-language magazines and newspapers or even to the German Historical Society's journal: "In the long run, the very richness and diversity of German-America, and the widening variety of perceptions of it by others, proved to be the weakness in that elaborate structure."[61]

By the early 1910s, German Americans were comfortable enough with their dual identities as both German and American that they could advocate dual ethnic identities as a strength versus a weakness. As John Higham observed: "Cultural pluralism would appeal to people who were already strongly enough positioned to imagine that permanent minority status might be advantageous. It was congenial to minority spokesmen confident enough to visualize themselves at the center rather than the periphery of American experience. Accordingly, cultural pluralism proved most attractive to people who were already largely assimilated. It was itself one of the products of the American melting pot."[62]

On the eve of World War I, German Americans in New York were comfortable and confident in their understandings of themselves as both German and American. Their community had survived the tragedy of the *General Slocum* disaster and the movement out of the old Kleindeutschland neighborhood to other districts, where Germans had created new German American communities. Their Vereine increasingly resembled English-speakers' clubs, in large part because of the influence German Americans had on Anglo American styles of socializing and recreation. German American political leaders more and more resembled politicians of other ethnicities, and not even the NGAA could convince German Americans to vote as an ethnic bloc. This question of what defined this community, what made a person German American beyond ancestry, would be hotly debated between 1914 and 1919. But in 1913, the German historian Otto Spengler could proclaim: "The future of German New York is brilliant. We can look forward with good confidence."[63]

6

Becoming Invisible

• •

German New Yorkers
during World War I

On Friday, July 31, 1914, the New York City waterfront hummed with activity. In Hoboken, on the New Jersey side of the Hudson, the North German Lloyd steamship the SS *Prinzess Irene*, and the Hamburg-America line's newest luxury liner, the SS *Vaterland*, were scheduled to sail the following day at 11:00 A.M. and noon, respectively, and hundreds of crew members and dock workers were working to get the massive ships ready for departure for Southampton, Cherbourg, Hamburg, and Bremen. Hundreds of tons of coal, food, and beverages, as well as mail and other freight, needed to be loaded on board for the ships' seven-day transatlantic voyages. Among the 2,700 passengers booked on the *Vaterland* were the Duchess of Marlborough, William A. Rockefeller, and Mrs. William G. Rockefeller. These and many other wealthy Americans were going to Europe for vacation and business. Another 750 third-class and 800 fourth-class immigrant passengers were also returning to Europe on the *Vaterland*, while the *Prinzess Irene* had room for 1,954 steerage passengers.

Nearly every day of the week a ship belonging to one of the German, Dutch, or Scandinavian steamship companies arrived or departed from the Hoboken piers, just as the British, French, and other European steamship companies sailed from their piers on the Manhattan side of the Hudson River. Passenger transportation and freight shipping to and from the Port of New York were the lifeblood of New York City, connecting the United States' largest manufacturing city to foreign markets, capital, and labor.

Men were going about their businesses on the docks and in the offices of the steamship lines when suddenly an announcement came from Hamburg America vice director William G. Sickel from his office at 45 Broadway: "In view of the uncertainty of the present European situation we have decided to postpone the sailing of the *Vaterland* tomorrow and the *Amerika* from Boston, August 1, and the *Imperator* from Hamburg, July 31. Due notice will be given of the eventual sailing dates."[1] North German Lloyd made a similar announcement about the sailing of the SS *Prinzess Irene* (destined for Genoa) and the SS *Kronprinz Wilhelm*, scheduled to sail from Hoboken to Bremen Tuesday, August 3. Then shipping executives made a further announcement, even more shocking: several steamships already at sea—the HAPAG ship the SS *President Grant* and the North German Lloyd ship the SS *Grosser Kurfürst* (already more than four hundred miles at sea after sailing on Thursday, July 30)—had been wired instructions to return to New York.

Within twenty-four hours more wireless orders were transmitted to German ships at sea on the Atlantic and in Caribbean: Germany had declared war on Russia, seek neutral harbors, and watch out for French warships. By the end of the first week of August, Germany had declared war on France and invaded Luxembourg and Belgium, and Great Britain had declared war on Germany. By August 7, the beginning of the great Battle of the Frontiers, nearly twenty German steamships crowded the piers of Hoboken, Manhattan, and Brooklyn, and shipping company managers were saying that no German ship would sail until the war in Europe had ended. Great Britain's blockade of Germany prevented ships from entering or leaving the North Sea and made it impossible for German ships to return to Germany for the duration of the war without risk of being captured and confiscated.[2]

So began a long period of waiting, from August 1, 1914, to April 6, 1917, in which the United States remained neutral from the slaughter in Europe, before finally entering the conflict on the side of Great Britain, France, and Russia. It was during this period of thirty-three months that Germans in New York City tested the boundaries of American identity and found, to their dismay, that Americanism was not defined by the exercise of American political values, such as free speech and association, but rather by the English language and public conformity to Anglo American values and behavioral practices.

To be German or German American in New York City in 1914–1918 was a time of reflection on the great immortal question, "Who am I?" The answer for many—as is often the case with existential questions—was not achieved easily or painlessly. For German immigrants who were citizens of the German Empire, the decision was made for them by the U.S. government when the

United States entered the war: they were alien enemies, to be viewed as potential terrorists, a fifth column of spies and saboteurs, and imprisoned. For German immigrants who had naturalized, U.S. citizenship protected them from the ignominious status of alien enemy but did not prevent them from experiencing prejudice, discrimination, or harassment because of their place of birth. In addition, Americans of German birth or heritage faced the emotional and psychological stresses of dual and conflicted loyalties in the face of Anglo Americans' demand for 100 percent Americanism (which meant taking the side of Great Britain and her allies).

In reaction, German Americans both reasserted (unsuccessfully) their loyalty and patriotism on Anglo American terms and deemphasized their Germanness, abandoning the German language and their beloved Vereine and denying their German heritage. A long process of disappearing into American culture rapidly turned into an effort to hide in plain sight or become invisible.

Austria-Hungary's declaration of war on Serbia on July 28, 1914, and the continent's rapid descent into war surprised many Americans, even those who had been following European events since Serbian nationalists had assassinated the heir to the Austria-Hungarian Empire, Franz Ferdinand, in Sarajevo, Bosnia-Herzegovina, on June 28, 1914.

By the end of the first week of August 1914, as German, French, British, and Belgian armies clashed along the Franco-German border, the piers of the Port of New York were crowded with mostly German ships unable to sail. HAPAG had its liners—the SS *Vaterland*, SS *Hamburg*, SS *Pennsylvania*, SS *President Grant*, SS *President Lincoln*, SS *König Wilhelm II*, SS *Prinz Joachim*, SS *Prinz Eitel Friedrich*, SS *Nassovia*, SS *Pisa*, SS *Allemania*, and SS *Grácia*—in dock in Hoboken or in rented berths in Brooklyn. North German Lloyd had the SS *Kaiser Wilhelm II*, the SS *George Washington*, the SS *Barbarossa*, the SS *Grosser Kurfürst*, the SS *Prinzess Irene*, and the SS *Friedrich der Grosse* also in New York. Four German oil tankers were in dock in Tompkinsville, New Jersey.[3]

A few British ships were also in New York when the war broke out: the White Star Line's SS *Adriatic* and Cunard's SS *Saxonia*. The British freight shipper Uranium Line had two ships—the SS *Uranium* and the SS *Principello*—and the Lamport & Holt Line had its SS *Vandyck* in New York Harbor.

Although there was a flurry of excitement at the announcement of war—immigrant military reservists flooded consulates with questions about their military obligations, and German and Austrian immigrants paraded through the streets of Hoboken before going to a beer garden to sing songs—the reality of a European conflict quickly set in.[4] Transatlantic travel almost completely ceased, as warring nations tightened borders and would-be immigrants and travelers were unable to leave Europe (1,218,480 immigrants entered the United States in 1914; only 326,700 did so in 1915).[5]

The militarization of the Atlantic affected thousands of travelers, including Americans in Europe trying to get back to the United States.[6] On August 12, 1914, Johanna Hager, who had been raising her three grandsons after they had been orphaned by the *General Slocum* accident, applied at the U.S. embassy in Berlin for an emergency passport. Hager, who had been born in Prussia in 1849 and had lived in the United States since 1879, said that she had been in Germany only for a few weeks and wanted to return home to New York "at once."[7] Another *General Slocum* survivor, the musician Joseph Eller and his second wife, Auguste, were also trapped in Germany. It was more than two years before they were able to return to the United States, via the Netherlands.[8]

One of the most famous German Americans to be stranded in Europe was the brewer George Ehret. Ehret had been suffering from ill health for the past five years and so had begun to take a six-month vacation in Germany to visit the many health spas there. In May 1914, Ehret sailed for Europe, intending to return, as usual, in November. But now Ehret found himself trapped, along with his daughter, Baroness Anna M. von Zedlitz. The American ambassador to Germany, James W. Gerard, refused to allow the eighty-three-year old Ehret to accompany him back to the United States, fearing that the brewer would die in his care. Ehret ultimately spent four years in Germany before finally being able to return to New York City in August 1918.[9]

With the end of transatlantic travel, waterfront jobs and other businesses, such as bars and boarding houses, that depended on sailors' custom began to suffer on both sides of the Hudson. Although light manufacturing was the largest area of employment in New York City, shipping and water-related transportation were still very important to the local economy. In New York and New Jersey, 9,000 men worked as sailors in the New York Harbor; another 23,500 longshoremen lived in New York and New Jersey. About 60,800 New York men worked as baggage and freight handlers while New Jersey had 16,500 men working such jobs.[10] These jobs dried up as the piers became disturbingly quiet.

With the outbreak of war, the question of American neutrality quickly emerged. German New Yorkers had long been divided over many issues, but neutrality was one issue that strongly united the city's German community. Although some Germans did support Germany in the war, most German Americans simply wanted the United States to remain out of the conflict. Here they were joined by many other Americans of a wide variety of ethnic and religious backgrounds, particularly Irish and Jewish. The combined German, Jewish, and Irish populations and their opposition to American entry on the side of Great Britain and her allies made New York City a hotbed of antiwar sentiment between 1914 and 1917.[11]

The loudest voices for neutrality were German-language newspapers, who sought to both inform their readers of the German side of the war and to lobby for neutrality. The *New Yorker Staats-Zeitung* published a daily column, in English, entitled The War Situation from Day to Day, as well as a German-language Kriegs-Bulletin (war bulletin).[12]

But information about what was happening in Europe became increasingly difficult to obtain after Great Britain cut Germany's transatlantic telegraph cables in early August 1914. This resulted in American newspapers becoming increasingly dependent on English-language news transmitted via British cables, and this information was heavily censored by the British government, which also incorporated its own propaganda into the material allowed to filter into the United States.[13]

The *New Yorker Staats-Zeitung* and other mainstream German-language press, such as the William Randolph Hearst–owned *New Yorker Herald*, came to view nearly all English-language coverage of the war (except for that of Irish papers) as British propaganda. But these German-language papers, in turn, became dependent on the German government via the German embassy in Washington and the consulate in New York as their primary sources of information about the war. The *Staats-Zeitung's* war coverage increasing strayed from providing an alternative perspective to pro-British journalism to uncritically repeating German government propaganda. To be able to reach (and hopefully influence) Germans in the United States, the German government bought $200,000 worth of stock in the *Staats-Zeitung* and paid $550,000 of its debts to keep the paper publishing. In return, publisher Herman Ridder became the loudest and most prominent German American voice for neutrality until his death in early November 1915.[14]

At the beginning of the war, there were few public demonstrations against it. New York City saw a small (about 1,500 participants) antiwar/pro-peace march at the end of August 1914 led by a coalition of women's groups.[15] But on June 24, 1915, an estimated 25,000 people packed the 12,000-seat Madison Square Garden to hear the former secretary of state and presidential candidate William Jennings Bryan and several other speakers denounce the war and urge that the United States remain neutral. Unlike the women's march for peace in 1914, this rally had been organized by German Americans and featured German-language speeches on several street corners outside of the Garden (although the speeches inside the Garden were given in English).[16]

Germans and German Americans also raised funds for the Red Cross and for charities for German war widows and orphans. One of the largest events was the German-American Bazaar for War Relief to the Central Powers, held for two weeks in December 1914 at the Seventy-First Regiment's Armory Hall on Park Avenue and East 34th Street. This huge fair—organized to resemble a Nürnberg Christmas market—attracted thousands of people and raised nearly $500,000.[17] A second, even larger bazaar was held in March 1916. This bazaar decorated Madison Square Garden as a medieval town square (but with streets named for Presidents Washington and Lincoln, among others), attracted one million visitors, and raised $760,000.[18] And a huge *Kriegshilfe* (war assistance) Volkfest was held in August 1916.[19] All of these events were aggressively promoted and extensively covered by the *Staats-Zeitung*.[20]

In November 1916, a more exclusive fundraiser for charities of the Central Powers was held on board the Hamburg-America luxury liner the SS *Vaterland*. The ball was attended by such notables as the publisher William Randolph Hearst, the Metropolitan Opera tenor Jacques Urlus, and 650 other elite members of the city's German American community.[21]

During the neutrality period, German Americans proudly asserted their rights as Americans to express their political opinions. This was in accordance with their long-standing belief in a pluralistic and ideological understanding of Americanism. When Anglo Americans increasingly attacked German Americans and Irish Americans as "hyphens" (Americans with divided loyalties), German Americans fought back, demanding to know why a hyphen was acceptable for Anglo-Saxons but not for German Americans. As the *Pittsburgh Volksblatt & Freiheits Freund* editor George Seibel declared at the German Day observations on August 31, 1916, in Johnstown, Pennsylvania: "The German-Americans believe in the hyphen, but they know that the hyphen is a mark of union, not of separation."[22]

German Americans also began to reach out to other attacked ethnic groups, and the National German-American Alliance formally joined with the Ancient Order of Hibernians in January 1917 to coordinate lobbying for neutrality.

The fight over the hyphen peaked during the fall 1916 presidential campaign, when President Woodrow Wilson campaigned on a platform of "he kept us out of war," referring to his refusal to ask for a declaration of war after a German U-boat sunk the British Cunard ocean liner the SS *Lusitania* on May 7, 1915, killing 1,198 people. But Wilson was also more than willing to attack Irish Americans, especially with the hyphen label. His most caustic comment about dual loyalties came in late September 1916 when the president publicly sparred with the Irish American editor Jeremiah A. O'Leary, the publisher of the *Bull*. After O'Leary criticized Wilson for "pro-British policies" for allowing American businesses to sell munitions and other supplies and to make loans to Great Britain, France, and Russia, Wilson responded in a widely circulated telegram: "I would feel deeply mortified to have you or anyone like you vote for me. Since you have access to many disloyal Americans and I have not, I will ask you to convey this message to them."[23] It was clear that the Anglophile president viewed any criticism of his foreign policy as unpatriotic and un-American, and German Americans voted in large numbers for Wilson's Republican opponent, the former Supreme Court justice and New York governor Charles Evans Hughes, who supported a neutral foreign policy regarding war.[24]

What was surprising for many German Americans during the political debate about neutrality was the swiftness of other Americans' rejection of Germans' assertions of Americanness. German Americans were right to be surprised: for years, American politicians and the mainstream English-language press had treated German culture as if it were American culture. The *New York Times*' society columnists covered the yacht races in Kiel as extensively as it did the sailing in Newport.[25] New York City mayors feted German political and military leaders whenever given the chance, as when Mayor William J. Gaynor hosted a city dinner in honor of German naval officers visiting New York City for Fleet Week in June 1912.[26]

There had also been a mantra chanted by many—both German American and not—in the mid-1910s that Kaiser Wilhelm II was a force for peace in Europe. (Given Wilhelm II's obsession with military—especially naval—power, calling him a "lover of peace" was rather delusional.)[27] For example, in 1909, at the end of the Hudson-Fulton celebrations, Mayor George B. McClellan, Jr. called the kaiser "the most potent force for the preservation of European peace."[28] In 1912, the *New York Times* and other large national papers praised Wilhelm for preventing Europe from going to war over France's annexation of Morocco (Wilhelm, in fact, nearly involved Germany in a war with both France and Great Britain), and prominent intellectuals, such as University of California president Benjamin Ide Wheeler, suggested that the kaiser should receive the Nobel Peace Prize for this foreign policy interjection.[29] Andrew Carnegie reiterated this idea as well with his endorsement of a book by the pacifist Alfred H. Fried called *The German Emperor and the Peace of the World*.[30]

But by the fall of 1914, mainstream English-language papers remembered previous foreign policy conflicts with Germany over colonial possessions in the Pacific and reinterpreted these tensions as examples of Germany's inherent aggressiveness and deceitfulness.[31] Reflecting the success of British propaganda (and the failure of German propaganda), the American press did a complete about-face and began calling Germans both in Germany and in the United States "Teutons" and "Huns," and the slurs and attacks grew sharper as tensions grew between the United States and Germany.[32]

The weakness and shallowness of Anglo Americans' prewar appreciation of German Americans' Americanness quickly became apparent. In early 1915, the Brooklyn Sängerbund was chosen to host the twenty-fourth annual national Sängerfest, scheduled to be held at the end of May. Such a major cultural event had been covered by both the German- and English-speaking press for decades and was recognized as an example of the high level of culture available in New York City. Both Democratic and Republican politicians understood the festival to be an enjoyable networking event where German American voters could be courted. In the case of the 1915 Sängerfest, President Wilson had promised to attend, as did New York governor Charles Whitman, New York City mayor John Purroy Mitchel, and Brooklyn borough president Lewis H. Pounds. But after the sinking of the SS *Lusitania* on May 7, 1915, these politicians sought to avoid associating themselves with anything that resembled German culture (or Kultur).[33]

It was clear from the tone of the English-language public commentary that German Americans' greatest sin was pride, specifically pride in assuming that they were American. German Americans had long asserted their Americanness with a type of arrogance that other groups, especially Anglo Americans, resented.

For decades, German Americans had told other Americans (and themselves) that they were just as American as anyone else (if not more so). Germans claimed that their hard work, ingenuity, and entrepreneurship had literally built the United States and that they had made significant contributions to American society and culture that few other groups could match.[34] Now the dominant English-speaking society said that German immigrants' contributions were not only not welcomed but were actively harmful to the United States. Kultur was not culture; it was now defined as autocracy and militarism. Kultur was also reduced to frankfurters, sauerkraut, and opera and quickly renamed (hot dogs, "liberty cabbage") or banned.

For Germans and especially German Americans, the hypernationalism of the war was not simply a question of political loyalty to the nation-state. Rather, 100 percent Americanism was an attack on culture and its inherent value (or lack thereof) to a society. Thus, this form of nationalism was impossible to debate politically or rationally.

Relations between Germany and the United States deteriorated in early 1917, and by February, it was clear that tensions were coming to a head. Germany announced it was resuming unrestricted submarine warfare on January 31, 1917, and the United States broke off diplomatic relations with Germany on February 3.

Then, on April 3, 1917, President Wilson asked Congress for a declaration of war against Germany and her allies. German Americans were shocked, especially after Wilson had campaigned on a peace and neutrality platform only six months earlier. As the *New Yorker Staats-Zeitung*'s new publisher Bernard H. Ridder, the son of Herman Ridder, wrote: "The address of the President, demanding a full and complete warfare against the German Imperial Government will come as a shock to millions of Americans of German ancestry." But Ridder continued: "The President need have no concern as to the loyalty of Americans of German ancestry."[35]

In New York City, the word of the president's request resulted in a wave of flag waving, singing of the "Star-Spangled Banner," and hints of the vigilantism that would mark the American war experience: the mobbing and beating of people who expressed antiwar sentiments.[36] Three days later, on April 6, 1917, Good Friday, the United States formally declared war on Germany.

With the declaration of war, the United States set into motion its tentative plans for mobilization. Two policies in particular had significant and long-lasting effects on Germans in New York City: the internment of alien enemies (citizens of countries now at war with the United States) and the seizure of ships and other property belonging to German companies.[37] The Wilson administration's decision to avoid using federal power and instead rely on state and local authorities to implement federal policies—plus its encouragement of volunteerism, on the part of the general public—also had significant consequences on German immigrants and German Americans, resulting in an oppressive atmosphere of coercive peer pressure, harassment, and vigilantism.[38]

The long build-up to war in the winter of 1916–1917 gave the federal government time to prepare (with British government assistance) lists of German and Austro-Hungarian citizens it considered potential threats to the war effort.[39] On the day that war was declared, April 6, Department of Justice agents arrested thirteen prominent Germans in New York and New Jersey, including Rev. Herman Bruckner of St. Matthew's German Lutheran Church in Hoboken.[40] The forty-four-year-old Bruckner was arrested at his home at the church's rectory on 8th Street while five hundred members of his congregation were at the church waiting for him to preside over a Good Friday service. Bruckner—who had taken over one of the largest German churches in Hoboken after his predecessor had suffered a nervous breakdown after being stranded in Germany in August 1914—was targeted because he was the president of the German Seaman's House in Hoboken and, it was alleged, had acted as an intermediary for imprisoned German sailors in Jamaica (then an English colony), transporting their mail and sending them such supplies as cigarettes. Bruckner had also drawn attention to himself in 1915 when he had sworn an affidavit to the German ambassador Johann Heinrich Graf von Bernstorff that he had seen guns on the SS *Lusitania* before she sailed on her ill-fated voyage to Great Britain.[41]

A few days later, more Germans were arrested, including Karl George Frank, the former head of the Sayville Wireless Company.[42] For the rest of 1917, prominent German businessmen were arrested and detained, including the banker Rudolph Hecht, the HAPAG auditor Heinrich S. Ficke, the Deutsche Bank executive Hugo Schmidt, and F. A. Borgermeister, the personal secretary of Heinrich Albert, the German embassy's financial attaché. Ultimately more than 6,300 German citizens were arrested under presidential warrants; several thousand others were detained without a warrant; and about one-third of these were interned, either at Ellis Island or in internment camps at Hot Springs, North Carolina; Fort Oglethorpe, Georgia; and Fort Douglas, Utah.[43]

The crews of the German shipping lines were also arrested and detained at Ellis Island, not only because they were aliens but also because they were employees of foreign corporations considered vital to the German war effort. The head of security for the Hamburg-America line, Paul Koenig; pier superintendents Captain Otto Wolpert and Captain Eno Bode; and fellow employee Henry von Staden were among those HAPAG employees arrested in the first days of the war. In total, four thousand German crew members were arrested and detained in internment camps.[44]

These arrests were not simply a dragnet of German citizens in the United States. Several employees of the German steamship companies had been involved in suspicious activity in 1914–1917. Koenig had been arrested in 1916 for conspiring to blow up the Welland Canal that connected Lake Ontario and Lake Erie. In June 1916, he had pled guilty to trying to buy information about Allied arms shipments but was released on his own recognizance until his trial, not yet underway in April 1917. Wolpert was under indictment for allegedly plotting to smuggle bombs onto Allied ships.[45] Another German citizen in Hoboken, Fritz Kolb, had been arrested in March 1917 and soon after convicted and sentenced to a maximum of five years in state prison for possessing explosives.[46] In the first few months of the war, other Germans in Hoboken were arrested for alleged espionage and bomb making.[47]

Using the argument that certain property, especially ships and piers, were vital to the German war effort and therefore forfeit, the United States confiscated several million dollars' worth of German property and businesses in the first weeks of war. In New York Harbor, the seizure of property began the same day war was declared. At dawn on April 6, 1917, three hundred customs officials and soldiers from the Twenty-Second U.S. Infantry seized twenty-seven German ships in the Port of New York, most of them docked at the Hoboken piers. Reflecting the longtime relationship between port authorities and the German captains, the port collector Dudley Field Malone hosted the officers from the Hamburg-America ships to breakfast at the Duke's House hotel while the North German Lloyd officers ate at the Hof Brau Haus before the Germans were taken to Ellis Island for internment.[48] Two weeks later, the federal government seized the piers belonging to the Hamburg-America and North German Lloyd lines, bringing three companies of soldiers over from New York in the middle of the night of April 19 to take control of the facilities.[49]

The United States had two goals in seizing the German ships: firstly, it intended to keep them out of their new enemy's hands, and secondly, the Americans hoped to convert the large luxury liners into troop transport ships, since the United States had no large Navy or merchant marine fleet of its own. But the German crews had disabled their vessels' engines; only the massive *Vaterland* was not damaged.[50] (On August 31, 1918, a record 46,214 soldiers shipped out of the Port of New York; the *Vaterland*, renamed *Leviathan*, alone carried 12,000 men.[51]) Ultimately, the United States salvaged twenty German liners and converted them into troop transports, and these ships, along with twenty-three others, made 936 transatlantic sailings to transport the American Expeditionary Force (AEF) to Europe.[52]

Although the military took over the piers in April 1917, it was not until the end of June 1918 that the federal government made the confiscation official. In late March 1918, the U.S. Senate voted unanimously, with little debate, to authorize the president to seize and sell the German piers under the Trading with the Enemy Act. The Senate also voted to authorize the president to seize and sell all German-owned or controlled property in the country to "extinguish every vestige of Junkerism from America forever."[53]

Besides seizing German property owned in the United States, the federal government also claimed property owned by businessmen who had long lived in the United States but who were still German citizens. In total, the alien property custodian A. Mitchell Palmer came to control property worth $1.5 billion organized into nearly 30,000 trusts. Palmer targeted the large German chemical and pharmaceutical industries that had plants in the United States. But the brewers were also targeted, most notably Hell Gate Brewery owner George Ehret. Even though Ehret was an American citizen and had two American-born sons, who were active in the business, the alien property custodian used the excuse of Ehret's presence in Germany as a reason to seize his entire estate (around $40 million) and placed it in a trust to be managed by lawyers and accountants controlled by the custodian. Ehret's property was not returned until after the war.[54] Ehret was lucky: most German-owned property—such as corporate assets, including patents; stocks and bonds; real estate; and other random items—was not returned but rather auctioned off or otherwise sold, with the proceeds going into U.S. Treasury coffers.[55]

Included in the extensive portfolio seized and managed by Palmer's office was property owned by wealthy American women who were married to German or Austro-Hungarian citizens. Under American law at the time, a woman's citizenship was tied to that of her husband's citizenship, and therefore, when a female U.S. citizen married a foreigner, she immediately lost her American citizenship and was assumed to have the citizenship of her husband. Among the more prominent of these mostly German American women was the brewer Frederick Schaefer's daughter, Rosa K. Schertel von Burtenbach, who had a trust fund of $200,000 from her father. Being related to the former president Theodore Roosevelt did not protect the Baroness Cornelia C. Zedlitz, the daughter of Charles Yates Roosevelt, from having her trust fund of $1 million and personal property of $200,000 seized by Palmer. Other prominent New Yorkers to have property seized were Cornelius Vanderbilt's daughter, the Countess Gladys Vanderbilt Szechenyi of Hungary, who had nearly $4 million in securities and income from a $5 million trust fund; the Baroness Clara Erhart von Truchsess, daughter of Pfizer cofounder Charles Erhart, who had an estate of more than $1 million in a trust fund and in securities; and the Baroness

Olivia Louise von Rothkirch, daughter of the insurance magnate William John Brown, who had a trust fund of $1 million.[56]

With the United States' entry into war, life for New York's and New Jersey's large German community immediately became very difficult. Citizens of Germany, Austria-Hungary, and the Ottoman Empire were required to register with the government as alien enemies. The government established extensive rules defining what alien enemies could and could not do, including not being allowed to own a radio, to be within half a mile of a military installation or factory contracting with the military (almost impossible, given New York City's geography), and to make statements or engage in activity designed to undermine the war effort.[57]

The most difficult of these rules were those that controlled where German citizens could live and work. In late May 1917, the Justice Department declared that all piers in the Port of New York were within a "barred zone" in which no alien enemy could live or work without a special permit. About 20,000 German New Yorkers applied for permits on the first day alone.[58] To be exempted from the barred zone, an alien enemy had to provide information about their employment and residence and submit affidavits from employers or "well-respected" Americans as to their character. The Justice Department investigated and ultimately granted 200,000 exemption passes. If an application was denied, the person had to quit and/or move immediately.[59]

The combination of not being allowed on the waterfront and discrimination resulted in at least 10,000 Germans losing their jobs. Thousands of teamsters, stevedores, and other dock workers had to find other work away from the waterfront; not even being a naturalized U.S. citizen protected German American dock workers. Other Germans lost their jobs when their businesses failed due to the lack of trade with Germany.[60]

Germans also suffered from countless acts of harassment, ranging from spitting and petty vandalism to more serious vigilantism, including being forced to publicly kiss the flag, and physical violence. The lynching of Robert Praeger in Collinsville, Illinois—and the acquittal of his killers—sent a powerful message to Germans in the United States: American equals English; keep quiet; stay out of sight.[61]

Helen Wagner, who lived on the Upper East Side during the war, remembered: "You couldn't walk the street with a German paper under your arm, you'd be abused from one end of the block to the other. . . . We kept speaking German at home, but we avoided it on the street."[62]

German Vereine also suffered discrimination in the form of being denied space for events (if they did not own their own meeting spaces) and by having their clubhouses repeatedly searched by police looking for "disloyal" material.[63]

Adding to Germans' sense of being under constant suspicion and surveillance by both the government and their neighbors was the English-language

FIG. 6.1 Henry Raleigh, *Hun or Home? Buy More Liberty Bonds* (Chicago: Edwards & Deutsch, [1918]). (Library of Congress.)

press's encouragement of mob behavior. In the summer of 1917, the *New York Herald* published a 112-page list of Germans registered as alien enemies in the city. The list included names and addresses and read like a city directory, with more than 39,500 names.[64] Hiding the fact that one was German became more difficult when a person's name was published in the newspaper as being an alien enemy.

Even prominent politicians were not exempt from scapegoating. The German-born state senator and Senate minority leader Robert F. Wagner Sr. was accused of "working in the interests of the German Government," by New York City mayor John Purroy Mitchel, who was in a power struggle with Wagner over the transfer of city land in Long Island to the federal government to build a fort.[65] Wagner, who had been born in Hesse and who still spoke with a German accent, was part of the liberal faction of Tammany Hall, while Mitchel, an Irish Catholic Republican, was a long-time Tammany foe. Although the federal government got its land, Mitchel's willingness to question Wagner's loyalty and patriotism because of his heritage showed the extent and tone of American wartime jingoism.

While their leaders frantically waved the American flag and loudly proclaimed their loyalty, other German immigrants and German Americans quickly assumed a low profile: they stopped speaking German (at least in public), stopped attending Vereine meetings and other events, and stopped publicly displaying aspects of German culture. Many singing societies canceled their traditional concerts, and other Vereine canceled their annual picnics, parties, and balls. For instance, the Sängverein Concordia of Brooklyn, observing its fiftieth anniversary in 1917, postponed its celebration until after the war, as did the United German Societies. The Mozart Verein canceled its summer events and limited other events to its clubhouse. Other major Verein events were canceled, such as the Sängerfeste of Brooklyn and Harlem and the New Yorker Schützenfest, all planned for June 1917. The Plattdeutschen and Bayerischen Volksfeste were held but now labeled as "American," with the purpose of raising money for the American Red Cross. The "seriousness" of the times caused some clubs to even cancel their children's Christmas festivals and pageants and their *Faschingsballs* before Lent.[66] The Metropolitan Opera canceled all performances of German opera.[67] "This course is adopted in line with the desire in Washington that meetings be avoided that might cause misunderstandings," explained a German American who was active in several Vereine.[68]

Many German organizations—including the Elks Lodge, the Bäckergewerkschaft (Baker's Union), and the Liederkranz—abandoned German in favor of English in meetings and announcements. The Brooklyn Gesangverein and the Flushing Männerchor also began to sing only in English.[69]

To try to prove their loyalty, Vereine and other German organizations offered their facilities to the state and federal governments for military use. Several shooting clubs gave their Union Hill Schützen Park shooting range in North Bergen to the government for troop target practice.[70] The Gesellschaft Harmonie also offered its clubhouse at 426 Broome Street to President Wilson to serve as a hospital or any other military purpose.[71] The Liederkranz also offered its clubhouse as an auxiliary to the German Hospital, and Columbia University's Deutsches Haus (which used to be a library and guest quarters for visiting professors) became the university's "war hospital."[72]

Several businesses founded by German immigrants in the nineteenth century hurried to change their names to avoid the stigma of being "German." The German Savings Bank of Manhattan renamed itself the Central Savings Bank; the German Savings Bank of Brooklyn changed its name to the Lincoln Savings Bank; and the Germania Life Insurance Company became the Guardian Life Insurance Company.[73]

In an effort to both publicly declare their loyalty and protect themselves legally, thousands of German and Austrian immigrants hurried to apply for citizenship, as it became clear that American citizens, even those of German or Austrian birth, would receive better treatment or be exempt from discriminatory measures.[74] In May 1918, President Wilson approved an act of Congress amending the naturalization laws, which allowed alien enemies who had begun the naturalization process before the war to complete the process. (Since April 1917, all naturalizations of Germans and Austrians had been halted to prevent citizens of a hostile nation from becoming American citizens.)[75]

In June 1917, the United States enacted the Espionage Act, which among its many requirements, called for a fine of up to $10,000 or twenty years in prison (or both) for anyone found guilty of disseminating information that undermined the U.S. war effort or supported those of its enemies. In addition, any publication found to be disseminating "treasonous" material would not be distributed through the mail, and violators would be fined and/or imprisoned.

This measure was applied frequently against socialist and other radical publications, especially those printed in German and other foreign languages. The *New Yorker Volkszeitung*—which had opposed the war from the beginning—lost its second-class mailing privileges, which required the paper to submit its editorial content daily to the post office for review. The paper's war-related content was often deemed "unmailable," and thus, the paper could not print it. Other types of censorship and delays caused the morning paper to not arrive on newsstands until the evening.[76]

Newspaper editors who had lobbied for neutrality before 1917 found themselves in political trouble during the war. Jeremiah O'Leary's anti-British *Bull* and George Viereck's *Fatherland* newspapers were among those papers raided by federal authorities and shut down.[77]

The next blow to the foreign-language press was the Trading with the Enemy Act. This law, passed in October 1917, required foreign-language publications to provide English translations of all material related to the government or the war. Thousands of foreign-language newspapers and magazines applied for exemptions, but few German-language papers received them. The *New Yorker Staats-Zeitung* was one of the lucky seventy-four German-language newspapers to receive an exemption, possibly because—despite its strong support for neutrality—the *Staats-Zeitung* had not opposed the Espionage Act. The translation and permit requirements caused many German newspapers to either drastically shrink in size and coverage or simply go out of business. New York had had twelve German-language publications before the war (three of them dailies), but neither the *Volkszeitung* nor the Hearst-owned *New Yorker Deutscher Journal* ever received a translation exemption permit. The *Journal*, in fact, closed in late April 1918.[78]

The wartime atmosphere of superpatriotism was used by some to pursue personal vendettas or to transform personal conflicts into questions of national security, loyalty, and patriotism. Neighbors turned on neighbors: the German immigrant and Hoboken resident Henry Latrell was badly beaten by his next-door neighbor, Joseph McDonald, for refusing to buy Liberty bonds in June 1918. Such violence was indirectly encouraged by such newspaper head-lines as the one reporting Latrell's assault: "Enemy Badly Battered, Registered German Alleged to Have Spoken Too Freely."[79] A longshoreman murdered a pressman in a bar fight, allegedly about the war, in July 1918.[80] That same sum-mer, the federal government seized the financial records of the Tietjen & Lang dry dock corporation after secretaries of two draft boards in Hoboken alleged that the company was aiding young men in evading the draft by giving them jobs at the dry dock.[81] Another German Hoboken resident, Ernest Hertel, was arrested for expressing the opinion that Kaiser Wilhelm was a better man than President Wilson at a Fourth of July picnic, and two Hoboken women swore out a complaint against a New York German resident for saying that Ameri-can ships would sink because of faulty riveting work done by German sympa-thizers at the Federal Shipping Company shipyard in Kearney, New Jersey.[82] The Brooklyn butcher Stephen Binder was sentenced to two years in jail for publishing an antiwar book. A socialist in Queens, Peter Grimm, was jailed for saying, "America ought never to have gone to war with Germany. It's only a war of the capitalists."[83]

This vigilante atmosphere was encouraged by political leaders at the high-est levels. In the fall of 1917, Mayor Mitchel ran for reelection as a prowar fusion candidate after he lost the Republican nomination to William M. Bennett. Seeking to distinguish himself as particularly patriotic in a hyperpatriotic atmo-sphere, Mitchel attacked Germans, Irish, and Jews as disloyal and un-American for their previous support for neutrality. Mitchel also attacked the loyalty and patriotism of the antiwar socialist Morris Hillquit.[84] Offended by Mitchel's slurs, many German Americans, Irish Americans, and Jewish Amer-icans voted for either the Tammany Hall Democrat John F. Hylan (who won by a landslide) or Hillquit (who came in a very close third).

The U.S. and New York City governments attempted to institute surveil-lance of thousands of German citizens in New York, announcing in early November 1917 their intention to monitor the activities of 25,000 alien ene-mies who held permits to do business or live within the barred zones.[85] But this plan required the local beat cop to be familiar with every German citizen within his area and was quickly found to be unworkable.

Faced with New York's lack of capacity to monitor all alien enemies, Presi-dent Wilson proclaimed on November 16, 1917, that alien enemies could not live, work, or even travel within one hundred yards of docks, piers, and water-fronts. Alien enemies who lived, worked, or owned property within the zone were ordered to move out. Thousands of Germans who lived on Riverside Drive along the Hudson River were evicted from their homes.[86] Even as people packed to move, Germans consoled themselves with the fact that the barred zone did not extend one hundred miles inland as the Secret Service had sought.[87]

Besides banning Germans from the new military zone, the permits that had previously allowed Germans to be on the waterfront were revoked. Alien enemies were not allowed to ride streetcars or railroads that passed through the zone, even if they were not getting off within the barred area. (They were still allowed to ride public ferries.)[88]

As mobilization and the military draft got underway, the surveillance and harassment of Germans in New York City intensified. There was a new registration of alien enemies, and this time women were required to register. By mid-February 1918, all male German citizens fourteen years of age and older were required to register with local police authorities. This registration required alien enemies to provide extensive information about their life and employment histories, as well as photographs and fingerprints.[89] Under the new regulations, alien enemies had to carry a registration card with them, had to get a permit for change of residence and employment, and had to report to federal or local authorities on a regular basis. Federal authorities estimated that 130,000 German men over the age of fourteen lived in the greater New York City metropolitan area, including northern New Jersey.[90]

The federal government's surveillance of Germans extended to sending naval and other military intelligence officers to loiter in the city's German restaurants and bars to spy on patrons' behavior. In April 1918, eleven Germans and Austrians were arrested in a German restaurant on East 84th Street for toasting the health of the kaiser, singing German military songs (such as "The Watch on the Rhine"), and celebrating the military "success of the Hun hordes."[91] That same month six German singers were fired from the Metropolitan Opera chorus because they were not American citizens.[92] Germans were also investigated by and expelled from the New York Athletic Club.[93]

The German language continued to be the main target of 100 percent Americanists. The Union League Club adopted a ban against the German language in the clubhouse and prohibited alien enemies from joining or even being on the premises.[94] The Democratic Club also banned both alien enemies and the speaking of German in its clubhouse.[95] The New York Board of Education decided in the spring of 1918 to eliminate German from all elementary schools, reduce German instruction in the high schools, and ban nine German textbooks.[96]

In the spring and summer of 1918, New Yorkers of all backgrounds experienced the terror of German submarines attacking American ships leaving New York Harbor; over the course of six months, six U-boats sank ninety-one American and European ships, most of them cargo ships. The attacks—which failed to sink any troop transport ships—furthered American paranoia that Germans in the city were aiding the German military in some way.[97] In August 1918, the barred zones were expanded to include large parts of the New Jersey shore to prevent Germans from somehow communicating with U-boats. There was also discussion of creating a coastal barred zone in Connecticut, which did not ulti-mately happen.[98]

Once American casualty lists began appearing daily in newspapers in the summer and fall of 1918, Americans became increasingly resentful that non-citizens did not have to serve in the military. (German citizens were exempt from the draft out of fear that they would betray the United States once in American uniform.) In September, the Justice Department—aided by local police and the private American Protective League—launched so-called slacker raids, in which thousands of young men were accosted at train stations, in the-aters, and on the street and arrested as "slackers" if they were not able to prove they had registered for conscription. The raids were very heavy-handed: in one raid in northern New Jersey, nearly 89,000 men were detained but only 750 were found to be in arrears with their draft boards. In Hoboken, 2,000 were held in the City Hall Armory, but only 100 of these were deemed "real slack-ers."[99] In New York City, more than 11,600 men were detained in Manhattan and the Bronx over a three-day period in September. This dragnet method sparked protests, and even some progovernment publications called the raids "amateur Prussianism in New York."[100]

Another hardship that came with the war that fall was the influenza epi-demic spread by soldiers traveling to Hoboken on their way to Europe. The epidemic—which traveled with the troops to Europe and then back to the United States on returning transports—affected one-quarter of the AEF and killed nearly 47,000 soldiers (almost as many who died in combat). Approxi-mately 675,000 Americans and 30,000 New Yorkers died of the flu in 1918–1919.[101]

Of the hundreds of thousands of New York men of German heritage to serve in the war, William Oettinger—who was the only one of his family on board the *General Slocum* to survive the disaster—was severely wounded on August 11, 1918, in France. He had become a chauffeur for a postal transfer company and had married in 1914. The grocer John Jurgen Roes, who survived the *General Slocum* accident as a nine-year-old boy while losing his German-born mother, Adele, also served overseas from September 1918 to July 1919. The first war vic-tim from Hoboken, Christopher Mohr, who died June 9, 1918, at Belleau Wood, was also the son of German immigrants. As always, death made no distinction in terms of ethnicity, race, religion, or class.

7

The Great Disappearing
Act, 1919–1930

● ●

In both the immediate aftermath of the war and for the rest of the 1920s, German New Yorkers struggled to find a new place in the sociocultural and political landscapes of the city. German Americans continued to hide or deny many aspects of their culture, and when they did become visible in public debates in the city, it was more as one of the many ethnic interest groups in the city than as a visible, organized community. So, while a German community existed in New York City into the 1930s, this community looked and behaved very differently from the one that had been so prominent before the war. German immigrants and German Americans disappeared into a larger ethnic group, "white American," which they had helped create after the war.[1]

By the time the armistice suspending World War I was declared on November 11, 1918, at 6:00 A.M. Eastern Standard Time, nearly all visible aspects of German culture in New York City had been eliminated. The performance of German music and theater had been banned; the German language was no longer taught in schools and universities; and German Vereine either did not meet or did so very quietly behind closed doors with no fanfare. German New Yorkers had spent the previous nineteen months making themselves invisible against the backdrop of a hyperaggressive Anglo American culture. By the end of the 1920s, while there were still many German immigrants and German Americans in New York City, the institutions and social activities that had made the German community so visible for so many decades were largely gone.

With the war now over, German New Yorkers were initially hopeful that life could return to "normal," meaning before the war. But the "opera riots" of 1919 quickly disabused them of this hope. Before the war, German opera, especially that of Richard Wagner, had dominated classical music in New York City and the United States. But Wagner was deemed emblematic of German Kultur and was therefore political, and thus his music disappeared from American stages during the war.[2]

In March 1919, as demobilization from the American Expeditionary Force continued at a brisk pace and thousands of returning soldiers passed through the Port of New York on their way home, the Rudolph Christians Producing Company announced that it would perform a series of comedic operas and operettas in German at the Lexington Theater. No tickets would be given away, and there would be no advertising. No Wagner would be on the program.[3]

Yet the backlash was immediate and fierce, with soldiers and sailors threatening violence against the theater if the productions occurred. The objections stemmed both from the fact that the operas would be sung in German and that the Versailles Treaty was still being negotiated. (The treaty was signed on June 28, 1919, and became effective January 10, 1920.)[4] Faced with the threat of violence by several thousand soldiers and sailors, Mayor John Francis Hylan forced the theater to postpone the performances "indefinitely" by threatening to revoke its license if there was any public disorder caused as a result of the performances.[5]

The manager of the production company, Max Winter, attempted to push back against this censorship, insisting that "there is absolutely no sort of propaganda in these plays." He also emphasized the fact that hundreds of thousands of Germans and German Americans in the city had also contributed to the war effort, suffering the death and injury of sons and buying war bonds, but were "barred from recreation in ordinary American theaters" because of the language barrier.[6]

Using language that would not have been possible a few months earlier, the president of the theater company, Ruldoph Christians, a recent German immigrant, used President Wilson's oft-repeated statement that "the war was not against the German people" to demand: "Why should the operas be interfered with by local authorities?"[7] But opponents had their way, and the production was canceled.[8]

Six months later, German opera again caused rioting in the city. The newly organized Star Opera Company attempted to put on light opera and operettas in German, again at the Lexington Theater. But veterans, now organized into the American Legion, continued to protest any theatrical performance given in German.[9] When the Star Opera Company performed a series of German operas, including Wagner's *Die Meistersinger von Nürnberg*, in late

October 1919 over mayoral objections, riots broke out between protesting ser-vice members and mounted police, resulting in several serious injuries.[10] Ger-man speakers showed their support for the production by buying tickets in large numbers, but many people stayed away from the actual performances, due to fear of violence, both inside and outside the theater.[11]

Eventually, the constant threat of violence requiring police presence at every performance wore the company and the theater down. The Bavarian-born jus-tice Leonard A. Giegerich ruled that performances in the German language would not be permitted in the city until the peace treaty went into effect, and the Star Opera Company declared bankruptcy in November 1919.[12] An attempt by the North German Society of Queens and the Plattdeutsch Verein of Long Island City to put on a performance of Richard Strauss's *Der Weisse Hirsch*, in Astoria in late November, was also shut down after protests by the Ameri-can Legion.[13] It was not until December 1920 that a performance of an opera in German (the innocuous *Hansel and Gretel* by Engelbert Humperdinck) was held at the Manhattan Opera House without the threat of mob violence.[14]

The protests and riots against German theater and opera in New York City in 1919 were loud and violent yet also revealed the shallowness of Anglo Amer-ican hostility toward German culture. The main argument against the Lexing-ton Theater's performances was that it was "too soon" for performances to be given in German and that it was offensive to servicemen to stage German the-ater while the United States was still technically at war with Germany. Such an argument implied that there was not anything inherently bad or morally objectionable about German opera, simply that English-speaking Americans insisted on their right to judge if and when it could be performed. Thus, the objection to German opera and theater was a continuation of English speak-ers demanding cultural and linguistic conformity and 100 percent American-ism. It was difficult for Anglo American cultural critics to assert that German classical music was inherently immoral or degenerate after they had claimed for most of the nineteenth century that it was, in fact, superior to American forms of popular music. The fight about opera was also an opportunity for the newly organized American Legion to flex its political muscles in New York City politics. By 1922, German opera, including that by Wagner, was being per-formed to full houses at the Metropolitan Opera House, with the only criti-cism coming from the theater critics.[15]

With opera and theater initially out of bounds, Vereine became more impor-tant as expressions and vehicles of German culture, yet German associational life suffered greatly during and immediately after the war. The great German disappearing act that had begun during the war and had centered on making Verein activities either invisible or nonexistent continued for most of the 1920s. Vereine both hid their activities and disappeared. There were fewer self-identified German organizations in New York in 1925 than in 1920 and far fewer than had existed before the war.[16] New York City had had an estimated two thousand German societies before the war, and most German (and some non-German) New Yorkers were members.[17] After the war, membership in Vereine dropped, in some cases, significantly. For example, the Nordamerikanische Turnerbund lost more than 3,600 members; the Verband des Staates New York lost around 500 members between 1917 and 1919.[18] Other Vereine merged, particularly the Liederkranz and Arion, in March 1919, and the Greenpoint and the Germania Sängerbunds, in an effort to stay alive because of the decline in dues-paying members.[19]

Many of those dropping their membership and participation in Vereine were Americans of German heritage rather than German immigrants. This ironically made the fewer remaining Vereine more German, as their members more often tended to be recent German immigrants who had immigrated in the 1920s.[20]

Although the wealthy Vereine, such as the Liederkranz, owned their own clubhouses, many smaller groups met in neighborhood bars or rented space in halls, such as the Turnhalle. The *Sammtisch* tradition of a club regularly meeting at a particular table in a bar or restaurant also began to die out, as Prohibition closed these places.[21]

Yes, German Americans continued to meet with friends and socialize, but these gatherings were more often informal than formal, and groups no longer chose to identify themselves as German to their neighbors and the larger community through the confident taking out of a short ad in the city directory or the newspaper. There was no more parading around the street on the way to or from a Verein celebration; the picnics and festivals that had attracted thousands were over. For Germans and German Americans seeking clearly identifiable German organizations, there were far fewer groups from which to choose.[22]

The Gesellschaft Harmonie, one of the oldest and most elite men's clubs in the city, attempted later to gloss over the traumas of the war by claiming that there had never been any conflict (which is doubtful):

The "World War" and the resulting business depression caused a great falling off in membership, in receipts and in social activities, which fortunately, was largely offset by the stimulation received from the Country Club. Despite the fact that our membership has always been mostly entirely of German descent, with many of the older members still under the influence of their early education and association and still devoted to their native language, literature, music and general culture, almost all of the older generation joined with the younger membership in staunch support of the attitude of our government and of American sentiment generally. No unpleasant incident took place and such consideration and forbearance were shown that the period was passed without any strain upon the pleasant inter-relations of the members.[23]

Surviving Vereine gradually began participating again in the city's cultural life in the mid-1920s, but there was tension between German Americans who wanted to reestablish the community's old institutions and those who simply wanted to enjoy socializing with other German Americans in an informal setting. The United German Societies reestablished Deutscher Tag (German Day) in New York City in 1921, but this was a much smaller event than it had been before the war and was only publicized in the German-language press.[24]

Raising money to be sent to Germany as charity was one way that German Americans could support Germany without being attacked by English speakers as being loyal to a foreign country. After the war, Germany suffered from several devastating strikes, high unemployment, and then the infamous inflation of 1923. In 1919, German American Vereine raised money and sent two hundred tons of foodstuffs to Germany, and then in 1922, German American newspapers papers sent 100 million marks to Germany to buy Christmas gifts for impoverished German families.[25] But sending money and foodstuffs to an economically devastated country could be—and was—positioned as Christian charity, not an act of political support for either the German people or the new Weimar Republic.

The debate about how visible and in what aspects of social life German Americans should be in the city came to the fore in the mid-1920s. In 1925, Bernard H. Ridder, the publisher of the now merged *New Yorker Staats-Zeitung* and the *New Yorker Herold Zeitung*, and Judge Charles A. Oberwager, president of the United German Societies, began lobbying to change the name of Lenox Hill Hospital (changed in May 1918) back to the German Hospital. The two argued that the name should be changed because virtually all of the hospital's staff was of German heritage and most spoke German. Oberwager also claimed that donations to the hospital had begun to fall after the name change. But few German Americans were interested in such a symbolic action, and the campaign failed.[26]

A few years later, however, the United German Societies, representing the members of 150 Vereine, successfully lobbied to establish a new German hospital by changing the name of the Stuyvesant Dispensary on Second Avenue to the German Polyclinic–Deutsche Poliklinik. The clinic had been called the German Dispensary before the war.[27] Clearly, to some German Americans, German-specific institutions still mattered.

But increasingly, German Americans participated in the city's social life as simply one of the many ethnic groups in the city rather than asserting a special status. When Gertrude Eberle, the daughter of German immigrants, became the first woman to swim the English Channel in August 1926, German Vereine participated in the ticker-tape parade held for her on Broadway, but they were barely visible among the two million people who attended the festivities.[28]

Politics was, ironically, one area where German Americans appeared to retain a sense of group identity, yet this too was ethereal. Americans of German birth or heritage had long been divided by religion and class and could only be organized as a voting bloc when central aspects of their identity (e.g., alcohol and language) were threatened by the English-speaking majority. But this was not often the case in the 1920s.

In 1920, New York State had 163,881 Germans who were either naturalized or who had begun the naturalization process; of the 215,310 German-born New Yorkers, 68 percent were naturalized.[29] The Steuben Society, founded in May 1919, sought to represent these new citizens politically and to replace the National German-American Alliance as the primary public face of the German American community. The goals of the society were to foster patriotism; educate people as to the role German immigrants had played in American history; warn citizens against political intrigues and oppose "aliens influenced government"; protect Germans against discrimination, insults, and misrepresentation; and encourage "race-pride."[30]

But the Steuben Society behaved like any other political interest group. It took the lead in lobbying against what it considered pro-Wilson candidates, supporting Al Smith for reelection as governor in 1922. The Steuben Society also supported Robert M. LaFollette, Sr. as a third-party candidate in 1924 because of his opposition to American entry into the war and his opposition to a pro-British/French foreign policy and the prescriptions of the Versailles Treaty on Germany.[31]

But German American voters did not need the Steuben Society to advise them about how to vote. German Americans distinguished between local Democrats, such as Al Smith and Franklin D. Roosevelt, and the national Democratic Party even after the hated Woodrow Wilson had left office. While German Americans in the Midwest supported the Republicans Warren G. Harding and Calvin Coolidge in 1920 and 1924, German Americans in New York City voted for Roosevelt (running for vice president in 1920).[32]

German Americans could not even be roused politically to fight against immigration restriction that would make it more difficult for Germans to immigrate to the United States. In May 1924, President Coolidge signed the Immigration Act of 1924 (also known as the Johnson-Reed Act), which established ethnic-based quotas for immigration, significantly restricted immigration from southern and eastern Europe, and totally barred immigration from Asian countries. As one of the largest immigrant groups for most of the nineteenth century, Germans had the largest quota of visas, more than 50,000 out of a total of 150,000. The United Kingdom had the next most, at 34,000.[33]

But Germans had not involved themselves much in the debate about immigration restriction between the war and 1924. Irish Catholics and Jewish Americans led the opposition, along with lobbyists for the Japanese government.[34]

Most of New York's members of Congress—especially the Democrats Emanuel Celler and Samuel Dickstein, both Jewish, and the Republican Fiorello LaGuardia—opposed the 1924 legislation but were not supported by many German American politicians. The Steuben Society claimed that the Johnson-Reed Act "discriminates against the admission of German immigrants" but did not fight particularly hard against the legislation, aware that many Americans were not interested in having any more German immigrants.[35]

In 1926, the longtime Tammany Democrat Robert F. Wagner Sr. was elected to the U.S. Senate, defeating the incumbent Republican senator James W. Wadsworth in a campaign that focused on Prohibition and the new restrictive immigration law that had been passed in 1924. (Wagner was against both.)[36] Wagner was the first German-born politician elected to high office in New York since 1894, when the Prussian-born Charles Adolph Schieren was elected mayor of Brooklyn and the Palatinate-born Isidor Straus of Macy's department store was elected to Congress, representing the Fifteenth District. Although Wagner enjoyed German American support and never hid his heritage (nor his German accent), he understood his constituency to be working-class New Yorkers of all backgrounds. One of his few acknowledgments to his German background was his membership in the German American Democratic club, the Roland Society.[37] But even this was not widely publicized: in a 1926 profile of Wagner on the eve of his election to the U.S. Senate, his membership in the city and state bar associations; the Manhattan, National Democratic, and City clubs; and the Phi Beta Kappa fraternity were all noted, but not the Roland Society.[38]

Another area in which the decline of the German community was particularly pronounced was in German churches. For most of the nineteenth century, German immigrants had founded many mostly Protestant German-language congregations, and Germans dominated the American Lutheran church, including in New York City. Most Lutheran congregations in New York City were German speaking and usually had German-born and German-educated pastors. But the anti-German feeling of the war extended to German-language churches, and many German congregations felt the social pressure to abandon German in favor of English.[39] In 1918, there was only one Lutheran church that explicitly identified itself as German in city directories, Trinity Lutheran on 139 Avenue B (although there were certainly still others that simply hid their use of German).[40]

Attendance at German parochial schools also suffered a significant drop during the war years and into the 1920s, as parents pulled their children out of German-language schools and presumably enrolled them in English-speaking public schools.[41]

By 1930, Yorkville was the recognized German neighborhood in New York City; the old Kleindeutschland district had been an eastern European Jewish

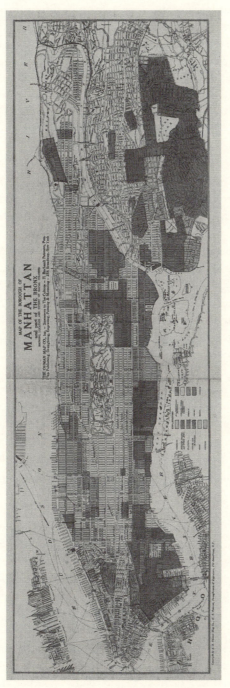
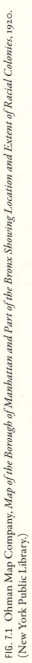

FIG. 7.1 Ohman Map Company, *Map of the Borough of Manhattan and Part of the Bronx Showing Location and Extent of Racial Colonies*, 1920. (New York Public Library.)

area for more than thirty years. But as in Kleindeutschland, Yorkville was both ethnically and socioeconomically diverse, with both a working class and a middle class, divided geographically by Third Avenue. More than 40 percent of the neighborhood was either German born or the children of German-born parents, a percentage that was comparable to Kleindeutschland in the 1860s and 1870s. The neighborhood had a large number of single women (60 percent of all females in the district) due to the many domestic servants living in the prosperous western section of the area. Families living west of Third Avenue were more likely to be headed by white-collar professionals, while more skilled craftsmen lived east of Third Avenue.[42]

The *New York Times* in 1926 described Yorkville as "gradually merging into a state of colorless impersonality."[43] But instead of calling the neighborhood "German," the paper instead concentrated on the area's "Central European" character, noting the large numbers of Czechs and Hungarians in the neighborhood.

Yet Yorkville was also shrinking in population, with fewer young couples and far fewer school children living in the neighborhood, as families moved out to other boroughs in search of less dense housing and a desire to live in a more "American" (i.e., less obviously German or immigrant) area. Queens— with its already established German communities in Astoria, College Point, and Ridgewood—was being rapidly developed by real estate speculators. But Germans moved to new communities in Corona and Elmhurst, leaving Astoria increasingly to Czech Americans.[44]

These changes in the neighborhood were attributed to modern life in a large city rather than pressures to integrate residentially. The *New York Times* observed: "It is one of the most conspicuous characteristics of immigrant life in America that the various racial groups are constantly shifting from one place to another and, driven by either rising rent or a desire for more comfortable quarters, travel en masse, driving before them other racial groups.'[45]

For most of the nineteenth century, it had been possible for German immigrants to live a German life in Kleindeutschland, but this life had always been narrow and limited. Kleindeutschland had always been more ethnically and linguistically diverse and less German than it appeared to outsiders, and any shopkeeper or entrepreneur who wanted to do business outside of a German-only-speaking customer base had to learn at least some English. Although Germans were a large minority in the city, they were still a minority and were never able to control the public or Catholic parochial school systems as they did in some other cities. Despite the brief introduction of German as a second language in the city schools in the 1870s, this meant that German American children were educated primarily—if not exclusively—in the English language, and thus, the preservation of German required active effort on the part of both parents and children. Germans' political divisions also meant that they were not able to dominate either of the main two political parties, as Irish Americans came to do so with the Democratic Party in New York City.

For decades, Germans and German Americans had defined the German language and participating in organized sociocultural activities with other Germans as being intrinsic to their identity as German. In the words of Milton Gordon, these activities were "essential and vital ingredients of the group's cultural heritage and derive[d] exactly from that heritage." But in the 1920s, it was clear that these sociocultural activities were what Gordon defined as "extrinsic," or "products of the historical vicissitudes of a group's adjustment to its local environment," which are "external to the core of the group's ethnic cultural heritage."[46]

The war caused German New Yorkers to question and reflect on what was essential to their community. If the German language and Verein Kultur were no longer central to being German, what exactly distinguished them from other white northern European ethnic groups in American society?

Although German New Yorkers pretended that language and Verein Kultur were not essential to being German, they were, in fact, what had distinguished Germans as an ethnic group from the city's many other immigrant groups. Geography—the tight density of Kleindeutschland as a German neighborhood—had also been underappreciated by German immigrants and German Americans as a type of glue that held their community together.

Yet German immigration had changed American culture enough in the nineteenth century that Germans' assimilation was not absorption by Anglo-America but rather a true merging and creating of a new white ethnic identity.[47] Being "German" became increasingly flexible and fluid for German Americans in the 1920s, something to put on when attending a Verein meeting or a Deutscher Tag event, but not something that dictated values like where one lived, who one married, or what kind of work one did. Even before World War I, German immigrants had the highest rate of naturalization (even higher than Irish immigrants) in the United States, and this continued after the war.[48] Only in cities with large, organized cultural institutions, such as New York City, was in-group marriage common: "Precisely where German immigrant cultural institutions were likely strongest, single-origin descendants are more prevalent and more likely to in-marry."[49] But people of the third generation were less likely to marry within their grandparents' ethnic group, and by the 1920s, out-of-group marriage was common among German Americans, including in New York City.[50]

German immigrants and German Americans had taken seriously the American value of liberty, the freedom to live as one pleased without government or other forms of interference. In the hypernationalistic 100 percent American environment of World War I, Anglo Americans strongly disagreed, insisting rather that personal and cultural liberty as Germans defined it was dangerous and that true Americanism was to be measured by outward displays of loyalty and conformity to Anglo American values and behaviors.

In response, German New Yorkers disappeared by abandoning what had been for decades intrinsic values of language maintenance and cultural practices. But the American culture and society German Americans assimilated into was one that they had significantly shaped over the course of nearly one hundred years of German immigration and cultural exchange. Just as Germans became more "American," so had other Americans become more "German," and nowhere was this more clearly seen than in New York City.

Acknowledgments

Writing a book requires a lot of help and support, and I have benefitted greatly from the help and support of many people.

I was privileged to receive a Fulbright Senior Scholar Fellowship to the University of Bremen in 2014–2015 to do preliminary research, and I was ably assisted by the Fulbright staff, by William McShane in Washington, DC, and by Catharina Hänsch and Silvija Stoljevska in Berlin. My colleagues at the time at Empire State College, SUNY, Stephen Flynn and Michael Merrill, also provided valuable assistance. At the University of Bremen, I benefitted from interactions with the members of the Faculty of English-speaking Cultures, particularly Sabine Broeck, Jana Geisler, Katja Müller, Irmgard Maassen, Anne Kirkham, and Inke Dubois. The University of Bremen International Office provided much logistical and emotional support, and for that I would like to thank Silke Prangemeier, Julia Holz, Janna Rodi Wilbers, and Sharon Mayer, as well as Janine Ludwig, Diethelm Knauf, Christine Rodewald, and Sarah Greger. Research for another project ended up being incorporated into this book, so I would like to thank Atiba Pertilla, Kelly McCullough, Claudia Winkler, and Uwe Spiekermann of the German Historical Institute in Washington, DC, for their support of my work.

I learned long ago that the key to historical research is not knowing where to look in libraries and archives but knowing who knows where to look. I would therefore like to thank Martina Faehnemann of the HAPAG archives, Barbara Koschlig and Helga Mügge of the Staatsarchiv Hamburg; Boris Löffler and Monika Marschalck of the Staatsarchiv Bremen; Simon Kursawe and Petra Schütz of the Deutsches Schiffahrtsmuseum, Bremerhaven, library; Jeffrey Dozik and Barry Moreno of the library at Ellis Island Liberty Island National Park; Diane DeFazio, Nancy Kandoian, Andrew McCarthy, and Antonio Vasquez of the New York Public Library; Rebecca Grabie of the New-York

Historical Society; and John Daggan of the Sutter Archives, Lutheran Synod of New York at Wagner College, Staten Island. My librarian friends David A. Smith, Jenny Furlong, and John Ward Beekman have always responded to frantic emails seeking help in little things like navigating complex library systems and databases and big things like renewing expired library cards remotely. I must also thank Alexander Gattig of the University of Bremen, Steve Morse of the Brooklyn genealogy blog located at https://stevemorse.org/, Jason M. Barr at Rutgers University–Newark, and S. Wright Kennedy at Columbia University for their valuable advice and assistance in dealing with U.S. census databases. The blogs *A Guide to Former Street Names in Manhattan* (http://www.oldstreets.com/index.asp), *Forgotten New York* (http://forgotten-ny.com/), and Maggie Blanck's located at http://www.maggieblanck.com/ were also useful tools, and I appreciate the hard work of these "amateur" historians.

Robert Foster of the Hoboken Historical Museum; Simone Blaschka of the Deutsches Auswandererhaus, Bremerhaven; and Ruth Schilling of the Deutsches Schifffahrtsmuseum, Bremerhaven, have long supported my work and my belief in the importance of using museums and their collections for historical research.

My husband, Scott McPherson, is not just a loving and supportive spouse and my biggest promoter; he is also an excellent copy editor, a Word and Excel wizard, and a fair critic. Katie Heidsiek also provided valuable feedback on an early draft of the manuscript.

I am sure I have missed some, so to my friends and colleagues in the United States and Germany, I will simply say, thank you / *vielen Dank*!

Christina A. Ziegler-McPherson
August 2020
Bremen, Germany

Notes

Introduction

1 Edward Albert, Prince of Wales and the future Edward VII of Great Britain, visited in 1860.

2 Daniel Patrick Moynihan and Michael Glazer, *Beyond the Melting Pot: The Negroes, Puerto Ricans, Jews, Italians, and Irish of New York City* (Cambridge, MA: Harvard University Press, 1963), 311–312.

3 For examples of other studies of immigrant communities in New York, please see Samuel L. Baily, *Immigrants in the Land of Promise: Italians in Buenos Aires and New York City, 1870–1914* (Ithaca, NY: Cornell University Press, 1999); Annie Polland and Daniel Soyer, *Emerging Metropolis: New York Jews in the Age of Immigration, 1840–1920* (New York: New York University Press, 2012); Jeffrey S. Gurock, *Jews in Gotham: New York Jews in a Changing City, 1920–2010* (New York: New York University Press, 2012); and Jeffrey S. Gurock, *The Jews of Harlem: The Rise, Decline and Revival of a Jewish Community* (New York: New York University Press, 2016). The history of Irish immigrants in New York is so extensive; it has its own bibliography: Ann M. Shea, *The Irish Experience in New York City: A Select Bibliography* (New York: New York Irish History Roundtable, 1995).

4 John Higham, *Strangers in the Land: Patterns of American Nativism, 1860–1925*, 3rd ed. (New Brunswick, NJ: Rutgers University Press, 1994), 196, notes studies and surveys by and of American intellectuals before World War I that attributed positive cultural and social attributes to Germans and ranked Germans even higher than the English and native-born white Americans.

5 My definition of assimilation comes from Russell Kazal, "Revisiting Assimilation: The Rise, Fall, and Reappraisal of a Concept in American Ethnic History," *American Historical Review* 100 (April 1995): 437–471.

6 Milton M. Gordon, *Assimilation in American Life: The Role of Race, Religion, and National Origins* (New York: Oxford University Press, 1964), 71.

7 John Higham, *Send These to Me: Immigrants in Urban America* (Baltimore: Johns Hopkins University Press, 1984), 175–197. Please also see Christina A.

Ziegler-McPherson, *Selling America: Immigration Promotion and the Settlement of the American Continent, 1607–1914* (Santa Barbara, CA: Praeger, 2017).

8 Kathleen Neils Conzen, "German-Americans and the Invention of Ethnicity," in *Americans and the Germans, An Assessment of a Three-Hundred-Year History*, vol. 1, *Immigration, Language, Ethnicity*, ed. Frank Trommler and Joseph McVeigh (Philadelphia: University of Pennsylvania Press, 1985).

9 This is what Milton Gordon called "intrinsic" versus "extrinsic" cultural traits or patterns: traits that are "essential and vital ingredients of the group's cultural heritage and derive exactly from that heritage" versus traits that are "products of the historical vicissitudes of a group's adjustment to its local environment" and are "external to the core of the group's ethnic cultural heritage." Gordon, *Assimilation in American Life*, 79–80.

10 Conzen, "German-Americans"; Charles Thomas Johnson, *Culture at Twilight: The National German-American Alliance, 1901–1918* (New York: Peter Lang, 1999).

11 Between 1830 and 1930, 5,875 million Germans immigrated to the United States. Table "Total Immigrants from each Region and Country, by Decade, 1820–2010," Scholastic.com, http://teacher.scholastic.com/activities/immigration/pdfs/by _region/region_table.pdf. The definition of "German" in this case refers to people who emigrated from the German Confederation and the German Empire.

12 Even today, one hundred years later and in the middle of a new mass migration movement from Latin America and Asia, German is still the largest self-claimed ethnic identity in the United States, with 49.2 million Americans, or approximately 16 percent of the country's 308 million residents, reporting some German ancestry in the 2011 American Community Survey conducted by the U.S. Bureau of the Census. "2011 American Community Survey 1-Year Estimates: Place of Birth for the Foreign-Born Population in the United States," Infoplease.com, http://www.infoplease.com/ipa/A0900547.html on September 24, 2014.

13 Stanley Nadel, *Little Germany: Ethnicity, Religion and Class in New York City, 1845–80* (Urbana: University of Illinois Press, 1990), 22–23; Hartmut Keil, "German Working-Class Radicalism in the United States from the 1870s to World War I," in *Struggle a Hard Battle, Essays on Working-Class Immigrants*, ed. Dirk Hoerder (DeKalb: Northern Illinois University Press, 1986), 74.

14 Guido Andre Dobbert, *The Disintegration of an Immigrant Community: The Cincinnati Germans, 1870–1920* (New York: Arno, 1980).

15 An average of 31 percent of Milwaukee's population was German in the late nineteenth century. Kathleen Neils Conzen, *Immigrant Milwaukee: Accommodation and Community in a Frontier City* (Cambridge, MA: Harvard University Press, 1976). Nadel, *Little Germany*, 22, table 1, "The German-born Population of Selected Cities, 1860–80," notes that Milwaukee's German population ranges from 35 percent in 1860 to 28 percent in 1880.

16 Audrey L. Olson, *St. Louis Germans, 1850–1920: The Nature of an Immigrant Community and Its Relationship to the Assimilation Process* (New York: Arno, 1980).

17 The German word for "the island" is *die Insel*, but here Stürenburg uses an English word spelled phonetically in German. Casper Stürenburg, "Das Friedesfest in New-York vom 9. Bis 11. April," in *Die Deutschen in Amerika und die deutsch-amerikanischen friedensfeste im jahr 1871* (New York: Verlags-expedition des Deutsch-amerikanischen conversations-lexicons, 1871), 38, refers to German New York as "Kleindeutschland." Peter Conolly-Smith, "Prose Pictures of Klein-deutschland: German-Language Local-Color Serials of the late Nineteenth

Century," in *Transnationalism and American Serial Fiction*, ed. Patricia Okker (New York: Routledge, 2012), 94.

18 Stanley Nadel, "Kleindeutschland: New York City's Germans, 1845–1880" (PhD diss., Columbia University, 1981), 42, table 1, "The German-born Population of Selected Cities, 1860–1880." On the use of the term *Germany* to apply to Klein-deutschland, see *Appleton's Dictionary of New York and Vicinity* (New York: D. Appleton, 1879), 90.

19 Nadel, "Kleindeutschland," 39–40; Edwin G. Burrows and Mike Wallace, *Gotham: A History of New York City to 1898* (New York: Oxford University Press, 1999), 745–748. These neighborhoods included Yorkville between 79th and 96th Streets east of Third Avenue in Manhattan; Long Island City, and Williams-burg, directly across the East River from the East Village in Brooklyn; Bushwick in the center of Brooklyn, and College Point in Queens.

20 Nadel, *Little Germany*, 41.

21 Nadel, 23–24. Nadel refers only to immigrants from Hamburg, but the two port cities are so similar that it is fair to extrapolate a similar migration pattern for people from Bremen.

22 Nadel, 103, 104–121.

23 Kenneth A. Scherzer, *The Unbounded Community: Neighborhood Life and Social Structure in New York 1830–1875* (Durham, NC: Duke University Press, 1992), 160.

24 Scherzer, *Unbounded Community*, 51, 75.

25 Scherzer, 95.

26 Scherzer, 55; Nadel, *Little Germany*, 37–39.

27 Nadel, 32. "German" is defined here as being from either the German Confedera-tion or the German Empire. Certainly, many other people in the neighborhood spoke German as their first or second language.

28 Ronald H. Bayor, *Neighbors in Conflict: The Irish, Germans, Jews and Italians of New York City*, 2nd ed. (Urbana: University of Illinois Press, 1988), 57–77; Birte Pfleger, ed., *Ethnicity Matters: A History of the German Society of Pennsylvania* (Washington, DC: German Historical Institute, 2006), 49; Frederick C. Luebke, *Bonds of Loyalty: German-Americans and World War I* (DeKalb: Northern Illinois University Press, 1974), 69.

29 La Vern J. Rippley, "Ameliorated Americanization: The Effect of World War I on German-Americans in the 1920s," in *Americans and the Germans, An Assessment of a Three-Hundred-Year History*, vol. 2, *The Relationship in the Twentieth Century*, ed. Frank Trommler and Joseph McVeigh (Philadelphia: University of Pennsylva-nia, 1985). Please also see Erik Kirschbaum, *The Eradication of German Culture in the United States: 1917–1918* (Stuttgart, Germany: Academic, 1986).

30 Joel Perlmann, "A Demographic Basis for Ethnic Survival? Blending across Four Generations of German-Americans," Levy Economic Institutes of Bard College, Working Paper 646 (December 2010), http://www.levyinstitute.org/pubs/wp_646.pdf; John R. Logan and Hyoung-jin Shin, "Assimilation by the Third Generation? Marital Choices of White Ethnics at the Dawn of the Twentieth Century," *Social Science Research* 41, no. 5 (September 1912), https://www.ncbi.nlm.nih.gov/pmc/articles/PMC3807942/#R26.

31 For instance, please see George U. Wenner, *The Lutherans of New York: Their Story and Their Problems* (New York: Petersfield, 1918), 79–90.

32 David Hackett Fischer, *Albion's Seed: Four British Folkways in America* (New York: Oxford University Press, 1889); Allan Kulikoff, *From British Peasants to*

Colonial American Farmers (Chapel Hill: University of North Carolina Press, 2000).

33 Scholars who argue most strongly that Germans assimilated into Anglo American culture look primarily at lifestyle practices, particularly in the area of recreation and entertainment, especially in New York. Please see Peter Conolly-Smith, *Translating America: An Immigrant Press Visualizes American Popular Culture, 1895–1918* (Washington, DC: Smithsonian Books, 2004); Sabine Haenni, *The Immigrant Scene: Ethnic Amusements in New York, 1880–1920* (Minneapolis: University of Minnesota, 2008), 57–93.

34 Dorothee Schneider, *Trade Unions and Community: The German Working Class in New York City, 1870–1900* (Chicago: University of Illinois Press, 1994); Nadel, *Little Germany.*

35 Lynne Tatlock and Matt Erlin, eds., *German Culture in Nineteenth-Century America: Reception, Adaptation, Transformation* (Rochester, NY: Camden House, 2005); Henry Geitz, Jürgen Heideking, and Jurgen Herbst, eds., *German Influences on Education in the United States to 1917* (Washington, DC: German Historical Institute, 1995); Bettina Goldberg, "The Forty-Eighters and the School System in America: The Theory and Practice of Reform," in *The German Forty-Eighters in the United States*, ed. Charlotte L. Barncaforte (New York: Peter Lang, 1989); Schneider, *Trade Unions and Community*; Nadel, *Little Germany*; Heike Bungert, Cora Lee Kluge, and Robert C. Ostergren, eds., *Wisconsin German Land and Life* (Madison, WI: Max Kade Institute, 2006); Kathleen Neils Conzen, "Phantom Landscapes of Colonization: Germans in the Making of a Pluralist America," in *The German-American Encounter: Conflict and Cooperation between Two Cultures, 1800–2000*, ed. Frank Trommler and Elliott Shore (New York: Berghahn Books, 2001).

Chapter 1   A Snapshot of Kleindeutschland in 1880

1 The New York State Board of Emigration Commissioners administered the Emigrant Landing Depot or Castle Garden between 1855 and 1890. A good explanation of the Castle Garden process can be found at Barry Moreno, "Castle Garden and Ellis Island: Doors to a New World," essay for exhibit, "Grüß Gott America, Good Bye Bayern," Haus der Bayerischen Geschichte, Augsburg, Germany, September 2003, http://www.hdbg.de/auswanderung/docs/moreno_kat_e.pdf.

2 There were multiple streetcar lines that served the eastern side of Manhattan, such as the East Belt Line, Avenue D Line, Avenue B Line, Avenue A line, Astoria Line, First Avenue Line, Second Avenue Line, Third Avenue Line, Fourth and Madison Avenues Line, all operated by separate private companies. Stephen L. Meyers, *Manhattan's Lost Streetcars* (Mount Pleasant, SC: Arcadia, 2005).

3 Chart, "Total Number of Immigrants per Year, 1820–2007"; U.S. Bureau of the Census, 1880, vol. 1, *Statistics of the Population of the United States*, table 16, "Foreign born Population of Fifty Principal Cities, Distributed According to Place of Birth, Among the Various Foreign Countries," 538–540; Nadel, *Little Germany*, 42.

4 Demographia, "New York (Manhattan) Sectors Population & Density 1800–1910," http://www.demographia.com/db-nyc-sector1800.htm.

5 Nadel, *Little Germany*, 31. Before the establishment of the German Empire (Kaiserreich) in 1871, there was the German Confederation.

6 Nadel, 37–39. Nadel also notes the important shift in migration from southern and western states toward immigration from Prussia and territories controlled by Prussia beginning in the 1870s (23–25).

7 Burrows and Wallace, *Gotham*, 745. This neighborhood has now been designated a series of historic districts by the New York City Landmark Preservation Commission. Please see East Village/Lower East Side Historic District Designation Report, October 9, 2012, http://www.nyc.gov/html/lpc/downloads/pdf/reports/2491.pdf; East 10th Street Historic District Designation Report, January 17, 2012, http://www.nyc.gov/html/lpc/downloads/pdf/reports/2492.pdf; and the East 17th Street/Irving Place Historic District Designation Report, 1998, http://www.nyc.gov/html/lpc/downloads/pdf/reports/EAST_17TH_STREET_-_IRVING_PLACE_-_HISTORIC_DISTRICT.pdf. *Trow's New York City Directory, compiled by H. Wilson, Vol. XCIII, for the year ending May 1, 1880, Vol. M–Z* (New York: John F. Trow, 1880), 18, "Churches, Jewish." It is estimated that New York had about 60,000 Jews in 1880, most of them German speaking. Cyrus Adler et al., eds, *Jewish Encyclopedia* (New York: Funk & Wagnalls, 1901–1906), 276. Also see Jeffrey S. Gurock, ed., *Central European Jews in America, 1840–1880: Migration and Advancement* (New York: Routledge, 1998), 316–317, which estimates about 30,000 German Jews in 1860.

8 Conzen, *Immigrant Milwaukee*, 127; Scherzer, *Unbounded Community*, 49; Ira Rosenwaike, *The Population History of New York City* (Syracuse, NY: Syracuse University Press, 1972), 43–44.

9 Jay P. Dolan, *The Immigrant Church: New York's Irish and German Catholics, 1815–1865* (Baltimore: Johns Hopkins University Press, 1975); Philip Gleason, *Conservative Reformers: German American Catholics and the Social Orders* (Notre Dame, IN: University of Notre Dame Press, 1968).

10 Nadel, *Little Germany*, 53–56.

11 U.S. Bureau of the Census, 1880, New York, New York, ED 71, FamilySearch.org, image 10 of 34, https://www.familysearch.org/ark:/61903/3:1:33SQ-GYBC-HH7; Claudius Torp, "Heinrich Engelhard Steinway," in *German-American Business Biographies, 1720 to the Present*, ed. William J. Hausman (Washington, DC: German Historical Institute, 2013), https://www.immigrantentrepreneurship.org/entry.php?rec=147.

12 Andrew S. Dolkart, "The Biography of a Lower East Side Tenement; 97 Orchard Street, Tenement Design, and Tenement Reform in New York City," Tenement Museum, accessed February 17, 2021, https://tenement.org/documents/Dolkart.pdf.

13 Nadel, *Little Germany*, 155–162.

14 There was also a German Club that met at 13 West 24th Street and was headed by Charles Unger in 1880, *Trow's New York Directory, 1880–81, Vol. M–Z*, 23–24; Rudolf Cronau, *Denkschrift zum 150. jahrestag der Deutschen Gesellschaft der Stadt New York, 1784–1934* (New York: German Society of New York, 1934); *One Hundred and Fifty Years, 1852–2002, the Harmonie Club* (New York: Harmonie Club, 2002).

15 New York City Landmark Preservation Commission (NYCLPC) historic designation report, Aschenbroedel Verein, November 17, 2009, 4, http://www.nyc

.gov/html/lpc/downloads/pdf/reports/AschenbroedelVerein.pdf. Mary Sue Morrow, "Somewhere between Beer and Wagner: The Cultural and Musical Impact of German Männerchör in New York and New Orleans," in *Music and Culture in America, 1861–1918*, ed. Michael Saffle (New York: Routledge, 2014), 81–86, counts at least 63 Männerchör in New York City (including the Bronx) founded during 1847–1890.

16 New York Liederkranz Society History Committee, *History of the Liederkranz of New York City, 1847–1947, and of the Arion, of New York* (New York: Drechsler, 1948), "Chronology," 142–147; Edwin M. Good, "William M. Steinway and Music in New York, 1861–1871," in *Music and Culture in America, 1861–1918*, ed. Michael Saffle (New York: Routledge, 2014), 3–28.

17 New York Liederkranz Society History Committee, *History of the Liederkranz*, 3, 19, 30, 147; Morrow, "Somewhere," 83–84; "The William Steinway Diary, 1861–1896," National Museum of American History, http://americanhistory.si.edu/steinwaydiary/.

18 "William Steinway Diary"; John Koegel and Jonas Westover, "Beethoven and Beer, Orchestral Music in German Beer Gardens Nineteenth-Century New York City," in *American Orchestras in the Nineteenth Century*, ed. John Spitzer (Chicago: University of Chicago Press, 2012), 153–155.

19 NYCLPC historic designation report, Aschenbroedel Verein, 3. Steinway was president of the Liederkranz in 1867, 1869, 1873, 1877, 1878–1879, 1880–1881, 1882–1883, 1885–1886, 1887–1888, 1892–1893, and 1896.

20 Arion would move to a new clubhouse before moving to Park Avenue and 59th Street in 1887. New York Liederkranz Society History Committee, *History of the Liederkranz*, 18, 142–147.

21 NYCLPC historic district designation report, 20, 99; Morrow, "Somewhere," 85.

22 Tom Goyens, *Beer and Revolution: The German Anarchist Movement in New York City, 1880–1914* (Chicago: University of Illinois, 2007), 168–171.

23 U.S. Bureau of the Census, 1880, vol. 1, *Statistics of the Population of the United States*, table 36, "Persons in Selected Occupations in Fifty Principal Cities, Etc: New York, New York," 892.

24 NYCLPC historic district designation report, 6; NYCLPC historic designation report, Aschenbroedel Verein.

25 *New York Times*, December 18, 1870, 5, estimates that 55 percent of MMPU members were German; 13 percent were French; 7 percent were Italian; 5 percent each were Polish, Belgian, Swedish, and Norwegian; 4 percent were English, Irish, and Dutch; while Spanish, Portuguese, and "American" were only 2 percent. Please also see John Spitzer, *American Orchestras in the Nineteenth Century* (Chicago: University of Chicago Press, 2012), 85–87.

26 Koegel and Westover, "Beethoven and Beer," 132–133, for pay figures.

27 Carl Wittke, *Refugees of Revolution: The German Forty-Eighters in America* (Philadelphia: University of Pennsylvania Press, 1952), 186; "The Turners," *New York Times*, September 20, 1853, 4.

28 This new clubhouse was built in 1872, before that, the Turnhalle was at 27 Orchard Street. *Trow's New York City Directory, compiled by H. Wilson, Vol. LXXXIV, for the year ending May 1, 1871* (New York: John F. Trow, 1871), 44. "Secret and Benefit Societies," notes the address. There were also the uptown Bloomingdale Turnverein lodge at 341 West 47th Street. Please also see Nora Probst, *The New York Turn Verein, finding aid of the archival documents*

(1850–2005), Max Kade Institute (New York, 2008), 4, https://maxkade.ku.edu /sites/maxkade.drupal.ku.edu/files/images/general/Turnverein-Collection /Finding%20Aid_N.Y.T.V.pdf. Please see "The Turners," *New York Times*, September 20, 1853, 4, explaining to English-speaking readers the activities and philosophy of the Turnverein.

29 The New York Turn Verein School educated 639 pupils and received $740,000 in public funds. See *Fifth Annual Report of the Board of State Commissioners of Public Charities of the State of New York, New York (State) Board of Charities, Annual Report*, vol. 5 (Albany: Argus, 1872), appendix, table 35, "List of Charity Week-day Schools aided by the State for the year ending September 30, 1871, with their location, number of scholars instructed, and the amount received by each," 166.

30 "Fire's Disastrous Work," *New York Times*, January 6, 1880, 1; "Incidents of the Fire," *New York Times*, January 6, 1880, 2; "The Turn Hall Fire," *New York Times*, January 7, 1880, 8; "The Fire in Turn Hall," *New York Times*, January 8, 1880, 5; "Capt. Winkel's Funeral," *New York Times*, January 15, 1880, 8.

31 NYCLPC historic designation report, German-American Shooting Club Society, June 26, 2001, http://s-media.nyc.gov/agencies/lpc/lp/2094.pdf; Nadel, *Little Germany*, 112–113.

32 Nadel, 110.

33 *Trow's New York Directory, 1880–81, Vol. M–Z*, 34, "Societies."

34 Nadel, *Little Germany*, 110–111.

35 Nadel, 107–108; Heike Bungert, *Festkultur und Gedächtnis, Die Konstruktion einer deutschamerikanischen Ethnizität, 1848–1914* (Paderborn, Germany: Ferdinand Schöningh, 2016).

36 Flyer for the Bremer Verein Freimarkt, October 1898, call no. IEK n.s.8, German pamphlets, not catalogued, New York Public Library (NYPL).

37 Please see Landsmannschaften Verein festival programs, call # IEK n.s. vols. 1–9, German pamphlets, not catalogued, NYPL.

38 Gompers was born in London to Jewish Dutch parents; the Gompers family emigrated in 1863, when Gompers was thirteen. Nadel, *Little Germany*, 122–136, 137–154; Schneider, *Trade Unions and Community*.

39 Nadel, *Little Germany*, 111–112; *Trow's New York City Directory, Vol. CI, for the year ending May 1, 1888* (New York: Trow City Directory, 1888), 46–49, "Secret and Benefit Societies." Gary L. Heinmiller, *Craft Masonry in Manhattan, New York County, New York, Vol. IV, Lodges Nos. 512 thru 698* (Onondaga and Oswego Masonic Districts Historical Societies, 2011), 37, 84–89.

40 Nadel, 92–95; Dolan, *Immigrant Church*, 68–86; Daniel Soyer, *Jewish Immigrant Associations and American Identity in New York, 1880–1939* (Cambridge, MA: Harvard University Press, 1997).

41 Dolan, *Immigrant Church*, 77–81; Gleason, *Conservative Reformers*.

42 Carl Wilhelm Schlegel, *Schlegel's German-American Families in the United States: Genealogical and Biographical, Illustrated* (New York: American Historical Society, 1916–1918), 1:355–362; Marion J. Barber, "Herman Ridder," in *Immigrant Entrepreneurship, German-American Business Biographies, 1720 to the Present*, ed. Giles R. Hoyt (Washington, DC: German Historical Institute, 2015), https://www.immigrantentrepreneurship.org/entries/herman-ridder/.

43 Nadel, *Little Germany*, 99–103. This church was located at 308 West Broadway and, while originally established as a German church, quickly became an Irish parish by the 1880s. See Dolan, *Immigrant Church*, 93–96.

44 *Trow's New York City Directory, compiled by H. Wilson, Vol. XCIII, for the year ending May 1, 1880, vol. M–Z* (New York: John F. Trow, 1880), 31–33, "Societies."

45 Stanley Nadel, "Jewish Race and German Soul in Nineteenth-Century America," in *Central European Jews in America, 1840–1880: Migration and Advancement,* ed. Jeffrey S. Gurock (New York: Routledge, 1998); Carl Wittke, *German-Language Press in America* (New York: Haskell House, 1973), 185.

46 NYCLPC historic designation report, Scheffel Hall, June 24, 1997, 3, http://www.nyc.gov/html/lpc/downloads/pdf/reports/scheffelhall.pdf.

47 George von Skal, *History of German Immigration in the United States and Successful German-Americans and their Descendants* (New York: Frederick T. Smiley, 1910), 81, 103.

48 Soyer, *Jewish Immigrant Associations.*

49 Dolan, *Immigrant Church*; Mary C. Kelly, *The Shamrock and the Lily: The New York Irish and the Creation of a Transatlantic Identity, 1845–1921* (New York: Peter Lang, 2005).

50 *Craft Masonry in Manhattan*; B. H. Meyer, "Fraternal Beneficiary Societies in the United States," *American Journal of Sociology* 6 (March 1901): 646–651; Mary Ann Clawson, *Constructing Brotherhood: Class, Gender, and Fraternalism* (Princeton, NJ: Princeton University Press, 1989).

51 Koegel and Westover, "Beethoven and Beer," 139–142.

52 U.S. Census, 1880, vol. 1, table 36, "Persons in Selected Occupations in Fifty Principal Cities, Etc.: 1880, New York, New York," 892.

53 Robert Graham, *Liquordom in New York City* (New York, 1883), 5.

54 Graham, *Liquordom*, 5.

55 Caroline Schneider's death from tuberculosis on June 18, 1885, was probably a major factor in John Schneider's decision to close the pub in 1886 and move across the street to 98 Orchard with his son Harry. Tenement House Museum, New York City, www.tenement.org, particularly http://tenement.org/blog/a-shop-life -anniversary/ and http://tenement-museum.blogspot.de/2010/02/questions-for -curatorial-schneiders.html.

56 Tenement House Museum blog, http://tenement.org/blog/a-shop-life -anniversary/ and http://tenement-museum.blogspot.de/2010/02/questions-for -curatorial-schneiders.html.

57 Nadel, *Little Germany*, 106.

58 Matthew Hale Smith, *Sunshine and Shadow in New York* (Hartford, CT: J. B. Burr, 1869), 216.

59 Koegel and Westover, "Beethoven and Beer."

60 James Dabney McCabe, *Lights and Shadows of New York Life: or, the Sights and Sensations of the Great City* (Continental Publishing Co., 1873), 550–554.

61 Koegel and Westover, "Beethoven and Beer," 144–146.

62 Koegel and Westover, 151–152, 155.

63 Koegel and Westover, 153–155.

64 Jürgen Eichoff, "The German Language in America," and Marion L. Huffines, "Language-Maintenance Among German Immigrants and Their Descendants in the United States," in *Americans and the Germans, An Assessment of a Three-Hundred-Year History*, vol. 1, *Immigration, Language, Ethnicity*, ed. Frank Trommler and Joseph McVeigh (Philadelphia: University of Pennsylvania, 1985), both note the role of institutions, especially churches, schools, and the press, in language maintenance but focus mainly on the Midwest and Texas.

65 NYCPLC historic designation report, Aschenbroedel Verein. The Germania
    Theater was based at Tammany Hall during 1874–1881, at Wallack's Theater at
    844 Broadway at Thirteenth Street during 1881–1882, and then at the former
    Church of St. Ann, East 8th Street near Broadway, until 1902.
66 Koegel and Westover, "Beethoven and Beer," 144.
67 McCabe, *Lights and Shadows*, 483.
68 John Koegel, *Music in German Immigrant Theater in New York City, 1840–1940*
    (Rochester, NY: University of Rochester Press, 2009), 30–36, 50; Gustav Kobbé,
    The Complete Opera Book (London, UK: Putnam, 1929), 117; "Amusements This
    Evening," *New York Times*, May 8, 1871, 4.
69 Michael Immerso, *Coney Island: The People's Playground* (New Brunswick, NJ:
    Rutgers University Press, 2002), 23–24, 130 for Feltman, 23 for Bauer; "Paul Bauer
    Is Dead," *New York Times*, January 3, 1889, 8; "Charles Feltman, Inventor of the
    Hot Dog," Coney Island History Project, https://www.coneyislandhistory.org
    /hall-of-fame/charles-feltman.
70 "Sketches of the People Who Oppose our Sunday Laws," *Harper's Weekly* 3,
    no. 146 (October 15, 1859): 657–658, is a good example.
71 Koegel and Westover, "Beethoven and Beer," 144.
72 Daniel Czitrom, *New York Exposed: The Gilded Age Police Scandal that Launched
    the Progressive Era* (New York: Oxford University Press, 2016).
73 Graham, *Liquordom*, 17–18; Koegel and Westover, "Beethoven and Beer," 136–137.
74 "Another Saloon Closed Up," *New York Times*, October 20, 1860, 2; "The Case of
    Lindenmuller on Appeal," *New York Times*, February 21, 1861, 2.
75 *Trow's New York City Directory, compiled by H. Wilson, Vol. LXXXIV*, 38,
    "Newspapers," lists twenty German-language newspapers; also see 28, "Magazines."
76 Albert Bernhardt Faust, *The German Element in the United States*, vol. 2 (Boston:
    Houghton Mifflin Company, Riverside Press, 1909), 143, 360–363; "Death of
    Joseph Keppler," *New York Times*, February 20, 1894, 1.
77 Wittke, *German-Language Press*, 170–174, 190; Fritz Leuchs, *The Early German
    Theatre in New York, 1840–1872* (1928, reprint, New York: AMS Press, 1966),
    xvi–xviii, 5.
78 *Trow's New York City Directory, 1871*, 38, "Newspapers"; also see 28,
    "Magazines."
79 Conolly-Smith, *Translating America*, 27; *Phillips' business directory of New York,
    1881*, 40–42, "Booksellers."
80 *Trow's New York Directory, 1880–81*, 6, "Bookseller"; Koegel, *Music*, 566, bibliogra-
    phy notes "Steiger, E., A Catalogue of the Best Plays in the German Language,
    Selected from the Dramatic Literature of Germany, France, England, Spain, etc.
    Steiger's Theater Catalog 24 (New York: E. Steiger, 1876)" and "Steiger's Catalog
    deutscher Bühnenstücke, Steiger's Dramatic Catalog 25 (New York: E. Steiger,
    1900).
81 Barbaralee Diamonstein, *The Landmarks of New York* (New York: Harry Abrams,
    1998), 107.
82 Leuchs, *Early German Theatre*, 7; P. Ramsey, *Bilingual Public Schooling in the
    United States: A History of America's "Polyglot Boardinghouse"* (New York:
    Springer, 2010), 40; *Phillips' business directory of New York, 1881*, 517–518, "Schools."
83 Ramsey, *Bilingual Public Schooling*, 40–41; A. Emerson Palmer, *The New York
    Public School, Being a History of Free Education in the City of New York* (London,
    UK: Macmillan, 1905), 170–171, 229.

84 Ramsey, *Bilingual Public Schooling*, 40–41.

85 This was out of a total of 4,803 teachers, or 7 percent of all New York City teachers. U.S. Census, 1880, table 36, "Persons in Selected Occupations in Fifty Principal Cities, Etc.: 1880, New York, New York," 892; Janet Nolan, *Servants of the Poor: Teachers and Mobility in Ireland and Irish America* (Notre Dame, IN: University of Notre Dame Press, 2004), 2, notes that one-third of New York City public school teachers were either Irish or Irish American by the early twentieth century. *Trow's New York Directory, 1880–81*, 8–9, "Schools, Primary Schools," lists principals and vice principals, few of whom had German names.

86 *Trow's New York Directory, 1880–81, Vol. M–Z*, 8–9, "Schools, Primary Schools." Public Schools: #2, 116 Henry; #4, 203 Rivington; #5, 222 Mott; #7, 60 Chrystie; #8, 66 Grand; #13, 239 East Houston; #19, 344 East 14th; #20, 160 Chrystie; #31, 198 Monroe; #34, 108 Broome; #36, 710 East 9th; #42, 30 Allen; #47, 36 East 12th. Primary Schools: #1, 105 Ludlow; #3, 100 Cannon; #5, 269 East 4th; #6, 15 East 3rd; #8, 62 Mott; #9, 42 1st; #12, 85 Roosevelt; #14, 73 Oliver; #20, 187 Broome; #22, 150 First Ave.; #23, 17 St. Mark's Pl.; #26, 538 East 12th; #36, 68 Monroe; #40, 100 Norfolk.

87 Christina A. Ziegler-McPherson, *Immigrants in Hoboken: One-Way Ticket, 1845–1985* (Charleston, SC: History Press, 2011), 47.

88 Ramsey, *Bilingual Public Schooling*, 40–41.

89 George U. Wenner, *The Lutherans of New York: Their Story and Their Problems* (New York: Petersfield, 1918), 134–143, see abbreviation "P.S." for "parochial school," lists eight Lutheran parochial schools in Manhattan, another four in the Bronx, twelve in Brooklyn, four in Queens, two in Staten Island, and a total of 1,612 students in parochial schools. The Manhattan parochial schools were St. Matthew, at 421 West 145th; Trinity, 139 Avenue B; St. Peter, East 54th at Lexington Avenue; Immanuel, 88th at Lexington Avenue; St. John, at 219 East 119th; St. Paul, at 147 West 123rd; Washington Heights at West 153rd; and Advent at Broadway at West 93rd.

90 Rudolph J. Vecoli, *The People of New Jersey* (Princeton, NJ: D. Van Nostrand, 1965), 118–119.

91 *Trow's New York City Directory, compiled by H. Wilson, Vol. XCIII*, 17–22, "Churches"; Richard Haberstroh, *The German Churches of Metropolitan New York: A Research Guide* (New York: New York Genealogical and Biographical Society, 2000). German immigrants organized five Baptist congregations (First German Baptist, 336 East 14th; German Baptist, Washington Avenue near 169th; Second German Baptist at 451 West 45th; St. Paul's, Third Avenue and East 60th; First Baptist of Harlem, East 118th near Second Avenue); two Methodist congregations (German Methodist Episcopal, 346 West 40th; and St. Paul's German Methodist Episcopal, 308 East 55th); a Presbyterian Church at 292 Madison Avenue; two Reformed congregations (German Reformed Protestant Church, 131 Norfolk; and German Evangelical Reformed Church, 97 Suffolk); and two missions, the Fourth German Mission at 244 West 40th and the German Evangelical Mission at 141 East Houston.

92 Nadel, *Little Germany*, 92–95; Haberstroh, *German Churches*, also identifies Our Lady of Sorrows, founded in 1867 at Pitt and Stanton Streets as German, but it is not identified specifically as German in *Trow's New York City Directory, 1880, vol. M–Z*, 17–22, "Churches." According to *Trow's*, other German Roman Catholic churches were St. Mary Magdalen, East 17th and Avenue B; Immaculate

Conception, East 151st and Third Avenue; St. Joseph's, Washington Avenue and
176th; St. Joseph's, East 87th and First Avenue; St. Joseph's, West 125th and Ninth
Avenue.

93 Other Lutheran churches were German Evangelical Trinity Lutheran at 732
Ninth Avenue; Trinity, 47 West 21st; Immanuel, East 83rd and Third Avenue;
Immanuel, East 87th and Third Avenue; St. James, 216 East 15th; St. John's, 81
Christopher; St. John's 217 East 119th; St. Lucas, 233 West 42nd; St. Marcus, 323
Sixth; St. Matthew's, Courtland Ave and 154th; St. Paul's, 226 Sixth Avenue;
St. Paul's, West 123rd and Seventh Avenue; St. Peter's, 474 Lexington Avenue;
St. Stephen's Mission, 359 Broome; and Trinity Lutheran, 139 Avenue B. *Trow's
New York City Directory, 1880, vol. M–Z,* 17–22, "Churches." Please also see
Haberstroh, *German Churches*; Dolan, *Immigrant Church*; Ed O'Donnell, *Ship
Ablaze: The Tragedy of the Steamboat General Slocum* (New York: Broadway, 2003).

94 Nadel, *Little Germany*, 91–103; George J. Manson, "The Foreign Element in New
York City—the Germans," supplement, *Harper's Weekly* 32, no. 1650 (August 4,
1888): 582–591, reported that one religious leader claimed that 50,000 Germans
were nonchurchgoers.

95 Lenox Hill Hospital, "Our History," https://www.northwell.edu/find-care
/locations/lenox-hill-hospital/about?id=102; Leuchs, *Early German Theatre*, 9.

Chapter 2   Climbing the Economic Ladder in Kleindeutschland in 1880

1 The Contract Labor Law of 1885 made it illegal to immigrate with a job contract
already in hand, but most immigrants arrived with a name or names of people to
contact about work.

2 Skal, *History of German Immigration*.

3 It is difficult to determine the unemployment rate for New York City in the 1880s,
but J. R. Vernon has estimated for the United States for the late nineteenth
century, and New York City was the largest economic area in the country.
J. R. Vernon, "Unemployment Rates in Postbellum America: 1869–1899," *Journal
of Macroeconomics* 16, no. 4 (Fall 1994): 701–714.

4 U.S. Bureau of the Census, 1880, vol. 2, Statistics of Manufactures, table 6,
"Manufactures of 100 Principal Cities, by Totals," 380.

5 U.S. Bureau of the Census, 1880, vol. 1, Statistics of the Population of the United
States, table 36, "Persons in Selected Occupations in Fifty Principal Cities, Etc:
New York, New York," 892. Note: the census separated tailoring, dressmaking,
and millinery from boot and shoe making.

6 Walter Kamphoefner, "The German Component to American Industrialization
(1840–1893)," in *Immigrant Entrepreneurship, German-American Business
Biographies, 1720 to the Present*, ed. William J. Hausman (Washington, DC:
German Historical Institute, 2014), https://www.immigrantentrepreneurship.org
/entry.php?rec=189; Hartmut Keil, "German Working-Class Radicalism in the
United States from the 1870s to World War I," in *Struggle a Hard Battle, Essays on
Working-Class Immigrants*, ed. Dirk Hoerder (DeKalb: Northern Illinois
University Press, 1986), 74–75.

7 1880 Census, vol. 1, table 36, 892; and vol. 2, table 6, 417. The garment industry
included tailors, dressmakers, and milliners, as well as cap, corset, shirt, and
artificial feather and flower makers. Leather goods outside of shoes and boots are
not included here.

8 The directory of the City of New-York for 1852–1853, compiled by Henry Wilson (New York: J. F. Trow, 1852), 300 lists "Hornthal & Whitehead, tailors, 295 Grand." The company was called Hornthal, Whitehead, Weissman & Co. by 1884. Please see "Meyer Whitehead," *New York Times*, May 22, 1890, Obituary, 5. An immigration record for "L Hornthal," age thirty, born in New York City in 1846, arriving in New York from Liverpool on the SS *Butannic* on September 30, 1876, suggests that Marx Hornthal had immigrated sometime before 1846. New York Passenger Lists, 1820–1891, electronic image 109 of 1020, Familysearch.org, https://www.familysearch.org/ark:/61903/3:1:939V-R394-87?i=108&cc=1849782. Please see also "Police Reports," *New York Times*, June 22, 1860, 8, noting embezzlement of Hornthal & Whitehead by a German employee.

9 "Mark Hornthal, tailor," lived at 199 ½ Division Street in 1845; Meyer Whitehead was not listed that year. *New-York City Directory for 1844 & 1845* (New York: John Doggett, 1845), 173. In 1852, Marx Hornthal lived at 27 Norfolk Street; Meyer Whitehead did not list a home address, *The Directory of the City of New-York for 1852–1853* (New York: J. F. Trow, 1852), 300. In 1865, Marx Hornthal still lived at 27 Norfolk Street, while Meyer Whitehead lived at 259 East Broadway near Montgomery on the Lower East Side. The store had moved to 19 Dey. *Trow's New York City Directory, compiled by H. Wilson, Vol. LXXVIII, for the Year ending May 1, 1865* (New York: J. F. Trow, 1865), 433.

10 "A Business Men's Union," *New York Times*, May 22, 1884, 5. Of the eighty firms listed in the Traders and Travelers' Union, only eleven had German-sounding names.

11 *Annual Report of the Directors of Mount Sinai Hospital, January 1886* (New York: Thalmessinger & Mendham, 1886), http://dspace.mssm.edu/bitstream/handle /123456789/4954/annualreportofdi1885moun.pdf?sequence=1&isAllowed=y. Also please see "Donations to the Hospital Fund," *New York Times*, January 6, 1882, 8, which notes contributions from Mrs. Marx Hornthal and Z. M. Hornthal for ten and twenty dollars, respectively.

12 The Mount Sinai Hospital, "About the Hospital, History," http://www.mountsinai .org/locations/mount-sinai/about/history.

13 Lewis Hornthal was married twice, once to Carrie Speyer on June 1, 1869, and then to Anna Smith on August 27, 1896; Anna Smith's parents were born in Virginia and New York. "New York, New York City Marriage Records, 1829–1940," database, *FamilySearch* (https://familysearch.org/ark:/61903/1:1:24CP-XL6: 10 February 2018), Lewis Hornthal and Anna Smith, 27 August 1896; citing Marriage, Manhattan, New York, New York, United States, New York City Municipal Archives, New York; FHL microfilm 1,493,576. Lewis Marx Hornthal received his MA from the College of the City of New-York in 1868. "College of the City of New-York," *New York Times*, July 3, 1868, 4. "Failures in Business," *New York Times*, February 6, 1885, 3; "Collecting Relief Funds, in the Trades," *New York Times*, June 5, 1889, 2. Please also see Daniel Soyer, *A Coat of Many Colors: Immigration, Globalization, and Reform in New York City's Garment Industry* (New York: Fordham University Press, 2005), 110–111.

14 The store was located at 425 Broome Street in 1876, Hornthal lived at 117 East 56th Street, and Whitehead lived at 122 East 70th Street. *Trow's New York City Directory, 1876–1877* (New York: J. F. Trow, 1877), 645, 1458; U.S. Census, New York, New York, ED 583, image 38 of 40, Familysearch.org, https://www .familysearch.org/ark:/61903/3:1:33S7-9YB5-SC8?i=37&cc=1417683; "Find a Grave Index," database, FamilySearch.org, https://familysearch.org/ark:/61903

/1:1:QVG1-48ZZ, "Marx Hornthal, Burial, Ridgewood, Queens, New York, Beth El Cemetery," citing record ID 132923463, http://www.findagrave.com; "Meyer Whitehead," *New York Times*, May 22, 1890, Obituary.

15 Jane Ziegelman, "97 Orchard," *New York Times*, July 27, 2010, Books; Census of 1850, Ward 10, FamilySearch.org, image 180 of 559, https://www.familysearch.org /ark:/61903/3:1:S3HT-63P9-P16?i=179&cc=1401638.

16 Lucas and Wilhelmina Glockner had three other children, besides now-grown Oscar: fifteen-year-old William, identified as a "colegian"; eight-year old Minnie; and six-year old Ida. Census of 1880, 25 Allen Street, Ward 10, Familysearch.com, image 18 of 56, https://www.familysearch.org/ark:/61903/3:1:33SQ-GYB5-9SY?i =17&cc=1417683. Glockner ultimately sold 97 Orchard Street in 1886 for $29,000. Tenement Museum, https://www.tenement.org/Virtual-Tour/vt_indfin.html.

17 All of the Steinway sons anglicized their names: Karl to Charles, Heinrich to Henry, Wilhelm to William. The eldest son, C. F. Theodore, remained in Germany and opened his own piano-making workshop. Heinrich Steinweg was already calling himself Henry Steinway by 1852. *New York City Directory for 1852–1853* (New York: Doggett and Rode, 1853), 488, although Schneider, *Trade Unions and Community*, 1–4, 6, says that the company and family names were anglicized later.

18 Nadel, *Little Germany*, 40, 73–74, 85–86. "Steinway & Sons, pianos, 84 Walker, 91 Mercer, & 85 Varick," *Trow's New York City Directory, for the Year ending May 1, 1857* (New York: J. F. Trow, 1857), 786.

19 Torp, "Heinrich Engelhard Steinway."

20 Torp.

21 Torp.

22 The Steinways (listed as "Steinway, Henry, piano manufacturer, 199 Hester") first appear in New York City directories in 1853. *New York City Directory for 1852–1853* (New York: Doggett and Rode, 1853), 488. By 1857, the home of Charles, Henry, and William Steinway is listed as 84 Walker Street. *Trow's New York City Directory, for the Year ending May 1, 1857*, 586; *Trow's New York City Directory, 1876–1877*, 1314.

23 Torp, "Heinrich Engelhard Steinway"; NYCLPC, Gramercy Park Historic District designation report, September 20, 1966, http://www.nyc.gov/html/lpc /downloads/pdf/reports/GRAMERCY_PARK_HISTORIC_DISTRICT.pdf.

24 Richard K. Lieberman, *Steinway and Sons* (New Haven, CT: Yale University Press, 1995), 79–85; James S. Lapham, "The German-Americans of New York City, 1860–1890" (PhD diss., St. John's University, 1977), 132–164, esp. 157.

25 Seven Beckert, "The Monied Metropolis: New York City and the Consolidation of the American Bourgeoisie, 1850–1896," in *Class: The Anthology*, ed. Stanley Aronowitz and Michael J. Roberts (Hoboken, NJ: John Wiley and Sons, 2017), 403; Stanley Nadel, "Those Who Would Be Free: The Eight-Hour Day Strikes of 1872," *Labor's Heritage*, 2, no. 2 (April 1990): 70–77; Lieberman, *Steinway and Sons*, 93–95; Lapham, "German-Americans," 34–35; "Steinway's Men on Strike," *New York Times*, February 18, 1880, 8; "The Piano Men's Victory," *New York Times*, March 25, 1880, 3; "Piano-Makers on Strike," *New York Times*, September 19, 1882, 8; "Collapse of the Strike in the Piano Trade," *New York Times*, November 25, 1882, 5; "Short Hour Notes," *New York Times*, May 2, 1886, 2; "End of the Piano Strike," *New York Times*, May 10, 1886, 8.

26 "German Society; the Yearly Report Election of Officers," *New York Times*, January 24, 1862; Torp, "Heinrich Engelhard Steinway."

27 New York Liederkranz Society History Committee. *History of the Liederkranz*; "William Steinway," *New York Times*, December 1, 1896, 4; Torp, "Heinrich Engelhard Steinway."

28 "William Steinway Diary," "Liederkranz Membership," http://americanhistory.si .edu/steinwaydiary/annotations/?id=629; "William Steinway Diary," "The Arion Society," http://americanhistory.si.edu/steinwaydiary/annotations/?id=761.

29 "Deutscher Liederkranz von New York," *New-Yorker Staats-Zeitung*, March 17, 1895, 1, http://americanhistory.si.edu/steinwaydiary/annotations/?id=757&popup =1&ajaxResetHistory=1. Although the quotation is in English here, since it originally appeared in the *Staats-Zeitung*, which was printed in German, it is assumed that the statement was originally made in German.

30 The Smithsonian transcription of Steinway's diary notes that Steinway did sometimes write in German, using the Fraktur script, but the diary is primarily written in English, from the first entry on April 20, 1861.

31 "William Steinway Diary," "The Steinway Family," http://americanhistory.si.edu /steinwaydiary/family/; "William Steinway Diary," "William and Regina Steinway's divorce," http://americanhistory.si.edu/steinwaydiary/annotations/?id =95; and "William Steinway Diary," "Regina Roos Steinway," http://american history.si.edu/steinwaydiary/annotations/?id=93. Regina Steinway died of typhoid in Nancy, France, in 1882. Although adultery was one of the few grounds for divorce in the nineteenth century, the fact that Steinway disinherited and disavowed his youngest son, Alfred, suggests that Steinway believed that Alfred had been fathered by another man. The diary also notes multiple affairs and marital tumult.

32 Mark Benbow, "German Immigrants in the United States Brewing Industry (1940–1895)," in *Immigrant Entrepreneurship, German-American Business Biographies, 1720 to the Present*, ed. William J. Hausman (Washington, DC: German Historical Institute, 2017), https://www.immigrantentrepreneurship.org /entry.php?rec=284; Kamphoefner, "German Component."

33 Schneider, *Trade Unions and Community*, 134–140; Dorothee Schneider, "The German Brewery Workers of New York City in the Late Nineteenth Century," in *Labor Divided: Race and Ethnicity in United States Labor Struggles, 1835–1960*, ed. Robert Asher and Charles Stephenson (New York: SUNY Press, 1990).

34 Schneider, *Trade Unions and Community*, 137, 141.

35 For example, George Ehret sang in the Liederkranz, while John Christian Glaser Hupfel was active in the Arion and Jung-Arion Societies, the Liederkranz and its Bachelor Circle, and the Beethoven Männerchor. Skal, *History of German Immigration*, 98, 103 (for Ehret), 115 (for Hupfel).

36 Benbow, "German Immigrants". Please also see *The Year Book of the United State Brewers' Association* (New York: United States Brewers Association, 1909).

37 Both John Christian Glaser Hupfel and his brother Adolph Glaser Hupfel were active in Democratic Party politics. Jacob Ruppert Jr. was a Tammany Democratic congressman in the early 1900s. Skal, *History of German Immigration*, 115 (for the Hupfel brothers), 121–122 (for Ruppert).

38 F. W. Salem, *Beer, Its History and Its Economic Value as a National Beverage* (Hartford, CT: F. W. Salem, 1880); George Ehret, *Twenty Five Years of Brewing, with an illustrated History of America Beer* (New York: Gast Lithograph & Engraving, 1891), 50.

39 Skal, *History of German Immigration*, 98–103; Christopher Gray, "A Park Ave. Mansion Built with Beer," *New York Times*, July 17, 2005. U.S. Bureau of the Census, 1880, New York, New York, ED 623, 98 4th Avenue at 94th Street, FamilySearch.org, https://www.familysearch.org/ark:/61903/3:1:33SQ-GYB6 -94H?i=16&cc=1417683.

40 "Anton Huepfel," *New York Times*, January 4, 1895, Obituary, 5; *Historical and Genealogical Record Dutchess and Putnam Counties New York* (Poughkeepsie, NY: A. V. Haight, 1912), 283–468, says that Adolph Glaser died in 1849. The Glasers changed their name to Hupfel in 1874. Kenneth Scott, *Petitions for Name Changes in New York City, 1848–1899, Special publications of the National Genealogical Society, no. 53* (Washington, DC: National Genealogical Society, 1984), 31, states: "Petition (6 Feb. 1874) of Adolph Glaser and his wife Magdalena. Adolph is in his 29th year, Magdalena in her 25th. They have no children. Adolph is the stepson of Anton Hupfel, a wealthy citizen of the U.S. Adolph wishes to change his name to Adolph Hupfel, as this would be to his advantage." "A Curious Record, Change of Names Sanctioned by the Court of Common Pleas," *New York Times*, January 2, 1875, 8, lists an Adolph, Magdalena, John Christian, and Anna Maria Glaser petitioning to change their names to Hupfel. John W. Leonard, *Who's Who in Finance, Banking and Insurance: A Biographical Dictionary of Contemporaries* (New York: Who's Who in Finance, 1925), 484.

41 *Gouldings New York City directory, 1877–1878* (New York: Lawrence G. Goulding, 1878), 682.

42 For John Christian Glaser Hupfel, U.S. Bureau of the Census, 1880, New York, New York, ED 477, FamilySearch.org, https://www.familysearch.org/ark:/61903 /3:1:33S7-9YBZ-YB7?i=28&cc=1417683. "J.C.G Hupfel Dies," *New York Times*, February 18, 1932, 19, says Hupfel lived at 148 East 37th Street and had since he was nine years old; for Adolph Glaser Hupfel, U.S. Bureau of the Census 1880, New York, New York, ED664, FamilySearch.org, https://www.familysearch.org/ark: /61903/3:1:33S7-9YBG-NB7?i=11&cc=1417683.

43 Skal, *History of German Immigration*, 115, says Hupfel was a member of the New York Produce Exchange, Brewers' Board of Trade, Associated Brewers, State Brewers and Malsters, North Side Board of Trade, New York Botanical Society, Wieland Lodge No. 714, F.& A.M., Freundschaft Lodge No. 4, Improved Order of the Knights of Pythias, Melrose Turn Verein, Arion Liedertafel, Central Turn Verein, German Hospital, Deutsche Gesellschaft, the Terrace Bowling Club (with his brother John Christian), the Manhattan Club, and the Schnorer Club (a social club in Morrisania) and was a director of the Union Railway.

44 "Skal, *History of German Immigration*, 115. "J.C.G Hupfel Dies," *New York Times*, February 18, 1932, 19, lists Hupfel's memberships as assistant treasurer, director of the Lenox Hill Hospital (formerly the German Hospital); vice president of the Isabella Home; a member of the Charity Organization Society, American Forestry Association, New York Zoological Society, "A.P.C.A., A.S. P.C.C.," Tammany Hall, Liederkranz, New York Athletic Club, Automobile Club of America, Terrace Bowling Club, Red Bank Yacht Club, and Rumson Country Club. Heinmiller, *Craft Masonry in Manhattan*, 37, 84–89.

45 Hermann Schluter, *The Brewing Industry and the Brewery Workers' Movement in America* (Reddich, UK: Read Books, 2017, originally printed by the International Union of United Brewery Workmen of America, 1910).

46 Schneider, *Trade Unions and Community*, 130–153; Schneider, "German Brewery Workers."

47 Skal, *History of German Immigration*, 121–122, 193–194.

48 Lapham, "German-Americans," 142–152; Schlegel, *Schlegel's German-American Families*, 98–108.

49 College Point had 4,192 people, with 1,675 residents being foreign born. U.S. Bureau of the Census 1880, Compendium of the Tenth Census, table 26, "Population of places of 4,000 inhabitants and over, by nativity: 1880 and 1870, New York," 459; Lapham, "German-Americans," 139, for number of employees at Enterprise Works.

50 Lapham, 135–136. Out of the more than 1,200 residents, 762 were Prussian born (74 percent) in 1880. 1880 Census, vol. 1, College Point, New York, 1–51, 59–90.

51 Lapham, 141, 143 (Poppenhusen's religiosity), 147–149 (social welfare programs). Although the Poppenhusen Institute claims to have founded the first kindergarten in the United States in 1870, Hoboken claims to have had the first kindergarten in 1861. Ziegler-McPherson, *Immigrants in Hoboken*, 47.

52 "William Steinway Diary," "Conrad Poppenhusen," http://americanhistory.si.edu /steinwaydiary/annotations/?id=809.

53 Lapham, "German-Americans," 137, 141.

54 "William Steinway Diary," "Conrad Poppenhusen," citing entry September 10, 1875.

55 Vincent F. Seyfried, *The Long Island Railroad: A Comprehensive History*, part 2, *The Flushing, North Shore and Central Railroad* (Garden City, NY: Vincent F. Seyfried, 1963); Lapham, "German-Americans," 139, although Lapham spells Funke's name Funk.

56 Schlegel, *Schlegel's German-American Families*, 98–108, says that Herman's wife was from College Point; 1880 Census, New York, Queens, College Point, ED 264, FamilySearch.org, https://www.familysearch.org/ark:/61903/3:1:33SQ-GYBX -9D8Y?i=31&cc=1417683, for Alfred Poppenhusen; and 1880 Census, New York, Queens, North Hempstead, Ed 292, https://www.familysearch.org/ark:/61903 /3:1:33S7-9YBW-F1H, for Herman Poppenhusen says his wife was born in New York to Prussian-born parents. In 1880, Herman Poppenhusen listed his occupation as "farmer," although he ran his father's railroad business in the late 1870s. U.S. Bureau of the Census 1870, New York, Queens, Flushing, FamilySearch.org, https://www.familysearch.org/ark:/61903/3:1:S3HT-6LHQ-DL3?i=72&cc =1438024, lists Herman and Alfred living with their brother Adolph Poppenhusen and his wife and young daughter. Please also see "William Steinway Diary," "Conrad Poppenhusen."

57 Carol X. Venzant, *Lawyers, Guns, and Money: One Man's Battle with the Gun Industry* (New York: St. Martin's Press, 2005), 60–61; Seyfried, *Long Island Railroad*.

58 Seyfried, *Long Island Railroad*; Lapham, "German-Americans," 145; "Conrad Poppenhusen's Bankruptcy," *New York Times*, August 4, 1878, 9.

59 "William Steinway Diary," "Conrad Poppenhusen." See also Seyfried, *Long Island Railroad*.

60 William Stevenson, "Charles Pfizer," in *Immigrant Entrepreneurship, German-American Business Biographies, 1720 to the Present*, ed. William J. Hausman (Washington, DC: German Historical Institute, 2011), https://www.immigrant entrepreneurship.org/entry.php?rec=31.

61 Stevenson, "Charles Pfizer."

62 1880 Census, vol. 1, table 36, 892, notes 2,638 doctors and surgeons, of which 1,898 were American and only 309 were German. Figures for the number of pharmacists and chemists are unavailable, but vol. 2, table VO. 417 417, notes that there were twenty-seven establishments manufacturing drugs and chemicals, and 218 notes that there were forty-four establishments making patent medicines and compounds.

63 Stevenson, "Charles Pfizer."

64 The family lived at 295 Washington Street, Brooklyn. U.S. Census of 1880, New York, Kings, Brooklyn, ED 49, FamilySearch.org, https://www.familysearch.org /ark:/61903/3:1:33SQ-GYBG-CRH?i=30&cc=1417683.

65 Stevenson, "Charles Pfizer."

66 Skal, *History of German Immigration*, 139–140.

67 Stevenson, "Charles Pfizer."

68 Ziegler-McPherson, *Immigrants in Hoboken*, 38, table 5, "Hoboken's German Population, 1880–1930."

69 Elka Park had a total of twenty-one homes and was built in 1890. The Elka Club, "About Us," http://elkaparkclub.com/index.php?option=com_content&view =article&id=49&Itemid=44. See also New York State Office of Parks, Recreation, and Historic Preservation, Elka Park National Registry of Historic Places application, #1024-0018, Nancy Todd, February 1993, http://pwa.parks.ny.gov /hpimaging/hp_view.asp?GroupView=2638. Skal, *History of German Immigration*, 149, says that Keuffel was an honorary president of the Elka Park Association.

70 Christina A. Ziegler-McPherson, "Wilhelm J. D. Keuffel," in *Immigrant Entrepreneurship, The German-American Business Biography, 1720 to the Present*, ed. Giles R. Hoyt (Washington, DC: German Historical Institute, 2014), http:// www.immigrantentrepreneurship.org/entry.php?rec=157. One daughter, Margarethe, married a man from German-speaking Switzerland.

71 David C. Hammack, *Power and Society: Greater New York at the Turn of the Century* (New York: Columbia University Press, 1987), 66.

72 Hammack, *Power and Society*, 65.

73 Hammack, 69. Sidney Ratner, *New Light on the History of Great American Fortunes: American Millionaires of 1892 and 1902* (New York: A. M. Kelley, 1953), 57–85. Ratner lists 1,103 millionaires in New York City. Of these an estimated 94 had German-sounding names (although only 66 are certainties).

Chapter 3   Decades of Change, 1880–1900

1 An analysis of a sample of New York–born residents with two German-born parents in the 1880 census shows that a tiny professional class—doctors, dentists, pharmacists, teachers, ministers, and insurance agents—continued to live in predominantly German wards, the old Kleindeutschland Tenth and Seventeenth Wards, but also just north on the East Side, in the Eighteenth, Nineteenth, and Twenty-First Wards, and just to the west of the Bowery, in the Fifteenth Ward. In general, however, the highest percentage of German Americans still lived in the Tenth (24 percent), with the Nineteenth (Yorkville) becoming the second most popular district, with 15 percent of German Americans living there. Steve Morse, "Tables of Enumeration Districts," http://bklyn-genealogy-info.stevemorse.org /Ward/Man.1880.ed.html.

2 Beckert, *Monied Metropolis*.

3 Rosenwaike, *Population History*, 73.

4 Rosenwaike, 83; New York State Census, 1875, table 18, "Showing how many of the Inhabitants of Each County, Town, City and Ward at the Census of 1874, were born in certain selected Counties, States and Foreign Countries, New York County," 37–38. In 1875, the Eleventh Ward had a total population of 63,855, of which 18,643 were German born, while the Seventeenth Ward had a total population of 101,075, with 34,708 being German born. In 1855, native Germans were 31 percent of the population of the Eleventh and Seventeenth Wards; the population of the Eleventh Ward was 45,038, of which 17,763 were German born, and the population of the Seventeenth Ward was 63,757, of which 16,223 were German born. New York State Census, 1855, Classification by Place of Birth, New York County, 111 (Eleventh Ward), 118 (Seventeenth Ward).

5 F. E. Pierce, *The Tenement-House Committee maps* (New York: Harper and Brothers, 1895), *Map No. 2, Map of City of New York showing the distribution of Principal nationalities by sanitary districts*, https://www.loc.gov/resource/g3804n .ct001463r?r=0.221,0.333,0.348,0.179,0; also Jason M. Barr, *Building the Skyline: The Birth and Growth of Manhattan's Skyscrapers*, "Population Density by Race and Ethnicity in 1890," http://buildingtheskyline.org/figure-pop-density-race -ethnicity-1890/; "Population Density by Race and Ethnicity in 1900," graphics, http://buildingtheskyline.org/figure-population-density-race-ethnicity-1900/.

6 This can be seen in Pierce, *Tenement-House Committee maps*; and Kate Holladay Claghorn, map to accompany report, "The Foreign Immigrant in New York City," in *Reports of the Industrial Commission* (Washington, DC: U.S. Government Printing Office, 1901), 15:465–492.

7 This is based on the estimate of 60,000 Jews in New York in 1878, given in Cyrus Adler et al., *Jewish Encyclopedia*, 278, plus an estimated German/German American community of about 530,000 in Rosenwaike, *Population History*, 73, table 26, "Country of Origin of Total Population of Foreign or Mixed Parentage, 1880, and of White Population, 1890," 74, table 27, "Country of Origin of the Native-born Population of Foreign or Mixed Parentage, New York City, 1880, and of the Native-born White Population, 1890." Tobias Brinkmann, "Jews, Germans, or Americans: German-Jewish Immigrants in the Nineteenth-Century United States," in *The Heimat Abroad: The Boundaries of Germanness*, ed. Krista O'Donnell, Renate Bridenthal, and Nancy R. Reagin (Ann Arbor: University of Michigan Press, 2005), 111–140; Tobias Brinkmann, "'We Are Brothers! Let Us Separate!' Jews and Community Building in American Cities during the 19th Century," *History Compass* 11, no. 10 (October 2013): 869–879; Polland and Soyer, *Emerging Metropolis*, 30–31.

8 "A Sensation at Saratoga," *New York Times*, June 19, 1877, 1.

9 "Funeral of Mr. Seligman," *New York Times*, May 4, 1880, 3; "The Late Mr. Seligman," *New York Times*, May 2, 1880, 9.

10 Elliott Ashkenazi, "Joseph Seligman," *Immigrant Entrepreneurship, the German-American Business Biography, 1720 to the Present*, ed. William J. Hausman (Washington, DC: German Historical Institute, 2013), https://www .immigrantentrepreneurshiorg/entry.php?rec=184; Brinkmann, "Jews, Germans, or Americans"; Hammack, *Power and Society*, 66–67.

11 Beckert, *Monied Metropolis*, 265–266; Hammack, *Power and Society*, 67. Also "Louis Keller's Funeral," *New York Times*, February 19, 1922, 22, notes Keller's family's Catholicism.

12 "William Steinway Diary," "Liederkranz Membership," March 29, 1881, http://
americanhistory.si.edu/steinwaydiary/annotations/?id=629.

13 "William Steinway Diary," "Liederkranz Membership."

14 Nadel, "Jewish Race," 313. Nadel argues that the Arion choir conductor Leopold
Damrosch was Jewish, and while Damrosch's father was Jewish, Damrosch was
baptized Lutheran when he married Helene von Heimburg.

15 *One Hundred and Fifty Years*, 15; Beckert, *Monied Metropolis*, 265–266, on
anti-Semitism.

16 "William Steinway Diary," "Liederkranz Membership," January 13, 1874 (regard-
ing Gunther); February 27, 1883 (regarding English-speaking members); "Ex-
Mayor C. Godfrey Gunther," *New York Times*, January 24, 1885, Obituary, 5.
Please also see New York Liederkranz Society History Committee, *History of the
Liederkranz*, for a full membership list.

17 Cronau, *Denkschrift zum 150*.

18 A sample from the 1920 U.S. census of more than 6,000 persons, which asked
about the mother tongues of residents, as well as their parents, shows that among
New Yorkers with German-born parents, virtually all spoke English, and many
spoke it as their native tongue. Please also see Renate Ludanyi, "German in the
USA," in *Language Diversity in the USA*, ed. Kim Potowski (Cambridge, UK:
Cambridge University Press, 2010), 146–163.

19 "Burned in a Brewery Vat," *New York Times*, January 7, 1881, 2; "Burned in the
Brewery Vat," *New York Times*, February 9, 1881, 8; "The Brewers in Trouble," *New
York Times*, June 7, 1881, 5; "The Strikers Still Firm," *New York Times*, June 8, 1881,
2; "The Brewers and Their Men," *New York Times*, June 9, 1881, 2; "Brewery
Workmen's Strike," *New York Times*, June 12, 1881, 12; "Labor Agitations," *New
York Times*, June 13, 1881, 5; "Miscellaneous City News," *New York Times*, June 18,
1881, 8; "Among the Strikers," *New York Times*, June 19, 1881, 12; "Miscellaneous
City News," *New York Times*, June 29, 1881, 2; Schneider, *Trade Unions and
Community*, 151.

20 Schneider, 149–152; Schneider, "German Brewery Workers," 189–208. "Der
Brauerausstand," *New Yorker Volkszeitung*, 1, and "Bekanntmachtung," *New
Yorker Volkszeitung*, 3, note conditions in the breweries and call for the continued
boycott of nonunionized breweries and support for union shops.

21 Beckert, *Monied Metropolis*, 403

22 Keil, "German Working-Class Radicalism," 79–87.

23 There is debate about how radical the CLU was and which groups controlled it.
Robert E. Weir, "A Fragile Alliance: Henry George and the Knights of Labor," in
"Commemorating the 100th Anniversary of the Death of Henry George," special
issue, *American Journal of Economics and Sociology* 56, no. 4 (October 1997):
421–439, calls the Knights of Labor within the CLU both Marxist and Irish. Weir
also notes that the Knights of Labor nationally was apolitical and its Irish
American leader, Terrence Powderly, opposed Knights of Labor lodges participating in electoral politics, but the New York lodge, District Assembly 49, was led by
the Marxist-turned-anarchist Victor Drury. Schneider, *Trade Unions and
Community*, 119–129, argues that the CLU had three factions: Irish Knights,
German socialists, and English-speaking socialists. Stan Nadel, "The German
Immigrant Left in the United States," in *The Immigrant Left in the United States*,
ed. Paul Buhle and Dan Georgakas (New York: SUNY Press, 1996), 59, claims
that German unions dominated the CLU and pushed it toward radicalism.

24 "Die Central Labor Union," *New Yorker Volkszeitung*, September 4, 1882, 1; "Die heutige Arbeiter-Demonstration," *New Yorker Volkszeitung*, September 5, 1882, 1; "Working Men on Parade," *New York Times*, September 6, 1882, 8.

25 Philipp Reick, *"Labor Is Not a Commodity!" The Movement to Shorten the Workday in Late Nineteenth-Century Berlin and New York* (Frankfurt: Campus Verlag, 2016), 74–78.

26 Nadel, "German Immigrant Left," 59.

27 CPI Inflation Calculator, https://www.officialdata.org/.

28 Mark Benbow, "German Immigrants"; Schluter, *Brewing Industry*, 101–105, 114–116; Schneider, *Trade Unions and Community*, 156–158.

29 Schneider, 156–166. Stuart Mack Blumin, *The Emergence of the Middle Class: Social Experience in the American City, 1760–1900* (Cambridge, UK: Cambridge University Press, 1989), 272, says that the average annual earnings of industrial wage earners in 1880 was $345, so $50 was a substantial fee.

30 Schneider, *Trade Unions and Community*, 121–122. "Warnung für Schreiner," *New Yorker Volkszeitung*, July 2, 1882, 3; "An den Pranger!," *New Yorker Volkszeitung*, July 3, 1886, 3.

31 Burrows and Wallace, *Gotham*, 1098–1100.

32 Schneider, *Trade Unions and Community*, 122–123; Keil, "German Working-Class Radicalism," 78–79, notes the *Volkzeitung* and New York German Socialists' concerns about George. "Central Labor Union," *New Yorker Volkszeitung*, November 3, 1886, 1, notes the labor endorsement, but it was not in the large banner headlines that the *Volkszeitung* usually printed for socialist candidates. For example, please see November 1, 1896, 1, with its endorsement of Charles H. Matchett, or November 2, 1897, 1, endorsement for Theodore Cuno.

33 For examples, please see *Report and Proceedings of the Senate Committee Appointed to Investigate the Police Department of the City of New York* (Lexow Committee hearing transcripts), vols. 1–5 (Albany, NY: James B. Lyon, State Printer, 1895); E. Vale Blake, *History of the Tammany Society* (New York: Souvenir, 1901), 122, claims that Germans were "inclined" against Tammany Hall because of its Irish American character, "but Tammany found a way to change all this by a special effort. Seeking out the most intelligent Germans of this district and encouraging their aspirations for political influence, selecting the best of this class for nominations to office, in preference to other races."

34 This was the case in 1871–1872, when Steinway and Ottendorfer organized Germans against the Tammany Hall boss William M. Tweed and again in the 1890s, with the creation of the German American Reform Union. Lapham, "German-Americans," 185–188, 221–250.

35 *New Yorker Volkszeitung* postelection coverage in the 1880s and 1890s regularly noted between 8,000 and 10,000 votes for socialist candidates.

36 Nadel, "Forty-Eighters," 51–66; Lapham, "German-Americans," 240, on Steinway and Schurz's support for Hewitt.

37 "Hewitt Elected Mayor," *New York Times*, November 3, 1886, 1; Lapham, "German-Americans," 241, table 29, "A Comparison of the Mayoralty Vote of 1874 and 1886 in the German Wards." Also "What the Figures Show," *New York Times*, November 4, 1886, 8, includes the following comment by a police official: "In my opinion from 1,200 to 15,000 Republicans cast their votes for George out of principle. This was specially noticed among the districts inhabited by Germans." Please also see Hammack, *Power and Society*, 112–115, 137.

38 Finding lists of members of the New York City Municipal Assembly and the Board of Aldermen is surprisingly difficult; I searched in city directories in the municipal government sections, looking in the City Register section for lists of city officials. A good source of whom German Americans considered important politically at the time can be found in Skal, *History of German Immigration*. Please also see Lapham, "German-Americans," 183–220, 221–250. Please also see Political Graveyard, "New York: State Assembly, 1880s," http://politicalgraveyard .com/geo/NY/ofc/asmbly1880s.html; and Political Graveyard, "New York: State Assembly, 1890s," http://politicalgraveyard.com/geo/NY/ofc/asmbly1890s.html.

39 Jacob Wund was the exception, getting elected in 1891, 1893, and 1895 from the AD 18, *Proceedings of the Board of Aldermen of the City of New York from January 4 to March 29, 1892*, vol. 205 (New York: Martin B. Brown, 1892), 3; *Proceedings of the Board of Aldermen of the City of New York from January 2 to March 28, 1893*, vol. 209 (New York: Martin Brown, 1893), 3–5; *Proceedings of the Board of Aldermen of the City of New York from January 7 to March 26, 1895*, vol. 217 (New York: Martin Brown, 1895), 3–4.

40 This is based on analysis of names as well as written biographies of assembly members. Political Graveyard, "New York: State Assembly, 1880s," http:// politicalgraveyard.com/geo/NY/ofc/asmbly1880s.html; Political Graveyard, "New York: State Assembly, 1890s," http://politicalgraveyard.com/geo/NY/ofc /asmbly1890s.html; Henry Phelps, *New York State Legislative Souvenir for 1893, with Portraits of the Members of Both Houses* (Albany: Phelps and Kellogg, 1893), 47; Henry Phelps, *New York State Legislative Souvenir for 1894, with Portraits of the Members of Both Houses* (Albany: Phelps and Kellogg, 1894), 57–58; *New York Evening Post, Tammany Biographies*, 3rd ed., rev. and enlarged (October 1894), 12.

41 "Four East Side Leaders," *New York Sun*, October 9, 1904, 8.

42 *New York Evening Post, Tammany Biographies*, 13, for quote; Skal, *History of German Immigration*, 147, for William Sohmer; 128–129, for Hugo Sohmer.

43 James J. Connolly, *An Elusive Unity: Urban Democracy and Machine Politics in Industrializing America* (Ithaca, NY: Cornell University Press, 2010), 84–85.

44 Terry Golway, *Machine Made: Tammany Hall and the Creation of Modern American Politics* (New York: W. W. Norton, 2014), 164.

45 "Four East Side Leaders," 8.

46 "Four East Side Leaders," 8.

47 Skal, *History of German Immigration*, 229–230. Skal says that Windolph was the Republican leader of the Eleventh AD for more than ten years, but no record of this could be found.

48 Moses King, *Notable New Yorkers of 1896–1899, a Companion Volume to King's Handbook of New York City* (New York: M. King, 1899).

49 "McFarland and Grosse," *New York Times*, March 10, 1894, 1; Lapham, "German-Americans," 238, 243; "Leonard Giegerich, Jurist, Dies at 72," *New York Times*, December 21, 1927, 25; "Ferdinand Eidman Dead," *New York Times*, May 6, 1910, 9; Charles G. Shanks, *The State Government for 1879* (Albany, NY: Weed, Parsons, 1879), 99–100.

50 "Anthony Eickhoff," *New York Times*, November 7, 1901, 9.

51 Hammack, *Power and Society*, 141.

52 "German-American Reformers," *New York Times*, January 21, 1893, 10; "Will Continue Its Good Work," *New York Times*, November 10, 1893, 5; "For Better City Government," *New York Times*, December 10, 1893, 5; "German-Americans

for Reform," *New York Times*, April 27, 1894, 8; "Straight or Fusion Ticket," *New York Times*, June 5, 1894, 9; "Arrayed against Tammany," *New York Times*, June 27, 1894, 4; "German Reformers Meet," *New York Times*, August 15, 1894, 1; "Not Concerned with Ballot Reform," *New York Times*, August 17, 1894, 5; "See a Charm in Seventy," *New York Times*, September 7, 1894, 1; "Wary of a Republican Trap," *New York Times*, September 7, 1894, 9; "Hewitt and the Foreigners," *New York Times*, September 18, 1894, 8; "German-Americans in Warm Debate," *New York Times*, September 19, 1894, 4; "They Will Pull Together," *New York Times*, September 20, 1894, 9; "Mr. Ottendorfer Resigns," *New York Times*, October 4, 1894, 1; "Republican Reformers," *New York Times*, October 5, 1894, 4; "Couldn't Agree upon Goff," *New York Times*, October 5, 1894, 1; "William L. Strong for Mayor," *New York Times*, October 6, 1894, 1; "Simply Ridiculous: The *Staats-Zeitung*'s View of Col. Strong's Nomination by the Seventy," *New York Times*, October 7, 1894, 4; "Gustav H. Schwab Angry," *New York Times*, October 9, 1894, 1; "Strong Demands Democrats," *New York Times*, October 9, 1894, 3; "Mr. Ottendorfer's Answer," *New York Times*, October 10, 1894, 1; "Accepted by the German Union," *New York Times*, October 12, 1894, 5; "The *Staats-Zeitung* for Strong," *New York Times*, October 12, 1894, 4; "The Seventy's Nominees Accept," *New York Times*, October 13, 1894, 5; "Mr. Strong on the Excise Law," *New York Times*, October 28, 1894, 16; "Strong and Goff Speak," *New York Times*, November 1, 1894, 1.

53 "Mr. Straus Likely to Retire," *New York Times*, October 19, 1894, 1; "Grant in Place of Straus," *New York Times*, October 20, 1894, 1; Hammack, *Power and Society*, 147–151.

54 "Strong!," *New York Times*, November 7, 1894, 1.

55 City Club of New York, *Annual Report of the Secretary, April 3, 1895*; "The People Warn Platt," *New York Times*, February 5, 1895, 1; "Reformers Rally Against Bosses," *New York Herald*, February 5, 1895, 4. By 1913, only two people were listed as being members of the GARU in Otto Spengler's *Das deutsche Element der Stadt New York, biographisches Jahrbuch der Deutsch-Amerikaner New Yorks und Umgebung* (New York: Spengler, 1913): 215 (Herman Ridder), and 221 (Herman Rosenthal). Skal's 1908 book, *History of German Immigration in the United States and Successful German-Americans and Their Descendants*, listed only 1 member, Theodore Sutro (153–154). Puck mocked both the GARU and the German American Citizens' Union in "August Schulze als Stumpredner," *Puck, illustrirtes humoristisches Wochenblatt* 20, no. 1 (September 4, 1895), 148.

56 Phelps, *New York State Legislative Souvenir for 1893*, 42–43; "New-York Citizens' Democracy," *New York Times*, May 25, 1893, 5; "Launching of a New Party," *New York Times*, July 13, 1893, 8.

57 "No Conference with the Mayor," *New York Times*, June 29, 1895, 1; "Vain Plea to the Mayor," *New York Times*, June 30, 1895, 9; "Must Change Excise Law," *New York Times*, July 3, 1895, 1, notes that members of the group included Liederkranz, Arion, Beethoven Männerchor, the Orpheon Society, the GARU, the Central Labor Federation, and the Personal Liberty League; "German-Americans Out," *New York Times*, September 7, 1895, 1; "Seek More Liberal Laws," *New York Times*, November 1, 1895, 1.

58 *New York Evening Post, Tammany Biographies*, 12.

59 *New York Evening Post, Tammany Biographies*, 12.

60 "No Conference with the Mayor," 1.

61 "German-Americans Out," *New York Times*, September 7, 1895, 1.

62 "Vain Plea to the Mayor," *New York Times*, June 30, 1895, 9.

63 "Mr. Strong on the Excise Law," *New York Times*, October 28, 1894, 16, quotes Strong as calling the excise law "antiquated, cumbersome, and impracticable" and says he would support lobbying the legislature to make the law more liberal.

64 "Für personliche Freiheit," *New Yorker Volkszeitung*, September 26, 1895, 3, reports 11,000 participants; "Reviewed by Roosevelt," *New York Times*, September 26, 1895, 9, says 30,000 participated. Gary Gerstle, *American Crucible: Race and Nation in the Twentieth Century* (Princeton, NJ: Princeton University Press, 2001), 49.

65 "Tammany!," *New York Times*, November 6, 1895, 1, which estimates that of 50,000 German voters, four-fifths had voted for Tammany Democrats. "Strong!," 1. "May Work with Tammany," *New York Times*, September 8, 1985, 16, notes how the decision of the GARU to possibly collaborate with Tammany Hall caused several prominent German Americans to quit the reform group.

66 Hammack, *Power and Society*, 151–157.

67 "Villagers Will Rule," *New York Times*, January 30, 1896, 1; "German-Americans Very Angry," *New York Times*, March 14, 1896, 5. Even Tammany Hall opposed the Republican-sponsored Raines Law, claiming that "it permits the opening of dives of all kinds, while closing the decent, quiet German beer saloons, and prohibiting restaurants from furnishing wine or beer with meals on Sunday." Blake, *History*, 170.

68 "Opposed to Seth Low," *New York Times*, August 23, 1897, 1.

69 Hammack, *Power and Society*, 153.

70 "Opposed to Seth Low," 1; "Germans Out for Mr. Low," *New York Times*, October 1, 1897, 1; "Germans Endorse Mr. Low," *New York Times*, October 16, 1897, 3; "Germans Cheer Seth Low," *New York Times*, October 26, 1897, 2; "G.A.R.U. Demonstration," *New York Times*, October 30, 1897, 11; Hammack, *Power and Society*, 115–117, 156, argues that the GARU initially endorsed Republican Charles A. Schieren, a former Brooklyn mayor, in 1894–1895, before supporting Low in 1901.

71 "Germans Endorse Mr. Low," 3, notes the platform plank demanding support of German in the schools. Hammack, *Power and Society*, 120–128, analyzes the various reform movements and political factions in city politics but largely ignores ethnicity as a factor.

72 At a meeting to decide whether to endorse Seth Low in 1897, one of the delegates, Leon Levi, attempted to speak in English and was attacked with demands that speeches be made in German, according to the constitution of the organization. After an intervention by Sheriff Tamsen, Levi was eventually allowed to speak in English. "Germans Endorse Mr. Low," 3.

73 Bungert, *Festkultur und Gedächtnis*, 544–564.

74 "German Day Celebrated," *New York Times*, October 5, 1891, 2; Bungert, *Festkultur und Gedächtnis*, also lists a 1902 Deutscher Tag as the first in her list of festivals.

75 "Vereine und Gesellschaften, Deutscher Tag," *New Yorker Volkszeitung*, November 2, 1902, 16; "First Celebration of German Day," *New York Times*, November 10, 1902, 2; "No German Day This Year," *New York Times*, May 27, 1917, 4; *Official Program of the Convention of the German American State Alliance of New York, and the Celebration of German Day, June 22, 23, and 24, 1907* (New-York Historical Society); Bungert, *Festkultur und Gedächtnis*.

76 Johnson, *Culture at Twilight*, 23.

77 Johnson, 11 (quote), 23 (on number of New York members).

78 Editions of *German American Annals*, also called *Americana Germanica*, can be found at HathiTrust Digital Library, https://catalog.hathitrust.org/Record /008572995?type%5B%5D=publisher&lookfor%5B%5D=German%20Historical %20Society&ft=.

79 Conzen, "German-Americans"; Johnson, *Culture at Twilight*.

80 Johnson.

81 Schlegel, *Schlegel's German-American Families*, 1.

82 Charles J. Hexamer, "Monument at Germantown," hearing before the Committee on the Library of the House of Representatives (Washington, DC: Government Printing Office, 1910), 5.

83 Hexamer, "Monument at Germantown," 8.

84 Johann Rittig, *Federzeichnungen aus dem Amerikanischen Stadtleben* (New York: Ernst Steiger, 1884); Casper Stürenburg, *Klein-Deutschland: Bilder aus dem New Yorker Alltagsleben* (New York: Ernst Steiger, 1885), also known as *Bilder aus dem Amerikanischen Leben von Deutschen in Amerika*. Please also see C. A. Honthumb, *Amerikanische Humoresken* (New York: E. Steiger, 1886); Reinhold Solger, *Anton in Amerika. Novelle aus dem deutsch-amerikanischen Leben* (New York: E. Steiger, 1872); Friedrich Kapp, *Geschichte der Deutschen im staate New York bis zum anfange des neunzehnten jahrhunderts* (New York: E. Steiger, 1884, originally published 1867), Gustav Philipp Körner, *Das deutsche Element in den Vereinigten Staaten von Nordamerika, 1818–1848* (New York: E. Steiger, 1884); Louis Viereck, *Leitfaden für deutsche Einwanderer nach den Vereinigten Staaten von Amerika* (New York: Deutsche Gesellschaft, 1903); Casper Stürenburg and Ernst Steiger, *Auskunft und Rath für Deutsch-Amerikaner in den wichtigsten Fragen des öffentlichen, Rechts-, Geschäfts- und Privat-Lebens / zusammengestellt und herausgegeben von C. Stürenburg und E. Steiger* (New York: E. Steiger, 1888).

85 Conolly-Smith, *Translating America*, 45.

86 "Die deutschen Einwanderer bringen weit mehr, als die irgend eines andern Volkes, vortreffliche Eigenschaften in unser Land mit sich: Gesundheit, gute Sitten, gesunden Menschenverstand und außer dem viele Habe." *New York Herald*, quoted in Joseph Pachmayr, *Leben und Treiben der Stadt New-York: mit Hinweis auf die Einwanderung und das deutsche Element: kulturhistorische Bilder* (Hamburg, Germany: H. Grüning, 1874), 123.

87 Hammack, *Power and Society*, 80–86, 84 (quote).

88 Hammack, *Power and Society*, 99, table 3-10, "Wage Earners' Support for Labor Unions, Lodges, and Religious Organizations, New York City, 1907," citing Robert Coit Chapin, *The Standard of Living among Workingmen's Families in New York City* (New York: Russell Sage Foundation, 1909), 45, 208. Interestingly, this study found low-medium financial support of Germans for labor unions, lodges, and churches or synagogues.

89 The ubiquitous honey-roasted nuts found on every other street corner in New York City are a standard festival food in Germany today. There are two competing claims for the inventor of Cracker Jack: Charles Frederick Gunther and Frederick William Rueckheim, both Chicago popcorn sellers in the 1870s. But recipes and advertisements for sugar-coated popcorn have been documented in the 1850s. Samantha Chmelik, "Frederick Rueckheim," in *Immigrant Entrepreneurship, German-American Business Biographies, 1720 to the Present*, ed. Jeffrey Fear

(Washington, DC: German Historical Institute, 2013), https://www
.immigrantentrepreneurshiorg/entry.php?rec=158; Neil Gale, "The History of
Charles 'Carl' Frederick Günther, known as 'The Candy Man' and 'The P. T.
Barnum of Chicago,'" *Digital Research Library of Illinois History Journal* (blog),
October 20, 2017, https://drloihjournal.blogspot.com/2017/10/the-history-of
-charles-carl-frederick.html; "Charles Feltman," Coney Island History Project,
http://www.coneyislandhistory.org/hall-of-fame/charles-feltman.

90 Joseph F. Kelly, *The Feast of Christmas* (Collegeville, MN: Liturgical, 2010) 94;
Johannes Marbach, *Die heilige Weihnachtszeit nach Bedeutung, Geschichte, Sitten
und Symbolen* (Frankfurt/Main, Germany: J. D. Saulerländer, 1859), 416. Initially,
the Christmas tree was a Protestant tradition, and the Vatican did not adopt the
custom until 1982.

91 Hermann Bokum, *The Stranger's Gift: A Christmas and New Year's Present*
(Boston: Light and Horton, 1836).

92 Morton Keller, "The World of Thomas Nast," https://cartoons.osu.edu/digital
_albums/thomasnast/keller.pdf.

93 Don Heinrich Tolzmann, *The German-American Experience* (Boston: Humani-
ties Press, 2000), 381–384. The *New York Daily Tribune* observed in 1868: "The
Easter Festival, once allowed to pass almost unnoticed by our Knickerbocker and
Puritan ancestors, is yearly more and more observed and was celebrated with
greater interest than has hitherto been manifested," according to Cindy Dell
Clark, *Flights of Fancy, Leaps of Faith: Children's Myths in Contemporary America*
(Chicago: University of Chicago Press, 1998), 33.

94 Alexis McCrossen, *Holy Day, Holiday: The American Sunday* (Ithaca, NY:
Cornell University Press, 2001), 42–43; Thomas Sowell, *Migrations and Cultures:
A World View* (New York: Basic Books, 1996); Koegel and Westover, "Beethoven
and Beer," 139–142.

95 "Sunday Baseball and Other Sins: America's Pastime and the Decline of Blue
Laws," PoliticalTheology.com, https://politicaltheology.com/sunday-baseball-and
-other-sins-americas-pastime-and-the-decline-of-blue-laws/. Please also see
"Baseball Men Exonerated," *New York Times*, August 22, 1917, S13.

96 Conolly-Smith, *Translating America*, 13, 81–82; Herold I. Casway, *The Culture and
Ethnicity of Nineteenth Century Baseball* (Jefferson, NC: McFarland, 2017), 10;
Larry R. Gerlach, "German Americans in Major League Baseball: Sport and
Acculturation," in *The American Game: Baseball and Ethnicity*, ed. Lawrence
Baldassaro and Richard A. Johnson (Carbondale: Southern Illinois University
Press, 2002), 28, notes that three of the members of the New York Knickerbocker
team that is considered to have played the first organized baseball game in 1845
were German and that the city also had two other German baseball teams in that
period.

97 Goldberg, "Forty-Eighters," 208; Tatlock and Erlin, *German Culture*; Geitz,
Heideking, and Herbst, *German Influence on Education*; Jurgen Herbst, *The
German Historical School in American Scholarship: A Study in the Transfer of
Culture* (Ithaca, NY: Cornell University Press, 1965); Thomas N. Bonner,
*American Doctors and German Universities: A Chapter in International Intellec-
tual Relations, 1870–1914* (Lincoln: University of Nebraska Press, 1963).

98 "Plans for Reception of Prince Henry," *New York Times*, February 5, 1902, 9; "The
Prince's Programme," *New York Times*, February 25, 2012, 2; "Prince Guest of
Honor," *New York Times*, February 26, 1902, 2. Business manager Herman Ridder

assumed the role of publisher of the *New Yorker Staats-Zeitung* in 1900, after Oswald Ottendorfer died.

99 "Prince Henry to the German Society," *New York Times*, March 9, 1902, 1.

100 "Gala Night at the Opera," *New York Times*, February 26, 1902, 2.

101 "Prince Henry's Welcome," *New York Times*, February 8, 1902, 8; "Prince Henry's Reception," *New York Times*, February 12, 1902, 9; "Prince Henry's Itinerary" and "Parade of the Germans," *New York Times*, February 15, 1902, 8; Bungert, *Festkultur und Gedächtnis*, 436–449.

102 "The Prince's Programme," 2; "City's Freedom Conferred," *New York Times*, February 26, 1902, 1.

103 "Parade of the Germans," *New York Times*, February 15, 1902, 8.

104 "Prince Welcomed by Chiefs of Industry," *New York Times*, February 27, 1902, 1.

105 "Mrs. C. Vanderbilt, Jr., the Prince's Hostess," *New York Times*, March 10, 1902, 1.

106 M. D. Learned, "German Day in New York," *German American Annals* 5 (1903): 32–38; the fact that the speech was specifically given in English is noted on 38; "Professor Learned Rede, Der Deutsche Verein als Pflegestette der Deutschen Kultur in Amerika," *German American Annals* 14 (1912): 249–255, focuses on observations in Brooklyn in 1912.

Chapter 4   Disappearing and Remembering

1 In the film, Gable's and Powell's characters have Irish and Anglo American names; they are rescued by an Irish Catholic priest and are ultimately taken in by a Russian Jew.

2 *Journal for the Seventeenth Annual Excursion, St. Mark's Evangelical Lutheran Church*, 323–327 Sixth Street, New York, Wednesday, June 15, 1904 (NYPL).

3 *Journal for the Seventeenth Annual Excursion*, 17, lists an advertisement for "E. Adickes, Fine Confectionery and Ice Cream Saloon, 49 Avenue A Between 3rd and 4th Streets." The Adickes family lived above the store according to the U.S. Bureau of the Census, 1900, ED 238 Borough of Manhattan, Election District 16 New York City Ward 10, New York County, New York. Note: the family's name was spelled "Adierkis." In his affidavit, Adickes corrects the spelling of family names ("Ernst" instead of "Ernest," adds umlaut for his mother-in-law, Margaret Stüve), "General Slocum Disaster, Evidence before the Committee on Claims of the House of Representatives on H.R. 4154, for the Relief of the Victims of the General Slocum Disaster," April 20, 1910, Committee on Claims, House of Representatives, 61st Congress, 2nd Session (Washington: Government Printing Office, 1910), 89 (statement of Ernst Adickes).

4 O'Donnell, *Ship Ablaze*, 75–76.

5 O'Donnell, 75–76. Vollmer's name is alternately spelled Ballmer and Bollmer in various sources but this is the spelling that appeared in city death records and on the family headstone in All Faiths Cemetery, Queens.

6 O'Donnell, *Ship Ablaze*, 75–76.

7 Edward T. O'Donnell and Elke Schönfeld, *Der Ausflug, das Ende von Little Germany, New York* (Hamburg, Germany: Marebuchverlag 2006), 132–133.

8 O'Donnell and Schönfeld, *Der Ausflug*, 142–145; J. S. Ogilvie, *History of the General Slocum disaster by which nearly 1200 lives were lost by the burning of the steamer General Slocum in Hell gate, New York harbor, June 15, 1904* (New York: J. S. Ogilvie, 1904).

9 "Slocum Disaster Brings Criminal Prosecution," *New York Times*, June 25, 1904, 3. Testimony of Max Schmittberger, "Report and proceedings of the Senate committee appointed to investigate the police department of the city of New York," vol. 5 (Albany, NY: James B. Lyon, State Printer, 1895), 4965–4966, 5311–5386.

10 "House to House Search for Missing," *New York Times*, June 19, 1904, 2.

11 O'Donnell and Schönfeld, *Der Ausflug*, 154–155; "The Slocum Dead Found by the Score," *New York Times*, June 21, 1904, 3.

12 "Vanguard of Dead Starts to the Tomb," *New York Times*, June 18, 1904, 2; "Death's Hand Heavy on Stricken Parish," *New York Times*, June 17, 1904, 2, notes that New York City had 169 Lutheran ministers, while Hudson County, New Jersey, had 25 Lutheran ministers.

13 O'Donnell and Schönfeld, *Der Ausflug*, 306–307.

14 "Directors Guilty, Says Slocum Jury," *New York Times*, June 29, 1904, 1; "Dr. Moldehnke's Funeral," *New York Times*, June 29, 1904, 2. The date of death could not be determined.

15 "Mournful Pomp of Death on East Side," *New York Times*, June 19, 1904, 3; "A Day of Funerals of the Slocum Dead," *New York Times*, June 19, 1904, 3; "Heaps of Flowers on Nameless Graves," *New York Times*, June 20, 1904, 5; "Many More Buried," *New York Times*, June 21, 1904, 3; "To Bury 52 Nameless Slocum Dead To-Day," *New York Times*, June 23, 1904, 5.

16 "Slocum Disaster Brings Criminal Prosecution," *New York Times*, June 25, 1904, 3.

17 Ogilvie, "History," 183, 189.

18 "Vanguard of Dead Starts to the Tomb," 2.

19 "City Will Raise Wreck of Slocum," *New York Times*, June 19, 1904, 2; "Slocum Commission Reports," *New York Times*, July 17, 1904, 7; "Slocum Fund Wound Up," *New York Times*, October 17, 1905, 5.

20 "Tammany Club Raises $600," *New York Times*, June 18, 1904, 3.

21 Sulzer introduced H.R. 2799 on December 4, 1905, and H.R. 3112 on December 5, 1905. 40 Cong. Rec. 7667–7670 (Washington, DC: Government Printing Office, 1906), 7667–7670. Sulzer also introduced H.R. 4154 on March 23, 1909, for the same purpose. "General Slocum Disaster."

22 Albin Boenhardt, Plaintiff, v. Jacob W. Loch, Louis W. Kaufmann, Hugo W. Hoffman, Emil C.J. Kraeling, John C. Haas and William S. Hackson, as Attorney-General of the State of New York, Defendants, Supreme Court, New York Special Term Nov. 1, 1907, 56 Misc. 406 N.Y. Misc. 1907.

23 William Peirce Randel. "The Flames of Hell Gate," *American Heritage Magazine* 30, no. 6 (October/November 1979): 62–75.

24 "Kick against Committee," *New York Times*, August 4, 1904, 12.

25 O'Donnell and Schönfeld, *Der Ausflug*, 375–377.

26 "Slocum Disaster Brings Criminal Prosecution," *New York Times*, June 25, 1904, 3; "No Step to Reinspect Harbor Steamboats," *New York Times*, July 2, 1904, 14; no headline, dateline Washington, July 15, *New York Times*, July 19, 1904, 14; "Gen. Slocum Indictments," *New York Times*, July 29, 1904, 1; "Jury Indicts Seven for Slocum Disaster," July 30, 1904, 12; "Punish the Guilty, Slocum Survivors Say" *New York Times*, September 29, 1904, 6; "Skippers Back Van Schaick," *New York Times*, January 20, 1906, 6. Pease was the captain of the Knickerbocker steamboat, the Grand Republic, and commodore of the company's fleet.

27 "Gen. Slocum Indictments," *New York Times*, July 29, 1904, 1; "Skippers Back Van Schaick," *New York Times*, January 20, 1906, 6; "Capt. Van Schaick's Own Story

of Slocum Fire," *New York Times*, January 26, 1906, 6; "Slocum Trial Near an End," *New York Times*, January 27, 1906, 2; "Slocum Sentence Affirmed," *New York Times*, February 13, 1908, 6; "Van Schaick Pardoned," *New York Times*, December 20, 1912, 24. Please also see "Punishment Demanded at the Slocum Graves," *New York Times*, June 16, 1906, 9.

28 "Steamboat Inspection May Begin This Week," *New York Times*, July 3, 1904, 8; "Slocum Suits for $800,000," *New York Times*, July 4, 1904, 5.

29 "Two Triple Funeral Services Held in Manhattan To-day," *Brooklyn Daily Eagle*, June 23, 1904.

30 This was due to a combination of blaming victims for supposedly damaging life preservers, falsifying company records stating when life jackets had been bought, and blaming the federal U.S. Steamboat Inspection Service, whose inspectors had certified the *General Slocum* as safe on May 5, 1904.

31 *Weekly Underwriter* 71 (July–December 1904): 448.

32 "Punish the Guilty, Slocum Survivors Say," *New York Times*, September 29, 1904, 6.

33 Among the more fanciful claims about the General Slocum accident is that survivors moved out of the Lower East Side to the Bronx to be closer to the spot where the boat sank. For instance, please see Ted Houghtaling, "Witness to Tragedy: The Sinking of the General Slocum," New-York Historical Society, *From the Stacks* (blog), http://blog.nyhistory.org/witness-to-tragedy-the-sinking-of-the -general-slocum/; Gilbert King, "A Spectacle of Horror—the Burning of the General Slocum," *Smithsonian Magazine*, https://www.smithsonianmag.com /history/a-spectacle-of-horror-the-burning-of-the-general-slocum-104712974/. Please see also the German Genealogy Group, "The Slocum, June 15, 1904: A Tragedy," http://www.germangenealogygroup.com/PDF/Slocum_Newsletter _Articles.pdf.

34 "How the Slocum Disaster Wiped Out a Population," *New York Times*, June 26, 1904, 28.

35 "How the Slocum Disaster Wiped Out a Population," 28.

36 *Annual Report of the Department of Public Charities of the City of New York for 1904* (New York: Martin B. Brown, 1905), 36; O'Donnell, *Ship Ablaze*, 298.

37 "William Hotz," U.S. Census, 1910, *FamilySearch* (https://familysearch.org/ark: /61903/1:1:M57H-J63 : accessed July 17, 2021), William J. Hotz in household of Sophie Frank, Manhattan Ward 19, New York, New York, United States; citing enumeration district ED 1005, sheet 1B, family 13, NARA microfilm publication T624 (Washington D.C.: National Archives and Records Administration, 1982), roll 1038; FHL microfilm 1,375,051.

38 "Real Estate Transfers," *New York Times*, May 24, 1904, 15, and "Real Estate Transfers," March 3, 1905, 14, list Schoett's purchase of real estate on 159th Street. Schoett identified himself as a "landlord" in the "United States Census, 1910," *FamilySearch* (https://familysearch.org/ark:/61903/1:1:M5WN-GQW : accessed July 17, 2021), Christian Schoett, Bronx Assembly District 33, New York, New York, United States; citing enumeration district (ED) ED 1518, sheet 1B, family 24, NARA microfilm publication T624 (Washington D.C.: National Archives and Records Administration, 1982), roll 1000; FHL microfilm 1,375,013.

39 For example, the husband of Amelia Abesser, Henry Abesser, remarried in 1905 and stayed in the family home at 128 East 4th Street at least until 1925. *New York City Directory, 1959*, 221, "H. Abesser, electrician, 128 E. 4th Street." Saloonkeeper George Feldhusen remarried after his wife Margaret died and stayed in the family

home on 50 West 8th Street through his second and third marriages until his death in 1915. "Mourns 11 Years; Kills Self," *Washington Post*, June 20, 1915, 20. The cigar manufacturer Ludwig Folke, who survived the accident but lost his wife, Annie, and mother, Dora, remarried in 1905 and stayed in the family home at 257 Avenue B at least until 1916 and possibly until his death in 1919. *New York City Directory, 1916*, "Folke, Ludwig A., 257 Av B, Cigars." "New York City Municipal Deaths, 1795–1949," database, *FamilySearch* (https://www.familysearch.org/ark: /61903/1:1:2WZ4-829 : accessed June 3, 2020), Ludwig A. Folke, 1919.

40 *Trow's New York City, Manhattan and Bronx City Directory, 1912, Vol. 125* (New York: Trow City Directory, 1912), 38–39.

41 The Stockermann family (Stöckermann) are listed as passengers on the HAPAG ship, SS *Graf Waldersee*, leaving Cuxhaven on January 31, 1903, and arriving in New York on February 16, 1903. "Hamburg Passenger Lists, 1850–1934," Ancestry.com, https://www.ancestry.com/search/collections/1068/?name= _Stockermann&arrival=_new+york+city&departure=1903-1-31_cuxhaven -lower+saxony-germany_31731&f-Self-Departure-Ship=Graf+Waldersee&name _x=_psx.

42 "Bertha Janck," New York Passenger Arrival Lists, 1892–1924, shows Jonck arriving in New York on the HAPAG ship, SS *Graf Waldersee* on April 23, 1904, from Cuxhaven, *FamilySearch* (https://www.familysearch.org/ark:/61903 /1:1:JF1Z-66Y : accessed March 2, 2021).

43 Jason Barr and Teddy Ort, "Population Density across the City: The Case of 1900 Manhattan," (August Rutgers University, 2013), Figure 2, "The distribution of heads of households based on birth country of parents in New York," located at http://andromeda.rutgers.edu/~jmbarr/skyscrapers/tenementsdraftv1_18aug2013 .pdf.

44 "A Blighted Oasis," *New York Times*, June 21, 1904, 6 (editorial).

45 Ogilvie, "History," 146.

46 "The East River Tragedy," *Evening Mail* editorial, in Ogilvie, "History," 245.

47 *Annual Report of the Department of Public Charities of the City of New York, 1904*, 43–105.

48 "Ernest and Anna Rueffer," U.S. Census, 1920, New York, Manhattan Assembly District 8, ED 639, New York, New York. *FamilySearch* (https://www .familysearch.org/ark:/61903/1:1:MJYY-C5K : accessed February 2, 2021).

49 "Joseph and Augusta Schaefer," U.S. Census, 1930, New York, Manhattan (Districts 0501–0750), New York, New York. *FamilySearch* (https://www .familysearch.org/ark:/61903/1:1:/x42G-2F3 : accessed July 17, 2021); Joseph Schaefer, Manhattan (Districts 0501-0750), New York, New York, United States; citing enumeration district (ED) ED 580, sheet 36A, line 13, family 732, NARA microfilm publication T626 (Washington D.C.: National Archives and Records Administration, 2002), roll 1561; FHL microfilm 2,341,296.

50 "Mary Illig," U.S. Census, 1930, New York, Manhattan (Districts 0001–0250), ED 214, *FamilySearch* (https://www.familysearch.org/ark:/ 61903/1:1:X4KT- LGT : accessed July 17, 2021), Mary Illig in household of Conrad Illig, Manhattan (Districts 0001-0250), New York, New York, United States; citing enumeration district (ED) ED 214, sheet 2A, line 10, family 33, NARA microfilm publication T626 (Washington D.C.: National Archives and Records Administration, 2002), roll 1555; FHL microfilm 2,341,290. Conrad Illig's death certificate in "New York City Municipal Deaths, 1795–1949," *FamilySearch* (https://www.familysearch.org

/ark:/ 61903/1:1:271H-MWQ : accessed June 3, 2020), Conrad Illig, 10 Jan 1907; citing Death, Manhattan, New York City, New York, United States, New York Municipal Archives, New York; FHL microfilm 1,323,140; Mary Illig's death certificate in "New York City Municipal Deaths, 1795–1949," *FamilySearch* (https://www.familysearch.org/ark:/61903/1:1:271H-MWQ : accessed June 3, 2020), Conrad Illig, 10 Jan 1907; citing Death, Manhattan, New York City, New York, United States, New York Municipal Archives, New York; FHL microfilm 1,323,140.

51 "Charles Schumacher," U.S. Census, 1930, New York, *FamilySearch* (https://familysearch.org/ark:/61903/1:1:X4KT-8MN : accessed July 17, 2021), Charles Schumacher, Manhattan (Districts 0001-0250), New York, New York, United States; citing enumeration district (ED) ED 214, sheet 13B, line 62, family 429, NARA microfilm publication T626 (Washington D.C.: National Archives and Records Administration, 2002), roll 1555; FHL microfilm 2,341,290.

52 Haberstroh, *German Churches*.

53 Haberstroh.

54 Harold Schiffman, "Language Loyalty in the German-American Church: The Case of an Over-Confident Minority," handout for LING 540, Language Policy, https://www.sas.upenn.edu/~haroldfs/540/handouts/gachurch/index.html.

55 *Report of the United States Commission of Investigation upon the Disaster to the Steamer "General Slocum"* (Washington, DC: U.S. Government Printing Office, 1904), 12; *Annual Report of the Department of Public Charities of the City of New York for 1904*, 130, "Percentage Table 'A', 863 Identified Dead, Lost on the 'General Slocum,' as to Age," and 132, "Percentage Table 'B', 924 Lives Lost on the 'General Slocum,' as to Sex." "1,000 Lives May Be Lost in Burning of the Excursion Boat Gen. Slocum," *New York Times*, June 16, 1904, 1; "Wreck Said to be Cleared of Bodies," *New York Times*, June 17, 1904, 1.

56 Three of the four Muller children—eleven-year-old Louis, nine-year-old Herman, and seven-year old Minnie—of 100 St. Mark's Place were also on the *General Slocum* and survived, all with injuries.

57 "A Labor Union Funeral," *New York Times*, June 25, 1904, 3.

58 O'Donnell, *Ship Ablaze*, 99.

59 Edward T. Devine, *The Principles of Relief* (New York: Macmillan, 1904), 452.

60 "Peter Kiesel," U.S. Census 1940, *FamilySearch* (https://familysearch.org/ark:/61903/1:1:KQPC-1WF : accessed January 20, 2020), Peter E Kiesel, Assembly District 6, Queens, New York City, Queens, New York, United States; citing enumeration district (ED) 41-1812, sheet 6B, line 64, family 172, Sixteenth Census of the United States, 1940, NARA digital publication T627. Records of the Bureau of the Census, 1790–2007, RG 29. Washington, D.C.: National Archives and Records Administration, 2012, roll 2754.

61 "Arthur Schumann," U.S. Census 1910, *FamilySearch* (https://familysearch.org/ark:/61903/1:1:M577-NZK : accessed 17 July 2021), Arthur R Schuman, Manhattan Ward 17, New York, New York, United States; citing enumeration district (ED) ED 1060, sheet 11A, family 222, NARA microfilm publication T624 (Washington D.C.: National Archives and Records Administration, 1982), roll 1033; FHL microfilm 1,375,046.

62 "Charles Bock" (spelled "Boch"), U.S. Census 1910, *FamilySearch* (https://familysearch.org/ark:/61903/1:1:M5HG-TPD : accessed July 17, 2021), Charles Boch, Queens Ward 2, Queens, New York, United States; citing enumeration

district (ED) ED 1191, sheet 15A, family 321, NARA microfilm publication T624 (Washington D.C.: National Archives and Records Administration, 1982), roll 1066; FHL microfilm 1,375,079.

63 "Robert Mettler," U.S. Census, 1910, *FamilySearch* (https://familysearch.org/ark: /61903/1:1:M59M-4J1 : accessed July 17, 2021), Robert Mettler, Manhattan Ward 19, New York, New York, United States; citing enumeration district (ED) ED 1098, sheet 8B, family 209, NARA microfilm publication T624 (Washington D.C.: National Archives and Records Administration, 1982), roll 1041; FHL microfilm 1,375,054.

64 "Slocum Survivor, Rev. Dr. Haas Dies," *New York Times*, October 1, 1927, 19.

65 "Gustav Doering," U.S. Census, 1910, *FamilySearch* (https://familysearch.org/ark: /61903/1:1:M5Q5-S2B : accessed July 17, 2021), Gustave Doering, Manhattan Ward 1, New York, New York, United States; citing enumeration district (ED) ED 1, sheet 8B, family 113, NARA microfilm publication T624 (Washington D.C.: National Archives and Records Administration, 1982), roll 1004; FHL microfilm 1,375,017.

66 "Mathias Bretz," U.S. Census 1910, *FamilySearch* (https://familysearch.org/ark: /61903/1:1:MRQQ-512 : accessed July 17, 2021), Mathias Bretz, Manhattan Ward 19, New York, New York, United States; citing enumeration district (ED) ED 1020, sheet 7B, family 164, NARA microfilm publication T624 (Washington D.C.: National Archives and Records Administration, 1982), roll 1039; FHL microfilm 1,375,052.

67 "William Oellrich," U.S. Census 1930, *FamilySearch* (https://familysearch.org /ark:/61903/1:1:X4LL-WDJ : accessed July 17, 2021), William Oellrich, Tusten, Sullivan, New York, United States; citing enumeration district (ED) ED 39, sheet 3B, line 58, family 79, NARA microfilm publication T626 (Washington D.C.: National Archives and Records Administration, 2002), roll 1653; FHL microfilm 2,341,387.

68 "Adolph Mollitor," New York City Marriage Records, 1829–1940, *FamilySearch* (https://familysearch.org/ark:/61903/1:1:24HR-J4G : accessed February 10, 2018), Adolph Molitor and Margaretha Hagenbucher, 27 Aug 1892; citing Marriage, Manhattan, New York, New York, United States, New York City Municipal Archives, New York; FHL microfilm 1,452,330.

69 "Henry Fischer," U.S. Census, 1930, *FamilySearch* (https://familysearch.org/ark: /61903/1:1:X7DH-3QV : accessed July 17, 2021), Henry Fischer, Bronx (Districts 1–250), Bronx, New York, United States; citing enumeration district (ED) ED 108, sheet 25A, line 22, family 678, NARA microfilm publication T626 (Washington D.C.: National Archives and Records Administration, 2002), roll 1466; FHL microfilm 2,341,201.

70 "Edward Schnitzler," New York City Marriage Records, 1829–1940, *FamilySearch* (https://familysearch.org/ark:/61903/1:1:244W-M9F : accessed February 10, 2018), Edward Schnitzler and Marie Appel, 20 Feb 1908; citing Marriage, Bronx, New York, New York, United States, New York City Municipal Archives, New York; FHL microfilm 1,940,311.

71 "Edward Muller," U.S. Census, 1920, New York, Queens, Queens Assembly District 1, ED 49, *FamilySearch* (https://www.familysearch.org/ark: /61903/1:1:MJ1B-79H : accessed February 2, 2021), Edward Muller, 1920. In his affidavit, Müller spells his name with the umlaut, "General Slocum Disaster," 40 (statement, Edward Müller).

72 "Frederick and Catherine Baumler," New York, New York City Municipal Deaths, 1795–1949, *FamilySearch* (https://www.familysearch.org/ark: /61903/1:1:2W25-MXM : 3 June 2020), Frederick Baumler in entry for Katherine Baumler, 1926. Although the Annual Report of the Department of Public Charities and other documents from the time identified the first Mrs. Baumler as "Margarite," her headstone at All Faiths Cemetery lists her name as: "Margaretha Fleischmann Baumler," so I have used that.

73 "Philip Borger," U.S. Census, 1910, *FamilySearch* (https://familysearch.org/ark: /61903/1:1:MP1M-V6J : accessed July 17, 2021), Philip Borger, Brooklyn Ward 26, Kings, New York, United States; citing enumeration district (ED) ED 970, sheet 7A, family 154, NARA microfilm publication T624 (Washington D.C.: National Archives and Records Administration, 1982), roll 979; FHL microfilm 1,374,992..

74 "Henry Siegwart" finds records of Henry marrying Louise Miller in 1905 and living in the Bronx between 1905 and 1940 with members of his wife's family. *FamilySearch* (https://www.familysearch.org/ark:/61903/1:1:MJGR-FK4 : accessed February 2, 2021), Henry Siegwart, 1920.

75 "Louis Geissler," U.S. Census 1910, *FamilySearch* (https://familysearch.org/ark: /61903/1:1:MP18-KX4 : accessed July 17, 2021), Louis Geisler, Manhattan Ward 12, New York, New York, United States; citing enumeration district (ED) ED 281, sheet 3A, family 48, NARA microfilm publication T624 (Washington D.C.: National Archives and Records Administration, 1982), roll 1013; FHL microfilm 1,375,026.

76 "Charles Timm," U.S. Census 1910, *FamilySearch* (https://familysearch.org/ark: /61903/1:1:MP17-4J9 : accessed July 17, 2021), Charles A Timm, Brooklyn Ward 28, Kings, New York, United States; citing enumeration district (ED) ED 873, sheet 15B, family 386, NARA microfilm publication T624 (Washington D.C.: National Archives and Records Administration, 1982), roll 981; FHL microfilm 1,374,994.

77 "Christian Schoett," U.S. Census 1910, *FamilySearch* (https://familysearch.org /ark:/61903/1:1:M5WN-GQW : accessed July 17, 2021), Christian Schoett, Bronx Assembly District 33, New York, New York, United States; citing enumeration district (ED) ED 1518, sheet 1B, family 24, NARA microfilm publication T624 (Washington D.C.: National Archives and Records Administration, 1982), roll 1000; FHL microfilm 1,375,013.

78 "General Slocum Disaster," 56 (statement of William Ehrlich), 7 (statement of Frank Weber).

79 "The General Slocum an Unlucky Craft," *New York Times*, June 16, 1904, 6; "Grief-Crazed Crowds View Lines of Dead," *New York Times*, June 16, 1904, 1; "Wreck Said to Be Cleared of Bodies," June 17, 1904, 1, 2, note the collective emotional upheaval.

80 "Death's Hand Heavy on Stricken Parish," *New York Times*, June 17, 1904, 2; "Boy Stricken Dumb," *Deaf Mutes Journal*, June 23, 1904.

81 "Brooklyn Arion in Berlin, Arion Singer in a Hospital," *New York Times*, July 10, 1908, 7.

82 "Raves of Slocum Disaster," *The Sun*, January 29, 1912; "Called for Lost Family," *New York Times*, January 29, 1912, 4.

83 "Death of Henry Heinz," *Brooklyn Daily Eagle*, November 17, 1916. Johanna Heinz of 97 Avenue A and her two daughters, Louise and Dina, died, but two boys, twelve-year old Henry (the one stricken mute) and seventeen-year-old George Heinz,

also of 97 Avenue A, survived. The boys, however, are not identified in Henry Heinz's affidavit, "General Slocum Disaster," 46–47 (Statement of Henry Heinz).

84 "Mr. Paul Liebenow, Slocum Survivor, Dies," *New York Herald*, February 1, 1910; please also see O'Donnell, *Ship Ablaze*, 76, 101–102; and O'Donnell and Schönfeld, *Der Ausflug*.

85 "East Side's Heart Torn by the Horror," *New York Times*, June 16, 1904, 3; "Grief-Crazed Crowds View Lines of Dead," 1.

86 O'Donnell, *Ship Ablaze*, 299.

87 "Grief Drove to Suicide," *New York Times*, June 18, 1905, 2.

88 "A Suicide in His Saloon," *New York Times*, August 28, 1906, 14.

89 "Mourns 11 Years; Kills Self," 20.

90 "McAdoo Orders Inquiry, Empty Benches in Schools," *New York Times*, June 17, 1904, 2; "To Bury 52 Nameless Slocum Dead Today, Mourn Their School Mates," *New York Times*, June 23, 1904, 5; "Graduates of School No. 24 Nearly All Killed in Slocum Disaster," *Brooklyn Daily Eagle*, June 23, 1904. The headline is inaccurate. "Punishment Demanded at the Slocum Graves," June 16, 1906, 9, notes that eighty students at PS 25 and PS 63 were either survivors or siblings of victims.

91 "Vanguard of Dead Starts to the Tomb," 2.

92 O'Donnell and Schönfeld, *Der Ausflug*, 276–277.

93 "McAdoo Orders Inquiry, Empty Benches in Schools," 2.

94 Nancy Foner, ed., *Wounded City: The Social Impact of 9/11 on New York City* (New York: Russell Sage Foundation, 2005); Ulrik F. Malt, "Traumatic Effects of Accidents," in *Individual and Community Responses to Trauma and Disasters: The Structure of Human Chaos*, ed. Robert J. Ursano, Brian G. McCaughey, and Carol S. Fullerton (Cambridge, UK: Cambridge University Press, 1995); Kathleen M. Wright and Paul T. Bartone, "Community Response to Disaster: The Gander Plane Crash," in *Individual and Community Responses to Trauma and Disasters: The Structure of Human Chaos*, ed. Robert J. Ursano, Brian G. McCaughey, and Carol S. Fullerton (Cambridge, UK: Cambridge University Press, 1995).

95 "800 at Slocum Memorial," *New York Times*, June 16, 1947, 23, notes that only nineteen survivors were still living. In 1954, when the New-York Historical Society had an exhibit about the accident, only twelve survivors attended. The *New York Times*, for instance, did not resume its coverage of the Slocum anniversary until 1923, and then its coverage was irregular, skipping 1924–1926, 1928–1931, 1933, 1935–1937, 1940, 1942–1946, and so on. O'Donnell and Schönfeld, *Der Ausflug*, 404.

96 "Slocum Survivors Pay Tribute to Dead," *New York Times*, June 16, 1934, 16.

97 O'Donnell and Schönfeld, *Der Ausflug*, 306; "Vanguard of Dead Starts to the Tomb," 2. "How the Slocum Disaster Wiped Out a Population," 28, notes that St. Mark's regular membership had dropped from 1,200–1,300 in the 1870s to a little more than 600 in 1904.

98 Zion St. Mark's Evangelical Lutheran Church, New York City, "Our History," http://www.zionstmarks.org/ourhistory.htm.

Chapter 5   A False Sense of Security, 1904–1914

1 Sulzer introduced H.R. 2799 on December 4, 1905, and H.R. 3112 on December 5, 1905. Please see 40 Cong. Rec. 7667–7670. Sulzer also introduced H.R. 4154 on March 23, 1909, for the same purpose.

2 "General Slocum Disaster," 35–89, lists the affidavits of survivors.

3 "General Slocum Disaster," 44 (statement of Jacob W. Hartmann), 39 (statement of Henry Mahlstedt), 42 (statement of Magnus Hartung), 42 (statement of Herman Heuer), 41 (statement of Lulu [Engel] Mann), 68 (statement of Charles Schwartz), 78 (statement of John H. Vassmer). In the *Annual Report of the Department of Public Charities of the City of New York for 1904*, Lulu Engel was described as "Lula Engel" but in her affidavit, she listed her name as "Lulu."

4 "General Slocum Disaster," 50 (statement of Gottlieb C. Klein), 49 (statement of John H. Klatthar), 52 (statement of Barbara Doerrhoefer), 53 (statement of Henry J. Cordes), 60 (statement of Fred Hauff).

5 "General Slocum Disaster."

6 "Carl Schurz Is Dead after a Week's Illness," *New York Times*, May 15, 1906, 9; "Carl Schurz Very Low," *New York Times*, May 11, 1906, 1; "The German Emperor Praises Carl Schurz," *New York Times*, May 17, 1906, 9; "Carl Schurz (1829–1906)," "German Ancestry Politicians in New York," Political Graveyard, http://politicalgraveyard.com/geo/NY/german.html.

7 "William Steinway Diary," "Carl Christian Schurz," http://americanhistory.si.edu/steinwaydiary/annotations/?id=802.

8 "Addresses in Memory of Carl Schurz," New York: Committee of the Carl Schurz Memorial, Carnegie Hall, New York, November 21, 1906. There are parks, schools, mountains, battleships, and at least one town named for Schurz in the United States, and there are also several streets and other landmarks in German cities named for Schurz. Both the United States and Germany have issued postal stamps with his name and portrait.

9 Skal, *History of German Immigration*; "German Ancestry Politicians in New York."

10 Daniel Czitrom, "Underworlds and Underdogs: Big Tim Sullivan and Metropolitan Politics in New York, 1889–1913," *Journal of American History* 78, no. 2 (September 1991): 536–558.

11 Skal, *History of German Immigration*, 306–307; Phelps, *New York State Legislative Souvenir for 1893*, 22; "Sulzer, William (1863–1941)," Political Graveyard, http://politicalgraveyard.com/bio/sullivant-summit.html#720.91.48.

12 "William Sulzer, Ex-Governor, 78," *New York Times*, November 7, 1941, 22; Gustav Myers, *The History of Tammany Hall* (New York: Boni and Liveright, 1917). See also Matthew L. Lifflander, *The Impeachment of Governor William Sulzer: A Story of American Politics* (New York: SUNY Press, 2012).

13 Skal, *History of German Immigration*, 268; "Wagner, Robert Ferdinand (1877–1953)," Political Graveyard, http://politicalgraveyard.com/bio/wagner.html#509.64.46. Wagner first became a Methodist in college and then converted to Roman Catholicism in 1946.

14 *Proceedings of the Board of Aldermen of the City of New York from January 6 to March 25, 1902*, vol. 1 (New York: Municipal Assembly, 1902), 1–6; *Proceedings of the Board of Aldermen of the City of New York from January 4 to March 23, 1904*, vol. 1 (New York: Board of Aldermen, 1904), 1–6; *Proceedings of the Board of Aldermen of the City of New York from January 1 to March 27, 1906*, vol. 1 (New York: Board of Aldermen, 1906), 1–8; *Proceedings of the Board of Aldermen of the City of New York from January 2 to March 28, 1911*, vol. 1 (New York: Board of Aldermen, 1911), 1; "Frederick Richter; Retired Deputy Commissioner of Plants and Structures Dies," *New York Times*, December 24, 1939, 14; "Max Greifenhagen, Ex-Sheriff, Dead," *New York Times*, October 30, 1932, 36.

15 Keith D. Revell, *Building Gotham: Civic Culture and Public Policy in New York City, 1898–1938* (Baltimore: Johns Hopkins University Press, 2005), 41.

16 *Proceedings of the Board of Aldermen of the City of New York from January 1 to March 27, 1917*, vol. 1 (New York: Board of Aldermen, 1917), 1.

17 Scholastic.com, table "Total Immigrants from each Region and Country, by Decade, 1820–2010," http://teacher.scholastic.com/activities/immigration/pdfs /by_region/region_table.pdf.

18 Thomas M. Henderson, *Tammany Hall and the New Immigrants: The Progressive Years* (New York: Arno Press, 1976), 74, states: "Between 1900 and 1910, the number of German immigrants in the city dropped from 322,000 to 278,000; even more dramatically, the number of second-generation Germans in the city dropped from 659,000 to 328,000. Comparative affluence and the new transit network worked to duplicate the pattern within the city; in 1910 only 42 per cent of the city's German immigrants lived in Manhattan, compared to 1900's 59 per cent. Only 35.6 per cent of the German second generation still resided in Manhattan."

19 U.S. Bureau of the Census, 1900, vol. 1, Statistics of Population, 801, table 8, "Population of incorporated cities, towns, villages and boroughs in 1900, 465"; table 34, "Foreign born population, distributed according to country of birth, by counties, 722"; table 35, "Foreign-born Population, Distributed according to country of birth, for cities having 25,000 inhabitants or more" (322,343 Germans). New York City had another 658,912 persons with German-born parents. See 876, table 59, "Total Persons having both parents born in specified countries" (678,912 persons with German parents).

20 Rosenwaike, *Population History*, 109–110.

21 U.S. Bureau of the Census, 1910, vol. 3, Population Reports by States, Nebraska–Wyoming: New York, section 2, chapter 1, 240, table 2, "Composition and Characteristics of the Population for Cities of 25,000 or more—cont." These figures come from adding "Foreign-born white: Born in—" to "Native white: Both parents born in—" for Manhattan and Brooklyn.

22 U.S. Bureau of the Census, 1910, vol. 3, Population Reports by States, Nebraska–Wyoming: New York, section 2, chapter 1, 216, table 13, "Foreign White Stock, by Nationality, for Cities of 100,000 or More." New York also had 76,025 Hungarian-born residents, virtually all of them living in Manhattan. Note also that table 13 includes native born with one foreign born parent in its calculations, while tables 1 and 2, which discuss the "composition and characteristics of the population for the state and for counties," only include native white with both parents foreign born in a particular country.

23 U.S. Bureau of the Census, 1910, vol. 3, Population Reports by States, Nebraska–Wyoming: New York, section 2, chapter 1, 253–256, table 5, "Composition and Characteristics of the Population for Wards (or Assembly Districts) of Cities of 50,000 or more—continued." These figures come from adding "Foreign-born white: Born in—Germany" to "Native white: Both parents born in—Germany."

24 These neighborhoods fall within AD 22 (27,848), AD 19 (23,086), and AD 20 (20,633). U.S. Census 1910, section 2, chapter 1, 256–258, table 5. These figures come from adding "Foreign-born white: Born in—Germany" to "Native white: Both parents born in—Germany."

25 U.S. Census 1910, section 2, chapter 1, 258, table 5. These figures come from adding "Foreign-born white: Born in—Germany" to "Native white: Both parents born in—Germany."

26 *Trow's General Directory of the Boroughs of Manhattan and Bronx, City of New York, Vol. CXXIV, for the year ending August 1, 1911* (New York: Trow City Directory, 1910), 46–50. Note: the Germania Music Verein is listed under "Trade Associations," on p. 91.

27 Nora Probst, *The New York Turn Verein: Finding Aid of the Archival Documents (1850–2005)* (New York, 2008), 5; NYCLPC historic designation report, Aschenbroedel Verein, November 17, 2009, 5.

28 *Trow's General Directory*, 46–50.

29 *Trow's General Directory*, 69–89.

30 *Trow's General Directory*, 69–89. Spengler, "Das New Yorker," 14, notes that the United German Societies was organized specifically for the prince's visit.

31 *Trow's General Directory*, 69–89.

32 Lenox Hill Hospital, "Our History," https://www.northwell.edu/find-care/locations/lenox-hill-hospital/about?id=102.

33 *Trow's General Directory*, 69–89.

34 *Trow's General Directory*, 69–89.

35 *Trow's General Directory*, 89–93.

36 Haberstroh, *German Churches*; Dolan, *Immigrant Church*; *Trow's New York City Directory, Vol. CI, for the year ending May 1, 1888* (New York: Trow City Directory, 1888), 19–26, "Churches." In 1910, there was only one German Catholic parish uptown: St. Joseph's, at 408 East 87th Street. *Trow's General Directory*, 37–46.

37 Haberstroh, *German Churches*.

38 *Trow's New York City Directory, Vol. CI*, 19–26, lists the following German Baptist Churches: First German, 336 East 14th; German, Washington Avenue and East 169th; Second German, 451 West 45th. See also *Trow's General Directory*, 37–46.

39 *Trow's General Directory*, 37–46. These German Methodist churches were in place by 1887, according to *Trow's New York City Directory, Vol. CI*, 19–26.

40 Haberstroh, *German Churches*.

41 *Trow's General Directory*, 37–46.

42 *Trow's General Directory*, 37–46, lists Dingeldeln Memorial at 429 East 77th; First Church of the Evangelical Association at 214 West 35th; German Evangelical Zion at 171 West 140th; St. Paul's at 159 East 112th; and Second Church of the Evangelical Assn, 424 West 55th.

43 *Trow's General Directory*, 37–46.

44 Ansche Cheshed Synagogue, https://www.anschechesed.org/about/history.

45 Haenni, *Immigrant Scene*, 57–93; Conolly-Smith, *Translating America*, 132–163; Koegel, *Music*.

46 Conolly-Smith, 152–160, 158 (quote).

47 "Atlantic Garden Changes Its Ways," *New York Times*, October 4, 1910, 5.

48 In the pre-1920s period of film, the use of title cards was limited, and as anyone who has seen a silent film knows, title cards are not needed to follow the plot of most silent films. Please also see Tessa Dwyer, "Universally Speaking: *Lost in Translation* and Polyglot Cinema," *Linguistica Antverpiensia* 4 (2005): 295–310.

49 Cristina Stanca Mustea, "Carl Laemmle." https://www.immigrantentrepreneurship.org/entries/carl-laemmle/; Frank Caso, "Marcus Loew." https://www.immigrantentrepreneurship.org/entries/marcus-loew/; Ian Baldwin, "Harry Cohn." https://www.immigrantentrepreneurship.org/entries/harry-cohn-man-mogul-and-myth/; Simon Joyce and Jennifer Putzi, "Adam Kessel." https://www.immigrantentrepreneurship.org/entries/adam-kessel/:

Kathleen A. Feeley, "Irving Thalberg." https://www.immigrantentrepreneurship
.org/entries/irving-thalberg/, all in *Immigrant Entrepreneurship, German-
American Business Biographies, 1720 to the Present*, Vol. 4, ed. Jeffrey Fear
(Washington, DC: German Historical Institute, 2011–2018); Conolly-Smith,
Translating America, 165.

50 *Bericht über das Festessen zur Feier des 118-jährigen Bestehens der Deutschen
Gesellschaft der Stadt New York, New York Turn Verein, Zur Jubelfeier seines 60
jahrigen Stiftungsfest, 1850–1910*, program, bound pamphlets, not cataloged, call
no. IEK n.s.: IEK n.c.5, NYPL.

51 Johnson, *Culture at Twilight*, 23. The NGAA held its fourth convention in New
York City in 1907. Please see *Vierten Konvention des Deutsch-Amerikanischen
National-Bundes der Ver. Staaten Von Amerika, Abgehalten vom 4. Bis 7. Oktober
1907 im Terrace Garden zu New York, N.Y.*

52 Pachmayr, *Leben und Treiben*, 127–128, 129–130.

53 Ernst Steiger, *Dreiundfünfzig jahre buchhändler in Deutschland und Amerika.
Erinnerungen und plaudereien, zur verbreitung in engerem kreise niedergeschrieben
von Ernst Steiger* (New York: Ernst Steiger, 1901), 288–289.

54 "Leider scheinen sich unsere ersten deutschen Vereine immer mehr zu amerikanisiren und gerade die Deutsch- Amerikaner und deren Nachwuchs scheinen
die Todtengräber der deutschen Sprache in Amerika zu werden. Viele Eltern sind
zu bequem, selbst mit ihren eigenen Kindern deutsch zu sprechen. Darum
gewinnt auch die englische Sprache immer mehr die Oberhand," from *Protokoll
der Vierten Konvention des Deutsch-Amerikanischen National-Bundes der Ver.
Staaten Von Amerika, Abgehalten vom 4. Bis 7. Oktober 1907 im Terrace Garden zu
New York, N.Y.*, 60, quoting "Bericht des Zweigverbandes des Deutsch-
Amerikanischen National-Bundes für das südliche Illinois für die vierte National-
Konvention des Deutsch-Amerikanischen National-Bundes in New York am 6.
Bis 8. Oktober 1907," speaker unidentified, most likely Edward V. P. Schneider-
hahn, a St. Louis attorney.

55 "Die Zukunft des deutschen Elements ist somit in Amerika geborgen! Die
Deutschen werden dort Deutsche bleiben, aber Deutsche andern Schlages sein. Sie
werden sich von ihren Brüdern in Europa unterscheiden in ihren Staatsideen, in
den Anschauungen über Bürgerrechte, in den Maßnahmen der Gemeinde, in der
Werthung der Manneskraft, in der politischen Freiheit und weltlichen Uneinge-
schränktheit. Alle diese Güter ihres Weltheiles werden sie abwägen gegen das
mindere Maß derselben diesseits des Oceans; aber nichts desto weniger wer den
sympathische Bande die beiden großen Volksstämme brüderlich umschließen."
Pachmayr, *Leben und Treiben*, 126.

56 Johnson, *Culture at Twilight*, 1.

57 Jürgen Eichhoff, "The German Language in America," in *America and the
Germans: An Assessment of a Three-Hundred-Year History*, vol. 1, *Immigration,
Language, Ethnicity*, ed. Frank Trommler and Joseph McVeigh (Philadelphia:
University of Pennsylvania Press, 1985), 228–230, citing Margarete Lenk, *Fünfzehn
Jahre in Amerika* (Zwickau, Germany: J. Hermann, 1911), 34, and Heinz Kloss,
"Deutsche Sprache ausserhalb des geschlossenen deutschen Sprachgebiets," in
Lexikon der Germanistischen Linguistike, 2nd ed., ed. Hans Peter Althaus, Helmut
Henne, and Herman Ernst Wiegand (Tübingen, Germany: Niemeyer, 1980), 54;
Marion L. Huffines, "Language-Maintenance Efforts among German Immigrants
and Their Descendants in the United States," in *America and the Germans, An*

Assessment of a Three-Hundred-Year History, vol. 1, *Immigration, Language, Ethnicity*, ed. Frank Trommler and Joseph McVeigh (Philadelphia: University of Pennsylvania Press, 1985), 249.

58 "Germans Celebrate Their Landing Here," *New York Times*, September 13, 1909, 8. Also please see "Honor Verrazzano at Hudson Festival," *New York Times*, July 25, 1909, 6, which has the subhead: "Americans Have Protested against the Number of German Organizations Asked to Participate." Please also see *Berichte und Anträge für die Sechste Konvention des Deutsch-Amerikanischen National-Bundes, 6. Bis 10. Oktober 1911 in Washington, D.C.* (New York: Bericht des D.A. Staats-Verbandes, 1911), 67.

59 Spengler, "Das New Yorker," 15.

60 For instance, please see *Der Detusche Vorkämpfer* (1907–1910: also called *New Yorker Echo* and *Rundschau zweier Welten*), a monthly magazine for German culture in the United States ("Monatsschrift für Deutsche Kultur in Amerika"). The journal was originally published by what was called the New Immigrants' Protective League, a German-speaking group organized by George S. Viereck.

61 James M. Bergquist, "German Communities in American Cities: An Interpretation of the Nineteenth-Century Experience," *Journal of American Ethnic History* 4, no. 1 (Fall 1984): 21, 22 (quote).

62 Johnson, *Culture at Twilight*; Higham, *Send These to Me*, 213.

63 "Die Zukunft des Deutschtums von New York ist glänzend. Wir können mit guter Zuversicht vorwärts blicken," in Spengler, "Das New Yorker," 15.

Chapter 6   Becoming Invisible

1 "Big German Lines Stop All Shipping," *New York Times*, August 1, 1914, 2.

2 "English Lines Stop Ships to Continent," *New York Times*, August 2, 1914, 3. Please also see telegrams, letters, reports, and other documents in files 621-1/95_416 Berichte der Filiale New York, 1914–1916, 621-1/95_417 Korrespondenzen mit der und über die Filiale New York, 1914–1917, 621-1/95_4825 D Vaterland, 1913–1920, 621-1/95_4680 D President Lincoln, 1907–1920, 621-1/95_4679 D President Grant, 1907–1920, HAPAG collection, 621-1/95 HAPAG-Reederei (1847–1970), Hamburg Staatarchiv, Hamburg, Germany.

3 "Battleship Florida Polices the Harbor," *New York Times*, August 7, 1914, 5, notes also that HAPAG had its ships SS *Amerika* and SS *Cincinnati* in Boston Harbor while North German Lloyd had the SS *Kronprinzessin Cecilie* at Bar Harbor, Maine, and the SS *Rhein* at Baltimore Harbor.

4 Barbara Wiedemann-Citera, *Die Auswirkungen des Ersten Weltkrieges auf die Deutsch-Amerikaner im Spiegel der New Yorker Staatszeitung, der New Yorker Volkszeitung und New York Times 1914–1926* (Frankfurt: Peter Lang, 1993), 44; "Ganz New York in Aufregung beim Eintreffen der ersten Kriegs-Depeschen," *New Yorker Staats-Zeitung*, August 3, 1914, 1; "Krieg zwischen England und Deutschland erklärt," *New Yorker Staats-Zeitung*, August 5, 1914, 1; "The War as Fought by Reservists in New York Cafes," *New York Times*, August 4, 1914, 5.

5 Table, "Total Number of Immigrants by Year, 1820–2007," Scholastic.com, http://teacher.scholastic.com/activities/immigration/immigration_data/.

6 Branden Little, "Evacuating Wartime Europe: US policy, Strategy, and Relief Operations for Overseas American Travelers, 1914–1915," *Journal of Military History* 79, no. 4 (October 2015): 929–958.

7 Emergency Passport Application (Form 1771–Consular), No. 07784, Johanna Hager, August 12, 1914; database with images, "U.S., Passport Applications, 1795–1925," Ancestry.com (https://www.ancestry.com/search/collections/1174: accessed July 28, 2021); National Archives, Washington DC, Record Group 59: General Records of the Department of State, Division of Passport Control, "Emergency Passport Applications, 1906–1925)," Volume 174 (Germany, 1914–1915), Application Nos. 6190 to 7816, Box 4585, ARC ID 1244183.

8 Eller applied for a passport for himself and his wife, Auguste, to travel to Germany in 1913. "United States Passport Applications, 1795–1925," Familysearch.org, https://www.familysearch.org/tree/person/sources/LYJW-1XJ. After being trapped in Europe by the war, the Ellers were finally able to sail from Rotterdam to New York on the SS *Noordam*, arriving on November 1, 1916. See "New York, Passenger and Crew Lists," Ancestry.com, https://www.ancestry.com/search/collections/7488/?name=Joseph_Eller&birth=1839_germany_3253&arrival=1916-11-1_new+york-usa_35&arrival_x=0-0-0_1-0&departure=_rotterdam-rotterdam-zuid+holland-netherlands_1024896&departure_x=_1-0&f-F0005959=Noordam&gender=m&name_x=_1. But tragically, Joseph died on November 13 at the age of seventy-eight. Please see "New York, New York City Municipal Deaths, 1795–1949," Familysearch.org, https://www.familysearch.org/ark:/61903/1:1:2WNJ-N8H?from=lynx1UIV8&treeref=LYJW-1XJ.

9 "George Ehret Dies, Famous as Brewer," *New York Times*, January 21, 1927, 15; "Ehret Expects to Get His Money Back," *New York Times*, August 13, 1918, 15.

10 U.S. Bureau of the Census, 1910, vol. 4, Population: Occupation Statistics, 571–583, table 8, "Total Males and Females 16 Years of Age and Over Engaged in Selected Occupations, Classified by Age Periods and Color or Race, Nativity, and Parentage, for Cities of 100,000 Inhabitants or More: 1910"; Geoffrey W. Clark, "An Interpretation of Hoboken's Population Trends, 1856–1970," in *Hoboken: A Collection of Essays*, ed. Edward Halsey Foster and Geoffrey W. Clark (New York: Irvington, 1975), 51.

11 "German Veterans Asked to Aid Bryan," *New York Times*, June 13, 1915, 2; Hugo Munsterberg, "The Impeachment of German-Americans," *New York Times*, September 19, 1915, 1; Wiedemann-Citera, *Die Auswirkungen*.

12 Herman Ridder, *Hyphenations: A Collection of Articles on the World War of 1914 which Have Appeared from Time to Time in the "New-Yorker Staats-Zeitung" under "The War Situation from Day to Day"* (New York: Max Schmetterling, 1915).

13 Eberhard Demm, "Censorship," *The International Encyclopedia of the First World War*, version 2.0, updated March 29, 2017, https://encyclopedia.1914-1918-online.net/article/censorship; Deian Hopkin, "Domestic Censorship in the First World War," *Journal of Contemporary History* 5, no. 4 (1970): 151–169; Thomas Fleming, *The Illusion of Victory: America in World War I* (New York: Basic Books, 2003), chap. 2.

14 Reinhard R. Doerries, *Imperial Challenge: Ambassador Count Bernstorff and German-American Relations, 1908–1917*, trans. Christa D. Shannon (Chapel Hill: University of North Carolina Press, 1989), 67–72, also 51–52, regarding Herman Ridder getting money from von Bernstorff; Ridder, *Hyphenations*. Another pro-neutrality publication, *The Vital Issue* (later called *Issues and Events*), was published by Franz Johann Dorl, noted in "Bar Riverside Drive to German Tenants," *New York Times*, November 23, 1917, 11. Herman Ridder died November 1, 1915. "Herman Ridder, Editor, Is Dead," *New York Times*, November 2, 1915, 11.

15 "Ask Mourning Display," *New York Times*, August 28, 1914, 7; "Protesting Women March in Mourning," *New York Times*, August 30, 1914, 11.

16 "Bryan Repeats His Peace Plea to Big Madison Sq. Garden Meeting," *New York Times*, June 25, 1915, 1; also "Plan Great Bryan Meeting," *New York Times*, June 13, 1915, 2; "Auf, in den Kampf für Frieden," *New Yorker Staats-Zeitung*, June 24, 1915, 1; "Aufrechterhaltung des Friedens mit der ganzen Welt und strengst Neutralität gefordert," *New Yorker Staats-Zeitung*, June 25, 1915, 1; Johnson, *Culture at Twilight*, 111–112.

17 "Bazar für Kriegsopfer eröffnet," *New Yorker Staats-Zeitung*, December 6, 1914, 1; "Bazar brachte über $338,000," *New Yorker Staats-Zeitung*, December 21, 1914, 1.

18 Conolly-Smith, *Translating America*, 125.

19 Gustav Scholer papers, box 2, folders Letters 1916 and Letters 1917, NYPL Manuscripts Division.

20 Wiedemann-Citera, *Die Auswirkungen*, 57–58. Also please see, as examples, in the *New Yorker Staats-Zeitung* "der "Wohlthähigkeit Bazar in Madison Square Garden," March 11, 1916, 9; "Der Riesen-Basar eröffnet," March 12, 1916, 1; "Gigantisches Werk der Nächstenliebe in Madison Square Garden," March 12, 1916, 2nd ed., 1; plus a special bazaar program in the March 12, 1916, Sonntagsblatt; "Brooklyn-Tag auf dem Basar," and "Deutscher herzen Hochflut!," March 13, 1916, 9; "Großartiges Fazit des Basars; $725,000 und 1,000,000 Besucher," March 24, 1916, 9 and "Gemeinde Freude über den unerwartet großen Erfolg," March 24, 1916, 10.

21 "War Charity Fete on the Vaterland," *New York Times*, November 5, 1916, 11. The *Times* reports that approximately $7,000 was raised and that tickets were a pricey $10 each. Tenor Urlus was Dutch and specialized in Wagnerian opera.

22 George Seibel, "The Hyphen in American History," address reproduced from the *New Yorker Staats-Zeitung*, September 4, 1916, Germans in the United States, bound pamphlets, not cataloged, call no. IEK n.s. IEK n.c.5, NYPL.

23 "Wilson Wants No Disloyal Vote Cast on His Side," *New York Times*, September 30, 1916, 1; Nancy Gentile Ford, *Americans All! Foreign-Born Soldiers in World War I* (College Station: Texas A&M University Press, 2001), 21–22; also Ross J. Wilson, *New York and the First World War: Shaping an American City* (New York: Routledge, 2016), 152.

24 S. D. Lowell, *The Presidential Election of 1916* (Carbondale: Southern Illinois University Press, 1980).

25 For examples, please see "Many Yachts for Kiel Regatta," *New York Times*, February 27, 1902, 10; "Yacht Race Off Again," *New York Times*, June 11, 1903, 7; "American Yachts Win," *New York Times*, June 29, 1904, 8; "Kaiser's Family at Kiel Regatta," *New York Times*, February 18, 1905, 10; "Longworths Again the Kaiser's Guests," *New York Times*, June 26, 1906, 7; "Kaiser's Cup Race Meeting," *New York Times*, February 26, 1905, 10.

26 List of attendees by table, Dinner given by the mayor of NY in honor of The Officers of His Imperial German Majesty's Squadron at the Waldorf Astoria, June 10, 1912, Germans in the United States, bound pamphlets, not cataloged, case no. IEK n.s.: n.s. 8, NYPL; "German Admiral Toasts President," "Germans Dine at Yacht Club," "Waiters Fail Again to Spoil Fleet Visit," *New York Times*, June 12, 1912, 24.

27 Christopher Clark, *The Sleepwalkers: How Europe Went to War in 1914* (New York: Harper Collins, 1912), has an excellent discussion of Kaiser Wilhelm II's approach to foreign policy.

28 "Farewell Dinner to the Admirals," *New York Times*, October 8, 1909, 6.

29 "Kaiser Is Now Well," *New York Times*, August 30, 1912, 5; "The Kaiser and Peace," *New York Times*, February 19, 1912, 8; "Churchill May Mar Haldane's Peace Aim," *New York Times*, February 10, 1912, 3; "Kaiser a 'Man of Peace,'" *New York Times*, January 6, 1912, 17.

30 "Carnegie Praises Kaiser," *New York Times*, September 19, 1912, 1; Alfred H. Fried, *The German Emperor and the Peace of the World* (New York: Hodder and Stoughton, 1912).

31 Zachary Smith, *Age of Fear: Othering and American Identity during World War I* (Baltimore: Johns Hopkins University Press, 2019), 9.

32 There are more than 1,500 articles in the *New York Times* that use the term *Teuton* and 430 that use the term *Huns* to describe Germans during 1914–1918. Gary S. Messinger, *British Propaganda and the State in the First World War* (Manchester, UK: Manchester University Press, 1992).

33 Conolly-Smith, *Translating America*, 194–196; "Auftakt zun 24 Nationalen Sängerfest," *New Yorker Staats-Zeitung*, May 30, 1915, 1; also "Grüße und Glückwünsche zum Sängerfest," May 30, 1915, 2nd ed., 1; the paper also reprinted the ten-page festival program in that issue.

34 For example, Pachmayr, *Leben und Treiben*, 119–126; and *Protokoll der Vierten Konvention*, 2, quoting the alliance president C. J. Hexamer, in which Hexamer stated: "Ja, der ist der beste Amerikaner, der nicht rastet und ruht bis 'amerikanisiren' gleichbedeutend mit 'germanisiren' sein soll. Es ist unsere vornehmste Pflicht—wo auch unsere Wiege stand, für deutsches Wissen, für deutsche Kunst, für deutsche Gemüthstiefe einzutreten, und gegen englische Heuchelei und Missgunst zu kämpfen." (Yes, he is the best American who does not rest and rest until "Americanization" is synonymous with "Germanization." It is our most noble duty—wherever our cradle stood, to stand up for German knowledge, for German art, for German depth of mind, and to fight against English hypocrisy and resentment.)

35 "German Press Views of the Address," *New York Times*, April 3, 1917, 4.

36 "Call for War Stirs All City," *New York Times*, April 3, 1917, 5; "Bar German Flag at Church Meeting," *New York Times*, April 5, 1917, 4.

37 Jörg Nagler, "Victims of the Home Front: Enemy Aliens in the United States during the First World War," in *Minorities in Wartime: National and Racial Groupings in Europe, North America and Australia during the Two World Wars*, ed. Panikos Panayi (Providence, RI: Berg, 1993); Jörg Nagler, *Nationale Minoritäten im Krieg, "Feindliche Ausländer" und die amerikanische Heimatfront während des Ersten Weltkriegs* (Hamburg, Germany: Hamburger Edition, 2000).

38 Robert D. Cuff, "Herbert Hoover: The Ideology of Voluntarism and War Organization During the Great War," *Journal of American History* 64, no. 2 (September 1977): 358–372.

39 Nagler, "Victims," 198.

40 "Wholesale Plot Arrests," *New York Times*, April 7, 1917, 1, 3; "Eight Taken Here as German Spies," *New York Times*, April 7, 1917, 3; "19 More Taken as German Spies," *New York Times*, April 8, 1917, 1; "Arrests of Spies Check Plotters," *New York Times*, April 9, 1917, 1.

41 "Eight Taken Here as German Spies," 3.

42 "19 More Taken as German Spies," 1.

43 Nagler, "Victims," 198, 206, 208; Robert C. Doyle, "Over There and Over Here: Enemy Prisoners of War and Prisoners of State in the Great War," in *The Enemy in*

Our Hands: America's Treatment of Enemy Prisoners of War from the Revolution to the War on Terror (Lexington: University Press of Kentucky, 2010); "Take Some Teutons from Ellis Island," *New York Times*, August 28, 1917, 7; "Germans Are Sent South," *New York Times*, November 4, 1917, 17; "Hecht Seeks Freedom," *New York Times*, December 9, 1917, 12; "Parole for Third Prominent German," *New York Times*, December 23, 1917, 4; "Interned German Gets Out on Parole," *New York Times*, December 12, 1917, 11.

44 Nagler, "Victims," 211.

45 "19 More Taken as German Spies," 1; Chad Millman, *The Detonators: The Secret Plot to Destroy America and an Epic Hunt for Justice* (New York: Little, Brown, 2008), 21–24, also discusses this, and on 41–44 and 56–58 discusses Koenig's espionage activities, as does Jules Witcover, *Sabotage at Black Tom: Imperial Germany's Secret War in America, 1914–1917* (Chapel Hill, NC: Algonquin Books of Chapel Hill, 1989), 59–66.

46 "German Arrested for Making Bombs," *New York Times*, March 6, 1917, 1; "All Spy Arrests Now Kept Secret," *New York Times*, April 13, 1917, 3; Witcover, *Sabotage at Black Tom*, 210.

47 "German in Jail Who Saw Troops Depart," *New York Times*, July 14, 1917, 3; "Arrested as Bomb Maker," *New York Times*, June 10, 1917, 4.

48 "27 Ships Taken Here," *New York Times*, April 7, 1917, 1; see also "Seizure of German Ships Takes Place without Difficulty," *Hudson Observer*, April 6, 1917, in World War I scrapbook, Hoboken Library, Hoboken, NJ. See also "Interned Germans Thirst in Captivity," *New York Times*, April 8, 1917, 6; "14 Austrian Liners Seized in Our Ports," *New York Times*, April 10, 1917, 3; "Stockade at Ellis Island," *New York Times*, April 12, 1917, 1.

49 "Army Put in Charge of Piers in Hoboken," *New York Times*, April 20, 1917, 1.

50 Howard B. Furer, "'Heaven, Hell or Hoboken': The Effects of World War I on a New Jersey City," *New Jersey History* 92, no. 3 (Autumn 1974): 149; "27 Ships Taken Here," 1; Albert Bushnell Hart, "Seizure of German Ships," *New York Times*, April 1, 1917, Opinion, SM1.

51 Daniel Van Winkle, *History of Municipalities of Hudson County, 1630–1923*, vol. 1, *Historical-Biographical* (Chicago: Lewis Historical, 1924), 318.

52 Van Winkle, *History of Municipalities*, 310–313. Van Winkle notes that the United States also had access to British, French, and Italian ships, for a total of 173 transatlantic liners.

53 "Wilson Asks Title to German Piers," *New York Times*, March 6, 1918, 7; "Move to Make Big German Concerns American-Owned," *New York Times*, March 8, 1918, 1; "Vote to Root Out Financial Power of Germany Here," *New York Times*, March 12, 1918, 1 (quote); also "Authorizes Sale of Hoboken Piers," *New York Times*, March 27, 1918, 15.

54 "George Ehret Dies, Famous as Brewer," *New York Times*, January 21, 1927, 15; *Report of the Alien Property Custodian* (Washington, DC: Government Printing Office, 1922), 677.

55 *Report of the Alien Property*, 13, notes that more than 150 corporations out of a total of 312 were either auctioned or sold for more than $54 million.

56 Frederick Franklin Schrader, *1683–1920* (New York: Concord, 1920), 233.

57 "Marshals Puzzled by Alien Question," *New York Times*, April 8, 1917, 2, notes the challenges of enforcing the proposed half-mile limit in Manhattan; "Make Exceptions for Enemy Aliens," *New York Times*, April 19, 1917, 7.

58 "Bar Enemy Aliens from Riverfronts," *New York Times*, May 7, 1917, 8; "Time Up for Teutons to Ask for Permits," *New York Times*, June 10, 1917, 12.

59 Nagler, "Victims," 198; see *New Yorker Staats-Zeitung*, May 27, 1917, 2; May 19, 1917, 6; May 20, 1917, 6a; and May 23, 1917, 1.

60 "Bar All German-Americans," *New York Times*, July 10, 1917, 2; "Waterfront Closed to Enemy Aliens," *New York Times*, July 11, 1917, 5; "Quiet Control of the Germans in New York," *New York Times*, July 29, 1917, 56.

61 Erik Kirschbaum, *Burning Beethoven: The Eradication of German Culture in the United States During World War I* (Berlin, Germany: Berlinca, 2015).

62 Steven H. Jaffe, *New York at War: Four Centuries of Combat, Fear, and Intrigue in Gotham* (New York: Basic Books, 2012), 207–208.

63 Wiedemann-Citera, *Die Auswirkungen*, 164–165.

64 "New York Herald's Complete and Alphabetical List of Names and Addresses of the German Alien Enemies Registered in New York City in the State Military Census," June 1917; "City's German List Holds 39,596 Names," *New York Times*, February 14, 1918, 8.

65 "Mayor Disavows Idea of Treason in Wagner Charge," *New York Times*, April 4, 1917, 1; "Senate Indorses Wagner, Ending Mitchel Inquiry," *New York Times*, April 5, 1917, 1.

66 Wiedemann-Citera, *Die Auswirkungen*, 163.

67 "Metropolitan Bars Operas in German," *New York Times*, November 3, 1917, 13; Conolly-Smith, *Translating America*, esp. chaps. 7 and 8, 217–242.

68 "Quiet Control of the Germans in New York," *New York Times*, July 29, 1917, 56.

69 Wiedemann-Citera, *Die Auswirkungen*, 164.

70 "Germans Here Quick to Back President," *New York Times*, April 7, 1917, 5; "Schuetzen Park Offered to Nation," *New York Times*, April 9, 1917, 4.

71 "Harmonie Club Offers Aid," *New York Times*, April 10, 1917, 15.

72 Wiedemann-Citera, *Die Auswirkungen*, 134.

73 Tyler Anbinder, *City of Dreams: The 400-Year Epic History of Immigrant New York* (New York: Houghton Mifflin Harcourt, 2016), 457.

74 "Teutons Rush for Papers," *New York Times*, April 3, 1917, 10.

75 Nagler, "Victims," 201.

76 Conolly-Smith, *Translating America*, 251–252.

77 Jaffe, *New York at War*, 204.

78 Wittke, *German-Language Press*, 209, 244; Conolly-Smith, *Translating America*, 249–251. Please also see Kevin Grieves, "'It Would Be for the Best to Suspend Publication': The German–American Press and Anti-German Hysteria During World War I," *American Journalism* 37 no. 1 (2020): 47–65.

79 "Enemy Badly Battered," *New York Times*, June 3, 1918, 11.

80 "Killed in Row over War," *New York Times*, July 16, 1918, 6.

81 "Books of Dry Dock Corporation Seized," *New York Times*, June 26, 1918, 13.

82 "Begin New Roundup of Enemy Aliens," *New York Times*, July 6, 1918, 7.

83 Jaffe, *New York at War*, 204.

84 John McClymer, "Of 'Mornin Glories' and 'Fine Old Oaks': John Purroy Mitchel, Al Smith, and Reform as an Expression of Irish American Aspiration," in *The New York Irish*, ed. Ronald H. Bayor and Timothy J. Meagher (Baltimore: Johns Hopkins University Press, 1997), 389–392.

85 "Police Will Watch 25,000 Enemy Aliens," *New York Times*, November 1, 1917, 7; "Roundup to Check Spy Menace Soon," *New York Times*, November 14, 1917, 3.

86 "Barred Zone Shut to Rich Germans," *New York Times*, November 22, 1917, 4; "Bar Riverside Drive to German Tenants," *New York Times*, November 23, 1917, 11; "Germans Leaving Barred War Zones," *New York Times*, November 24, 1917, 3; "Teuton Women Here May Be Registered," *New York Times*, November 19, 1917, 18, says an estimated 10,000 Germans lived or did business within two blocks of the waterfront.

87 "Enemy Aliens May Be Moved Inland," *New York Times*, November 6, 1917, 1.

88 "Soldiers to Guard All Docks and Piers Here," *New York Times*, November 18, 1917, 1; "Soldiers Arrest 200 in Raid in Hoboken, " *New York Times*, November 20, 1917, 1; "New Enemy Migration," *New York Times*, November 22, 1917, 4; "Barred Zone Shut to Rich Germans," *New York Times*, November 22, 1917, 4; "Military Guard Put in Control of River Fronts," *New York Times*, November 25, 1917, 1; "No Soldiers Sent to Guard Piers," *New York Times*, November 26, 1917, 1.

89 "Soldiers to Guard All Docks and Piers," 1; "Teuton Women Here May Be Registered," *New York Times*, November 19, 1917, 18; "All Germans Here under New Watch," *New York Times*, November 20, 1917, 4; "Plan to Register 500,000 Germans," *New York Times*, December 31, 1917, 4; "Start Registration of Germans Feb. 4," *New York Times*, January 12, 1918, 8; "City's German List Holds 39,596 Names," *New York Times*, February 14, 1918, 8.

90 "All Germans Here under New Watch," 4; Nagler, "Victims," 199–200.

91 "Gloating Germans Arrested in a Raid," *New York Times*, April 2, 1918, 6.

92 "Six Opera Aliens Dropped," *New York Times*, April 30, 1918, 11.

93 "Two More Germans Expelled by N.Y.A.C.," *New York Times*, April 11, 1918, 24; "N.Y. Athletic Club Expels Pro-German," *New York Times*, March 30, 1918, 11.

94 "Bars German in Club," *New York Times*, April 13, 1918, 18.

95 "Democratic Club Bans German," *New York Times*, April 3, 1918, 19.

96 Jaffe, *New York at War*, 206–207.

97 Jaffe, 208–212.

98 "Will Shut Enemy Spies from Coast," *New York Times*, August 15, 1918, 14.

99 "Seize 20,000 Here in Slacker Search," *New York Times*, September 4, 1918, 1; "60,187 Men Taken in Slacker Raids," *New York Times*, September 8, 1918, 9.

100 H. C. Peterson and Gilbert C. Fite, *Opponents of War, 1917–1918: The Story of the Persecution of Antiwar Groups* (Madison: University of Wisconsin Press, 1957), 231–232; Paul L. Murphy, *World War I and the Origin of Civil Liberties in the United States* (New York: W. W. Norton, 1979); Jennifer Fronc, *New York Undercover: Private Surveillance in the Progressive Era* (Chicago: University of Chicago Press, 2009), 147; "Amateur Prussianism in New York," *New York World*, September 6, 1918, 8.

101 Francesco Aimone, "The 1918 Influenza Epidemic in New York City: A Review of the Public Health Response," *Public Health Reports* 125, no. S3 (2010): 71–79. Please also see "Grip Now Sweeping Forty-Three States," *New York Times*, October 4, 1918, 24; "Copeland Satisfied by Influenza Tour," *New York Times*, October 30, 1918, 10; "What New York Looked Like during the 1918 Flu Pandemic," *New York Times*, April 2, 2020.

Chapter 7   The Great Disappearing Act, 1919–1930

1 Russell Kazal, *Becoming Old Stock: The Paradox of German American Identity* (Princeton, NJ: Princeton University Press, 2004).

2 In 1914–1915, thirty-four out of fifty-nine operas performed in New York City were written by Wagner. Wiedemann-Citera, *Die Auswirkungen*, 35, 176; Koegel, *Music*.

3 "Hylan Puts Stop to Opera in German," *New York Times*, March 11, 1919, 1.

4 "Ask Hylan to Stop German Opera," *New York Times*, March 8, 1919, 11; "Soldiers Rebel at German Opera," *New York Times*, March 9, 1919, 1; "Veterans to Fight Opera in German," *New York Times*, March 10, 1919, 1; "Hylan Puts Stop to Opera in German," 1; Wiedemann-Citera, *Die Auswirkungen*, 222–233.

5 "Hylan Puts Stop to Opera in German," 1.

6 "Ask Hylan to Stop German Opera," 11.

7 "Hylan Puts Stop to Opera in German," 1. Christians immigrated around 1914 or 1915.

8 "Hylan Puts Stop to Opera in German," 1.

9 "Plan German Opera Here," *New York Times*, July 17, 1919, 14; "To Give German Operas," *New York Times*, August 22, 1919, 11; "Singer of German Silenced by Legion," *New York Times*, September 24, 1919, 18; "Sees End to German Opera," *New York Times*, September 25, 1919, 7; "New York County Legion Posts Meet," *New York Times*, October 2, 1919, 17; "Anti-German Opera Drive," *New York Times*, October 16, 1919, 34; "Hearing on German Opera," *New York Times*, October 20, 1919, 13; Wiedemann-Citera, *Die Auswirkungen*, 222–233; J. E. Vacha, "When Wagner Was Verboten: The Campaign against German Music in World War I," *New York History* 64, no. 2 (April 1983): 171–188.

10 "Opera in German Given in Defiance of Hylan and Mob," *New York Times*, October 21, 1919, 1; "Hylan Bars Opera," *New York Times*, October 22, 1919, 1; "Police Club Mob at German Opera," *New York Times*, October 23, 1919, 1.

11 "Police Club Mob at German Opera," 1; "Give German Opera to Small House," *New York Times*, October 24, 1919, 17; "German Opera Sung Again," *New York Times*, October 25, 1919, 11.

12 "May Abandon Opera in German Tongue," *New York Times*, October 26, 1919, 21; "City Wins in Fight on German Opera," *New York Times*, October 28, 1919, 17; "Drop German Opera until Peace Comes," *New York Times*, October 29, 1919, 17; "Star Opera Company Fails," *New York Times*, November 25, 1919, 24.

13 "German Opera Is Dropped," *New York Times*, November 27, 1919, 8.

14 "Revive 'Hansel and Gretel,'" *New York Times*, December 26, 1920, 9.

15 "Mme. Jeritz in 'Lohengrin,'" *New York Times*, January 7, 1922, 19, "Wagner 'Ring' Revival for the Manhattan," *New York Times*, September 9, 1922, 14.

16 For instance, compare the number of German-named or self-identified organizations in *R. L. Polk's & Co's Trow General Directory of New York City, Embracing the Boroughs of Manhattan and the Bronx, 1916, Vol. 129* (New York: Trow Press, 1916) to *R. L. Polk & Co's 1920 Trow's New York City Directory, Boroughs of Manhattan and Bronx, Vol. 132* (New York: R. L. Polk, 1920). Please also see Peter C. Weber, "Ethnic Identity during War: The Case of German-American Societies during World War I," *Nonprofit and Voluntary Sector Quarterly* 43, no. 1 (2014): 185–206.

17 John A. Hawgood, *The Tragedy of German-America* (New York: G.P. Putnam's Sons, 1940), 294.

18 Wiedemann-Citera, *Die Auswirkungen*, 174–175.

19 Wiedemann-Citera, 174.

20 Bayor, *Neighbors in Conflict*, 57–77.

21 Wiedemann-Citera, *Die Auswirkungen*, 181, 203.

22 This phenomenon was not limited to New York City; please see Heinrich Tolzmann, *The Cincinnati Germans after the Great War*, American University Studies Series 9, History, vol. 16 (New York: Peter Lang, 1987), 197–198.

23 *One Hundred and Fifty Years*, 26.

24 Wiedemann-Citera, *Die Auswirkungen*, 210. "Honor ZR-3 Crew," *New York Times*, October 27, 1924, 12, is the first mention of German Day in the *New York Times* since 1916.

25 Wiedemann-Citera, 181; "Gift to German Children," *New York Times*, December 4, 1922, 10.

26 Wiedemann-Citera, 189–192; "Fight for Old Name," *New York Times*, January 23, 1925, 12; "Favor Restoring 'German Hospital," *New York Times*, February 25, 1925, 11.

27 "German Societies May Back Hospital," *New York Times*, January 26, 1927, 22; "Act on German Hospital," *New York Times*, February 18, 1927, 11; "Act to Give New York New German Hospital," *New York Times*, March 18, 1927, 2.

28 Wiedemann-Citera, *Die Auswirkungen*, 294–295; "Gertrude Ederle, the First Woman to Swim across the English Channel, Dies at 98," *New York Times*, December 1, 2003.

29 Schrader, *1683–1920*, 98–101.

30 Hawgood, *Tragedy of German-America*, 299–300.

31 Frederick C. Luebke, "German Immigrants and American Politics: Problems of Leadership, Parties, and Issues," in *Germans in America: Retrospect and Prospect. Tricentennial Lectures Delivered at the German Society of Pennsylvania in 1983*, ed. Randall M. Miller (Philadelphia: The German Society of Pennsylvania, 1984), 70; "Comes Out for Smith," *New York Times*, October 8, 1922, 5; "The Steuben Society Bloc," editorial, *New York Times*, September 12, 1924, 20; "Protest Promise to Aid La Follette," *New York Times*, September 21, 1924, 3; "2 Dead Presidents Bitterly Assailed," *New York Times*, August 31, 1924, 2.

32 Luebke, "German Immigrants," 69; Tolzmann, *Cincinnati Germans*, 163. Please see "The German-American Vote," *New York Times*, November 1, 1920, 13, and "A German-American Vote," *New York Times*, January 1, 1921, 7, for differences in German American voting decisions. The German American Societies endorsed Al Smith for president in 1928, believing him to oppose Prohibition and favor a less pro-British foreign policy regarding Germany. "Societies Back Smith," *New York Times*, September 23, 1928, 8.

33 Quotas for the Comprehensive Immigration Law (1924), Archive.org, https://web .archive.org/web/20090228084926/http://www.civics-online.org/library /formatted/texts/immigration1924.htm; Hawgood, *Tragedy of German-America*, 300.

34 James R. Barrett, *The Irish Way: Becoming American in the Multiethnic City* (London, UK: Penguin, 2012), 274–276.

35 "Dr. Wise Attacks New Quota Bill," *New York Times*, January 7, 1924, 3; "LaGuardia Resents Alien Blocs Charge," *New York Times*, February 22, 1924, 12; "New Yorkers Fight Immigration Bill as Racially Unfair," *New York Times*, February 25, 1924, 1; Chin Jou, "Contesting Nativism: The New York Congressional Delegation's Case against the Immigration Act of 1924," *Federal History* (2011): 66–79; Kristofer Allerfeldt, "'And We Got Here First': Albert Johnson, National Origins and Self-Interest in the Immigration Debate of the 1920s," *Journal of Contemporary History* 45, no. 1 (January 2010): 7–26.

36 "City Elects Wagner," *New York Times*, November 3, 1926, 1; "Wagner's Story Rise of an Immigrant Boy," *New York Times*, November 3, 1926, 6; "Love of Battle Sees Wagner Through," *New York Times*, November 14, 1926, 3.

37 Luebke, "German Immigrants," 63.

38 "Wagner's Story Rise of an Immigrant Boy," 6.

39 For instance, see letter to the editor from Dor Nils Hammerstrand, "German in the Churches," *New York Times*, February 7, 1918, 10, and "Describes Plots by German Spies to Incite Negroes," *New York Times*, December 15, 1918, 1, 10, about how the Lutheran church was supposedly a propaganda arm of the German government.

40 *R. L. Polk & Co's Trow General Directory of New York City Boroughs of Manhattan and Bronx, Vol. 130* (New York: R. L. Polk, 1918), 18–19; *R. L. Polk & Co's 1920*, 18–19; Haberstroh, *German Churches*, also shows the merger and closure of many German Lutheran churches. This also occurred in Philadelphia. Kazal, *Becoming Old Stock*.

41 *Evangelisch-Lutherisches Ministerium des Staates New York und angrezender Staaten und Lander, Einhundertneunundzwanzigste Versammlung 1919*, report, Evangelisch-Lutherischen Zions Kirche, Rochester, NY, 16–20 Juni 1919, Parochial-Berichte und Statistik, 1918–1919, pp. 78–92, Lutheran Synod, Sutter Archives, Horrimann Library, Wagner College, Staten Island, NY.

42 Rosalind Tough and Sophia M. Robison, "Yorkville: American Community and Melting Pot," *Journal of Land and Public Utility Economics* 19, no. 3 (August 1943): 257–258; Agnes Bretting, "'Little Germanies' in New York," *Deutschamerikanische Gesellschaften* (Stuttgart, Germany: Franz Steiner, 1992), 76, notes that the neighborhood was more German American than German.

43 "Alien Yorkville Re-enters the Union," *New York Times*, October 19, 1926, 6.

44 Tough and Robison, "Yorkville," 257; "Alien Yorkville Re-enters the Union," 6; Bretting, "'Little Germanies,'" 90.

45 "Alien Yorkville Re-enters the Union," 6.

46 Gordon, *Assimilation in American Life*, 79–80.

47 Kazal, *Becoming Old Stock*.

48 Hawgood, *Tragedy of German-America*, 290–291.

49 Perlmann, "Demographic Basis," 32 (quote), 33.

50 Kazal, *Becoming Old Stock*.

Bibliography

Primary Sources

GOVERNMENT DOCUMENTS—FEDERAL

40 Cong. Rec. 7667–7670. Washington, DC: Government Printing Office, 1906.

"General Slocum Disaster, Evidence before the Committee on Claims of the House of
Representatives on H.R. 4154, for the Relief of the Victims of the General Slocum
Disaster," April 20, 1910, Committee on Claims, House of Representatives,
61st Congress, 2nd Session. Washington, DC: Government Printing Office, 1910.

"List of German Officers and Crewmen Interned at Ellis Island or Hot Springs, North
Carolina," file 54261-154, box 54261147A to 54261158, record group 85, entry 9,
National Archives, Washington, DC.

Report of the Alien Property Custodian. Washington, DC: Government Printing
Office, 1922.

*Report of the United States Commission of Investigation upon the Disaster to the Steamer
"General Slocum."* Washington, DC: Government Printing Office, 1904.

Testimony of Max Schmittberger. "Report and proceedings of the Senate committee
appointed to investigate the police department of the city of New York," vol. 5
(Albany, NY: James B. Lyon, State Printer, 1895), 4965–4966, 5311–5386.

U.S. Bureau of the Census, Seventh–Fourteenth Annual Censuses, 1850–1930.
Washington, DC: Government Printing Office.

GOVERNMENT DOCUMENTS—NEW YORK STATE AND CITY

Albin Boenhardt, Plaintiff, v. Jacob W. Loch, Louis W. Kaufmann, Hugo W.
Hoffman, Emil C. J. Kraeling, John C. Haas and William S. Jackson, as Attorney-
General of the State of New York, Defendants. Supreme Court, New York Special
Term Nov. 1, 1907, 56 Misc. 406 N.Y. Misc. 1907.

Annual Report of the Department of Public Charities of the City of New York for 1904.
New York: Martin B. Brown, 1905.

New York City Landmark Preservation Commission. East 10th Street Historic
District Designation Report, January 17, 2012.

———. East 17th Street/Irving Place Historic District Designation Report, 1998.

———. East Village/Lower East Side Historic District Designation Report, October 9, 2012.

———. Gramercy Park Historic District Designation Report, September 20, 1966.

———. Historic Designation Report, Aschenbroedel Verein, November 17, 2009.

———. Historic Designation Report, German-American Shooting Club Society, June 26, 2001.

———. Historic Designation Report, Scheffel Hall, June 24, 1997.

New York City Marriage Records, 1829–1940.

New York State Board of Charities. *Fifth Annual Report of the Board of State Commissioners of Public Charities of the State of New York.* Albany, NY: Argus, 1872.

New York State Office of Parks, Recreation, and Historic Preservation. Elka Park National Registry of Historic Places application, #1024-0018, Nancy Todd, February 1993.

New York State Census, 1875.

Proceedings of the Board of Aldermen of the City of New York from January 6 to March 25, 1890. Vol. 197. New York: Martin Brown, 1890.

Proceedings of the Board of Aldermen of the City of New York from January 5 to March 31, 1891. Vol. 201. New York: Martin Brown, 1891.

Proceedings of the Board of Aldermen of the City of New York from January 4 to March 29, 1892. Vol. 205. New York: Martin B. Brown, 1892.

Proceedings of the Board of Aldermen of the City of New York from January 2 to March 28, 1893. Vol. 209. New York: Martin Brown, 1893.

Proceedings of the Board of Aldermen of the City of New York from January 4 to March 27, 1894. Vol. 213. New York: Martin B. Brown, 1894.

Proceedings of the Board of Aldermen of the City of New York from January 7 to March 26, 1895. Vol. 217. New York: Martin Brown, 1895.

Proceedings of the Board of Aldermen of the City of New York from January 7 to March 31, 1896. Vol. 221. New York: Martin Brown, 1897.

Proceedings of the Board of Aldermen of the City of New York from January 6 to March 25, 1902. Vol. 1. New York: Municipal Assembly, 1902.

Proceedings of the Board of Aldermen of the City of New York from January 4 to March 23, 1904. Vol. 1. New York: Board of Aldermen, 1904.

Proceedings of the Board of Aldermen of the City of New York from January 1 to March 27, 1906. Vol. 1. New York: Board of Aldermen, 1906.

Proceedings of the Board of Aldermen of the City of New York from January 2 to March 28, 1911. Vol. 1. New York: Board of Aldermen, 1911.

Proceedings of the Board of Aldermen of the City of New York from January 1 to March 27, 1917. Vol. 1. New York: Board of Aldermen, 1911.

Proceedings of the Board of Aldermen of the Municipal Assembly of the City of New York from January 1 to March 27, 1900. Vol. 1. New York: Municipal Assembly, 1900.

Report and Proceedings of the Senate Committee Appointed to Investigate the Police Department of the City of New York (Lexow Committee hearing transcripts). Vols. 1–5. Albany, NY: James B. Lyon, State Printer, 1895.

CITY DIRECTORIES

Gouldings New York City directory, 1877–1878. New York: Lawrence G. Goulding, 1878.

New-York City Directory for 1844 & 1845. New York: John Doggett, 1845.

New York City Directory for 1852–1853. New York: Doggett and Rode, 1853.

Phillips' business directory of New York, 1881. New York: W. Phillips, 1881.

R. L. Polk's & Co's Trow General Directory of New York City, Embracing the Boroughs of Manhattan and the Bronx, 1916, Vol. 129. New York: Trow Press, 1916.

R. L. Polk & Co's 1918 Trow General Directory of New York City Boroughs of Manhattan and Bronx, Vol. 130. New York: R. L. Polk, 1918.

R. L. Polk & Co's 1920 Trow's New York City Directory, Boroughs of Manhattan and Bronx, Vol. 132. New York: R. L. Polk, 1920.

R. L. Polk & Co's 1925 Trow's New York City Directory, Boroughs of Manhattan and Bronx, Vol. 137. New York: R. L. Polk, 1925.

Trow's General Directory of the Boroughs of Manhattan and Bronx, City of New York, Vol. 124, for the year ending August 1, 1911. New York: Trow City Directory, 1910.

Trow's New York City Directory, 1876–1877. New York: J. F. Trow, 1877.

Trow's New York City Directory, compiled by H. Wilson, Vol. 78, for the Year ending May 1, 1865. New York: J. F. Trow, 1865.

Trow's New York City Directory, compiled by H. Wilson, Vol. 84, for the year ending May 1, 1871. New York: John F. Trow, 1871.

Trow's New York City Directory, compiled by H. Wilson, Vol. 93, for the year ending May 1, 1880, vol. M–Z. New York: John F. Trow, 1880.

Trow's New York City Directory, for the Year ending May 1, 1857. New York: J. F. Trow, 1857.

Trow's New York City Directory, Vol. 101, for the year ending May 1, 1888. New York: Trow City Directory, 1888.

Trow's New York City, Manhattan and Bronx City Directory, 1912, Vol. 125. New York: Trow City Directory, 1912.

Trow's New York Directory, 1880–1881, Vol. 94, for the year ending May 1, 1881. New York: Trow City Directory, 1881.

NEWSPAPERS

Brooklyn Daily Eagle

New York Times

New Yorker Staats-Zeitung

New Yorker Volkszeitung

New York Evening Post, Tammany Biographies, 3rd ed., rev. and enlarged. October 1894.

New York Herald

Washington Post

Evening Mail

The Sun

PRIMARY DOCUMENTS

"Addresses in Memory of Carl Schurz." New York: Committee of the Carl Schurz Memorial, Carnegie Hall, New York, November 21, 1906.

Adler, Cyrus, Max J. Kohler, Cyrus L. Sulzberger, and D. M. Hermalin, eds. "New York." In *Jewish Encyclopedia*. New York: Funk & Wagnalls Company, 1901–1906. Accessed September 4, 2017, http://www.jewishencyclopedia.com/articles/11501 -new-york#anchor30.

Annual Report of the Directors of Mount Sinai Hospital. New York: Thalmessinger and Mendham, January 1886.

Appleton's Dictionary of New York and Vicinity. New York: D. Appleton, 1879.

"August Schulze als Stumpredner." *Puck, illustrirtes humoristisches Wochenblatt* 20, no. 1 (September 4, 1895): 148.

Bericht über das Festessen zur Feier des 118-jährigen Bestehens der Deutschen Gesellschaft der Stadt New York, New York Turn Verein, Zur Jubelfeier seines 60 jahrigen Stiftungsfest, 1850–1910. Program, bound pamphlets, not cataloged. Call no. IEK n.s.: IEK n.c.5, New York Public Library.

Bericht über das Festessen zur Feier des 118-jährigen Bestehens der Deutschen Gesellschaft der Stadt New York: am 8. März 1902 im Hotel Waldorf-Astoria. New York: Deutsche Gesellschaft, 1902.

Berichte und Anträge für die Sechste Konvention des Deutsch-Amerikanischen National-Bundes, 6. Bis 10. Oktober 1911 in Washington, D.C. New York: Bericht des D. A. Staats-Verbandes, 1911.

Blake, E. Vale. *History of the Tammany Society*. New York: Souvenir, 1901.

Bokum, Hermann. *The Stranger's Gift: A Christmas and New Year's Present*. Boston: Light and Horton, 1836.

Bremer Verein Freimarkt, October 1898. German pamphlets, not catalogued. Call no. IEK n.s.8, New York Public Library.

Chapin, Robert Coit. *The Standard of Living among Workingmen's Families in New York City*. New York: Russell Sage Foundation, 1909.

City Club of New York. *Annual Report of the Secretary, April 3, 1895*.

Claghorn, Kate Holladay. Map to accompany report, "The Foreign Immigrant in New York City." In *Reports of the Industrial Commission*, vol. 15, 465–492. Washington, DC: Government Printing Office, 1901.

Cronau, Rudolf. *Denkschrift zum 150. jahrestag der Deutschen Gesellschaft der Stadt New York, 1784–1934*. New York: German Society of New York, 1934.

Der Deutsche Vorkämpfer [The German pioneer, also known as New Yorker echo and Rundschau zweier Welten]. New York: Viereck Pub., 1907–1910.

Devine, Edward T. *The Principles of Relief*. New York: Macmillan, 1904.

Ehret, George. *Twenty Five Years of Brewing, with an illustrated History of America Beer*. New York: Gast Lithograph & Engraving, 1891.

Evangelisch-Lutherisches Ministerium des Staates New York und angrezender Staaten und Lander, Einhundertneunundzwanzisgste Versammulung 1919. Report, Evangelisch-Lutherischen Zions Kirche, Rochester, NY, 16–20 Juni 1919, Parochial-Berichte und Statistik, 1918–1919, 78–92, Lutheran Synod, Sutter Archives, Horrimann Library, Wagner College, Staten Island, NY.

Faust, Albert Bernhardt. *The German Element in the United States*. Vol. 2. Boston: Houghton Mifflin, Riverside Press, 1909.

Fried, Alfred H. *The German Emperor and the Peace of the World*. New York: Hodder and Stoughton, 1912.

Graham, Robert. *Liquordom in New York City*. New York, 1883.

Gustav Scholer Papers. New York Public Library, Manuscripts Division.

Heinrich, Charles. "Prince Henry of Prussia in America, Historical Review of His Royal Highness' American Travels." *German American Annals* 2, no. 5 (1903): 270–271.

Hexamer, Charles J. "Monument at Germantown." Hearing before the Committee on the Library of the House of Representatives. Washington, DC: Government Printing Office, 1910.

Historical and Genealogical Record Dutchess and Putnam Counties New York. New York: A. V. Haight, 1912.

Honthumb, C. A. *Amerikanische Humoresken*. New York: E. Steiger, 1886.

Jahresbericht der Direction der Hamburg-Amerika Aktien-Gesellschaft, bestimmt für die General-Versammlung der Actionaire am 30. März 1882. Bremerhaven, Germany: Deutsches Schiffahrtsmuseum Bibliothek, 1882.

Journal for the Seventeenth Annual Excursion, St. Mark's Evangelical Lutheran Church, 323–327 Sixth Street, New York, Wednesday, June 15, 1904. New York Public Library.

Kapp, Friedrich. *Geschichte der Deutschen im staate New York bis zum anfange des neunzehnten jahrhunderts*. New York: E. Steiger 1884. Originally published in 1867.

King, Moses. *Notable New Yorkers of 1896–1899, a Companion Volume to King's Handbook of New York City*. New York: M. King, 1899.

Körner, Gustav Philipp. *Das deutsche Element in den Vereinigten Staaten von Nordamerika, 1818–1848*. New York: E. Steiger, 1884.

Landsmannschaften Verein festival programs. German pamphlets, not cataloged. Call no. IEK n.s. vols 1–9, New York Public Library.

Learned, M. D. "German Day in New York." *German American Annals* 5 (1903): 32–38.

Lening, Gustav. "Die Emigranten Schwindler." In *Die Nachtseiten von New York und dessen Verbrecherwelt, von der Fünften Avenue bis zu den Five Points*, 2nd ed., 533. New York: S. Bickel, 1881.

Leonard, John W. *Who's Who in Finance, Banking and Insurance: A Biographical Dictionary of Contemporaries*. New York: Who's Who in Finance, 1925.

"List of attendees by table, Dinner given by the mayor of NY in honor of The Officers of His Imperial German Majesty's Squadron at the Waldorf Astoria, June 10, 1912." Germans in the United States, bound pamphlets, not cataloged. Call no. IEK n.s.: n.s. 8, New York Public Library.

Manson, George J. "The Foreign Element in New York City—the Germans." Supplement, *Harper's Weekly* 32, no. 1650 (August 4, 1888): 582–591.

Marbach, Johannes. *Die heilige Weihnachtszeit nach Bedeutung, Geschichte, Sitten und Symbolen*. Frankfurt/Main, Germany: J. D. Saulerländer, 1858.

McCabe, James Dabney. *Lights and Shadows of New York Life: or, the Sights and Sensations of the Great City*. New York: Continental Publishing, 1873.

Meyer, B. H. "Fraternal Beneficiary Societies in the United States." *American Journal of Sociology* 6 (March 1901): 646–651.

Myers, Gustav. *The History of Tammany Hall*. New York: Boni and Liverright, 1917.

"New York Herald's Complete and Alphabetical List of Names and Addresses of the German Alien Enemies Registered in New York City in the State Military Census." *New York Herald*, June 1917.

New York Liederkranz Society History Committee. *History of the Liederkranz of New York City, 1847–1947, and of the Arion, of New York*. New York: Drechsler, 1948.

New York Turn Verein. *Zur Jubelfeier seines 60 jahrigen Stiftungsfest, 1850–1910*. Germans in the United States, bound pamphlets, not cataloged. Call no. IEK n.s.: IEK n.c.5, New York Public Library.

Official Program of the Convention of the German American State Alliance of New York, and the Celebration of German Day, June 22, 23, and 24, 1907. New-York Historical Society.

Ogilvie, J. S. *History of the General Slocum disaster by which nearly 1200 lives were lost by the burning of the steamer General Slocum in Hell gate, New York harbor, June 15, 1904*. New York: J. S. Ogilvie, 1904.

One Hundred and Fifty Years, 1852–2002, the Harmonie Club. New-York Historical Society. New York: Harmonie Club, 2002.

Pachmayr, Joseph. *Leben und Treiben der Stadt New-York: mit Hinweis auf die Einwanderung und das deutsche Element: kulturhistorische Bilder*. Hamburg: H. Grüning, 1874.

Palmer, A. Emerson. *The New York Public School, Being a History of Free Education in the City of New York*. London, UK: Macmillan, 1905.

Phelps, Henry P. *New York State Legislative Souvenir for 1893, with Portraits of the Members of Both Houses*. Albany, NY: Phelps and Kellogg, 1893.

——. *New York State Legislative Souvenir for 1894, with Portraits of the Members of Both Houses*. Albany, NY: Phelps and Kellogg, 1894.

Pierce, F. E. *The Tenement-House Committee Maps*. New York: Harper and Brothers, 1895.

"Professor Learneds Rede, Der Deutsche Verein als Pflegestette der Deutschen Kultur in Amerika." *German American Annals* 14 (1912): 249–255.

Protokoll der Vierten Konvention des Deutsch-Amerikanischen National-Bundes der Ver. Staaten Von Amerika, Abgehalten vom 4. Bis 7. Oktober 1907 im Terrace Garden zu New York, N.Y. New York: National German-American Alliance, 1907.

Ridder, Herman. *Hyphenations: A Collection of Articles on the World War of 1914 which Have Appeared from Time to Time in the New-Yorker Staats-Zeitung under "The War Situation from Day to Day."* New York: Max Schmetterling, 1915.

Rittig, Johann. *Federzeichnungen aus dem Amerikanischen Stadtleben*. New York: Ernst Steiger, 1884.

Salem, F. W. *Beer, It's History and Its Economic Value as a National Beverage*. Hartford, CT: F. W. Salem, 1880.

Schlegel, Carl Wilhelm. *Schlegel's German-American Families in the United States: Genealogical and Biographical, Illustrated*. Vols. 1–3. New York: American Historical Society, 1916–1918.

Schluter, Hermann. *The Brewing Industry and the Brewery Workers' Movement in America*. Reddich, UK: Read Books, 2017, originally printed by the International Union of United Brewery Workmen of America, 1910.

Schrader, Frederick Franklin. *1683–1920*. New York: Concord, 1920.

Seibel, George. "The Hyphen in American History." Address reproduced from the *New Yorker Staats-Zeitung*, September 4, 1916. Germans in the United States, bound pamphlets, not cataloged. Call no. IEK n.s. IEK n.c.5., New York Public Library.

Shanks, Charles G. *The State Government for 1879*. Albany, NY: Weed, Parsons, 1879.

Shaw, William H. *History of Essex and Hudson Counties, New Jersey*. Vol. 2, *Charles B. Brush, City of Hoboken*. Philadelphia: Everts and Peck, 1884.

Smith, Matthew Hale. *Sunshine and Shadow in New York*. Hartford, CT: J. B. Burr, 1869.

Solger, Reinhold. *Anton in Amerika. Novelle aus dem deutsch-amerikanischen Leben*. New York: E. Steiger, 1872.

Spengler, Otto. "Das New Yorker Deutschtum von heute." In *Das deutsche Element der Stadt New York, biographisches Jahrbuch der Deutsch-Amerikaner New Yorks und Umgebung*, 13–15. New York: Spengler, 1913.

Steiger, Ernst. *Dreiundfünfzig jahre buchhändler in Deutschland und Amerika. Erinnerungen und plaudereien, zur verbreitung in engerem kreise niedergeschrieben von Ernst Steiger*. New York: Ernst Steiger, 1901.

Steiger's Catalog deutscher Bühnenstücke. New York: E. Steiger, 1900.

Steiger's Dramatic Catalog 25. New York: E. Steiger, 1900.

Steiger's Theater Catalog 24. New York: E. Steiger, 1876.

Stürenburg, Casper. "Das Friedesfest in New-York vom 9. Bis 11. April." In *Die Deutschen in Amerika und die deutsch-amerikanischen friedensfeste im jahr 1871*, 38–66. New York: Verlags-expedition des Deutsch-amerikanischen conversations-lexicons, 1871.

———. *Klein-Deutschland: Bilder aus dem New Yorker Alltagsleben.* New York: Ernst Steiger, 1885.

Stürenburg, Casper, and Ernst Steiger. *Auskunft und Rath für Deutsch-Amerikaner in den wichtigsten Fragen des öffentlichen, Rechts-, Geschäfts- und Privat-Lebens / zusammengestellt und herausgegeben von C. Stürenburg und E. Steiger.* New York: E. Steiger, 1888.

The Year Book of the United State Brewers' Association. New York: United States Brewers Association, 1909.

Thiess, K. "Die Entwicklung der Hamburg-Amerika Linie von 1847 bis 1901." In *Jahrbücher fur Nationalökonomie und Statistik [Journal of Economics and Statistics]*, Folge III, Band 21 [Series 3, Vol. 21]: 816–826. Jena, Gustav Fischer, 1901.

Tough, Rosalind, and Sophia M. Robison. "Yorkville, American Community and Melting Pot." *Journal of Land and Public Utility Economics* 19, no. 3 (August 1943): 257–258.

Van Winkle, Daniel. *History of Municipalities of Hudson County, 1630–1923.* Vol. 1, *Historical-Biographical.* Chicago: Lewis Historical, 1924.

Viereck, Louis. *Leitfaden für deutsche Einwanderer nach den Vereinigten Staaten von Amerika.* New York: Deutsche Gesellschaft, 1903.

Vierten Konvention des Deutsch-Amerikanischen National-Bundes der Ver. Staaten Von Amerika, Abgehalten vom 4. Bis 7. Oktober 1907 im Terrace Garden zu New York, N.Y. New York: National German-American Alliance, 1907.

von Skal, George. *History of German Immigration in the United States and Successful German-Americans and Their Descendants.* New York: Frederick T. Smiley, 1910.

Wenner, George U. *The Lutherans of New York: Their Story and Their Problems.* New York: Petersfield Press, 1918.

World War I newspaper scrapbook. Hoboken Library, Hoboken, New Jersey.

Secondary Sources

Aimone, Francesco. "The 1918 Influenza Epidemic in New York City: A Review of the Public Health Response." *Public Health Reports* 125, no. S3 (2010): 71–79.

Albion, Robert Greenhalgh. *The Rise of New York Port, 1815–1860.* New York: Charles Scribner's Sons, 1939.

Allerfeldt, Kristofer. "'And We Got Here First': Albert Johnson, National Origins and Self-Interest in the Immigration Debate of the 1920s." *Journal of Contemporary History* 45, no. 1 (January 2010): 7–26.

Anbinder, Tyler. *City of Dreams: The 400-Year Epic History of Immigrant New York.* New York: Houghton Mifflin Harcourt, 2016.

Ashkenazi, Elliott. "Joseph Seligman." In *Immigrant Entrepreneurship, German-American Business Biographies, 1720 to the Present*, Vol. 2, edited by William J. Hausman. Washington, DC: German Historical Institute, 2013. Accessed February 27, 2018, https://www.immigrantentrepreneurship.org/entry.php?rec=184.

Baily, Samuel L. *Immigrants in the Land of Promise: Italians in Buenos Aires and New York City, 1870–1914*. Ithaca, NY: Cornell University Press, 1999.

Baldwin, Ian. "Harry Cohn." In *Immigrant Entrepreneurship, German-American Business Biographies, 1720 to the Present*, Vol. 4, edited by Jeffrey Fear. Washington, DC: German Historical Institute, 2011. Accessed February 19, 2019, https://www.immigrantentrepreneurship.org/entries/harry-cohn-man-mogul-and-myth/.

Barber, Marion J. "Herman Ridder." *Immigrant Entrepreneurship, the German-American Business Biography, 1720 to the Present*, Vol. 3, edited by Giles R. Hoyt. Washington, DC: German Historical Institute, 2015. Accessed June 27, 2021, https://www.immigrantentrepreneurship.org/entries/herman-ridder/.

Barr, Jason, and Teddy Ort. "Population Density across the City: The Case of 1900 Manhattan*." (2014).

Barr, Jason M. *Building the Skyline: The Birth and Growth of Manhattan's Skyscrapers*. Accessed March 22, 2028. http://buildingtheskyline.org/figure-pop-density-race-ethnicity-1890/ and http://buildingtheskyline.org/figure-population-density-race-ethnicity-1900/.

Barrett, James R. *The Irish Way: Becoming American in the Multiethnic City*. London, UK: Penguin, 2012.

Bayor, Ronald H. *Neighbors in Conflict: The Irish, Germans, Jews and Italians of New York City*. 2nd ed. Urbana: University of Illinois Press, 1988.

Beckert, Sven. "The Monied Metropolis: New York City and the Consolidation of the American Bourgeoisie, 1850–1896." In *Class: The Anthology*, edited by Stanley Aronowitz and Michael J. Roberts, 393–411. Hoboken, NJ: John Wiley and Sons, 2017.

Benbow, Mark. "German Immigrants in the United States Brewing Industry 1940–1895." In *Immigrant Entrepreneurship, German-American Business Biographies, 1720 to the Present*, Vol. 2, edited by William J. Hausman. Washington, DC: German Historical Institute, 2017. Accessed November 3, 2017, https://www.immigrantentrepreneurship.org/entry.php?rec=284.

Bergquist, James M. "German Communities in American Cities. An Interpretation of the 19th Century Experience." *Journal of American Ethnic History* 4 (1984/1985): 9–30.

Blumin, Stuart Mack. *The Emergence of the Middle Class: Social Experience in the American City, 1760–1900*. Cambridge, UK: Cambridge University Press, 1989.

Bonner, Thomas N. *American Doctors and German Universities: A Chapter in International Intellectual Relations, 1870–1914*. Lincoln: University of Nebraska Press, 1963.

Bretting, Agnes. "Deutsche Siedlungsviertel in New York City 1830–1930." In *Auswanderung und Schiffartsinteressen/"Little Germanies" in New York/Deutscha-merikanishe Gesellschaften*, edited by Michael Just, Agnes Bretting, and Hartmut Bickelmann, 57–104. Stuttgart, Germany: Franz Steiner, 1992.

———. "Organizing German Immigration: The Role of State Authority in Germany and the United States." In *Americans and the Germans, An Assessment of a Three-Hundred-Year History, Vol. 1: Immigration, Language, Ethnicity*, edited by Frank Trommler and Joseph McVeigh, 25–40. Philadelphia: University of Pennsylvania, 1985.

———. *Soziale Probleme deutscher Einwanderer in New York City 1800–1860. Social Problems of German Immigrants in New York City, 1800–1860*. Stuttgart, Germany: Peter Steiner, 1981.

Brinkmann, Tobias. "Jews, Germans, or Americans: German-Jewish Immigrants in the Nineteenth-Century United States." In *The Heimat Abroad: The Boundaries of Germanness*, edited by Krista O'Donnell, Renate Bridenthal, and Nancy R. Reagin, 11–40. Ann Arbor: University of Michigan Press, 2005.

———. "'We Are Brothers! Let Us Separate!' Jews and Community Building in American Cities during the 19th Century." *History Compass* 11, no. 10 (October 2013): 869–879.

Bungert, Heike. *Festkultur und Gedächtnis, Die Konstruktion einer deutschamerikanischen Ethnizität, 1848–1914*. Paderborn, Germany: Ferdinand Schöningh, 2016.

Bungert, Heike, Cora Lee Kluge, and Robert C. Ostergren, eds. *Wisconsin German Land and Life*. Madison, WI: Max Kade Institute for German-American Studies, 2006.

Burrows, Edwin G., and Mike Wallace. *Gotham: A History of New York City to 1898*. New York: Oxford University Press, 1999.

Caso, Frank. "Marcus Loew." In *Immigrant Entrepreneurship, German-American Business Biographies, 1720 to the Present*, Vol. 4, edited by Jeffrey Fear. Washington, DC: German Historical Institute, 2011. Accessed February 19, 2019, https://www.immigrantentrepreneurship.org/entries/marcus-loew/.

Casway, Herold I. *The Culture and Ethnicity of Nineteenth Century Baseball*. Jefferson, NC: McFarland, 2017.

Cecil, Lamar. *Albert Ballin: Business and Politics in Imperial Germany, 1888–1918*. Princeton, NJ: Princeton University Press, 1967.

Chmelik, Samantha. "Frederick Rueckheim." In *Immigrant Entrepreneurship, German-American Business Biographies, 1720 to the Present*, Vol. 4, edited by Jeffrey Fear. Washington, DC: German Historical Institute, 2013. Accessed September 4, 2019. https://www.immigrantentrepreneurship.org/entry.php?rec=158.

Clark, Christopher. *The Sleepwalkers: How Europe Went to War in 1914*. New York: Harper Collins, 1912.

Clark, Cindy Dell. *Flights of Fancy, Leaps of Faith: Children's Myths in Contemporary America*. Chicago: University of Chicago Press, 1998.

Clark, Geoffrey W. "An Interpretation of Hoboken's Population Trends, 1856–1970." In *Hoboken: A Collection of Essays*, edited by Edward Halsey Foster and Geoffrey W. Clark, 47–62. New York: Irvington, 1975.

———. "The Progressives vs. The Political Machine in Hoboken, 1911–1915." In *Hoboken: A Collection of Essays*, edited by Edward Halsey Foster and Geoffrey W. Clark, 63–80. New York: Irvington, 1975.

Clawson, Mary Ann. *Constructing Brotherhood: Class, Gender, and Fraternalism*. Princeton, NJ: Princeton University Press, 1989.

Coffman, Edward M. *The War to End All Wars: The American Military Experience in World War I*. Oxford: Oxford University Press, 1968.

Cohn, Raymond L. *Mass Migration under Sail: European Immigration to the Antebellum United States*. Cambridge, UK: Cambridge University Press, 2009.

Connolly, James J. *An Elusive Unity: Urban Democracy and Machine Politics in Industrializing America*. Ithaca, NY: Cornell University Press, 2010.

Conolly-Smith, Peter. "Prose Pictures of Kleindeutschland: German-Language Local-Color Serials of the late Nineteenth Century." In *Transnationalism and American Serial Fiction*, edited by Patricia Okker, 84–110. New York: Routledge, 2012.

———. *Translating America: An Immigrant Press Visualizes American Popular Culture, 1895–1918*. Washington, DC: Smithsonian Institution, 2004.

Conzen, Kathleen Neils. "German-Americans and the Invention of Ethnicity." In
     Americans and the Germans: An Assessment of a Three-Hundred-Year History, vol. 1,
     Immigration, Language, Ethnicity, edited by Frank Trommler and Joseph
     McVeigh, 131–147. Philadelphia: University of Pennsylvania, 1985.
———. *Immigrant Milwaukee: Accommodation and Community in a Frontier City.*
     Cambridge, MA: Harvard University Press, 1976.
———. "Immigrants, Immigrant Neighborhoods, and Ethnic Identity." *Journal of*
     American History 66, no. 3 (December 1979): 603–615.
———. *Making Their Own America: Assimilation Theory and the German Peasant*
     Pioneer. German Historical Institute, Annual Lecture Series, no. 3. Providence, RI:
     Berg, 1990.
———. "Phantom Landscapes of Colonization: Germans in the Making of a Pluralist
     America." In *The German-American Encounter: Conflict and Cooperation between*
     Two Cultures, 1800–2000, edited by Frank Trommler and Elliott Shore, 7–21. New
     York: Berghahn Books, 2001.
Cudahy, Brian J. *Over and Back: The History of Ferryboats in New York Harbor.* New
     York: Fordham University Press, 1990.
Cuff, Robert D. "Herbert Hoover: The Ideology of Voluntarism and War Organ-
     ization during the Great War." *Journal of American History* 64, no. 2 (Septem-
     ber 1977): 358–372.
Czitrom, Daniel. *New York Exposed: The Gilded Age Police Scandal that Launched the*
     Progressive Era. New York: Oxford University Press, 2016.
———. "Underworlds and Underdogs: Big Tim Sullivan and Metropolitan Politics in
     New York, 1889–1913." *Journal of American History* 78, no. 2 (September 1991):
     536–558.
Deltas, George, Richard Sicotte, and Peter Tomczak. "Passenger Shipping Cartels and
     Their Effect on Trans-Atlantic Migration." *Review of Economics and Statistics* 90,
     no. 1 (February 2008): 119–133.
Demm, Eberhard. "Censorship." In *The International Encyclopedia of the First World*
     War, version 2.0, updated March 29, 2017. https://encyclopedia.1914-1918-online
     .net/article/censorship.
Diamonstein, Barbaralee. *The Landmarks of New York.* New York: Harry Abrams,
     1998.
Dobbert, Guido Andre. *The Disintegration of an Immigrant Community: The*
     Cincinnati Germans, 1870–1920. New York: Arno, 1980.
Doerries, Reinhard R. "German Transatlantic Migration from the Early 19th Century
     to the Outbreak of World War II." In *Population, Labour and Migration in*
     19th and 20th Century Germany, edited by Klaus J. Bade, 115–134. Oxford: Oxford
     University Press, 1987.
———. *Imperial Challenge: Ambassador Count Bernstorff and German-American*
     Relations, 1908–1917. Translated by Christa D. Shannon. Chapel Hill: University of
     North Carolina Press, 1989.
Dolan, Jay P. *The Immigrant Church: New York's Irish and German Catholics,*
     1815–1865. Baltimore: Johns Hopkins University Press, 1975.
Dolkart, Andrew S. "The Biography of a Lower East Side Tenement; 97 Orchard
     Street." Tenement Museum. Accessed February 17, 2021. https://tenement.org
     /documents/Dolkart.pdf.
Doyle, Robert C. "Over There and Over Here: Enemy Prisoners of War and Prisoners
     of State in the Great War." In *The Enemy in Our Hands: America's Treatment of*

Enemy Prisoners of War from the Revolution to the War on Terror, 159–178. Lexington: University Press of Kentucky, 2010.

Dwyer, Tessa. "Universally Speaking: *Lost in Translation* and Polyglot Cinema." *Linguistica Antverpiensia* 4 (2005): 295–310.

Eichhoff, Jürgen. "The German Language in America." In *Americans and the Germans: An Assessment of a Three-Hundred-Year History*, Vol. 1, *Immigration, Language, Ethnicity*, edited by Frank Trommler and Joseph McVeigh, 223–240. Philadelphia: University of Pennsylvania, 1985.

Feeley, Kathleen A. "Irving Thalberg." In *Immigrant Entrepreneurship, German-American Business Biographies, 1720 to the Present*, Vol. 4, edited by Jeffrey Fear. Washington, DC: German Historical Institute, 2011. Accessed February 19, 2019, https://www.immigrantentrepreneurship.org/entries/irving-thalberg/.

Fischer, David Hackett. *Albion's Seed: Four British Folkways in America*. Oxford: Oxford University Press, 1889.

Fisher, James T. *On the Irish Waterfront: The Crusader, the Movie, and the Soul of the Port of New York*. Ithaca, NY: Cornell University Press, 2009.

Fleming, Thomas. *The Illusion of Victory: America in World War I*. New York: Basic Books, 2003.

Foner, Nancy, ed. *Wounded City: The Social Impact of 9/11 on New York City*. New York: Russell Sage Foundation, 2005.

Ford, Nancy Gentile. *Americans All! Foreign-Born Soldiers in World War I*. College Station: Texas A&M University Press, 2001.

Fronc, Jennifer. *New York Undercover: Private Surveillance in the Progressive Era*. Chicago: University of Chicago Press, 2009.

Furer, Howard B. "'Heaven, Hell or Hoboken': The Effects of World War I on a New Jersey City," *New Jersey History* 92, no. 3 (Autumn 1974): 147–169.

Gale, Neil. "The History of Charles 'Carl' Frederick Günther, Known as 'The Candy Man' and 'The P. T. Barnum of Chicago.'" *Digital Research Library of Illinois History Journal* (blog), October 20, 2017. https://drloihjournal.blogspot.com/2017/10/the-history-of-charles-carl-frederick.html.

Geitz, Henry, Jürgen Heideking, and Jurgen Herbst, eds. *German Influences on Education in the United States to 1917*. Washington, DC: German Historical Institute, 1995.

Gerlach, Larry R. "German Americans in Major League Baseball: Sport and Acculturation." In *The American Game: Baseball and Ethnicity*, edited by Lawrence Baldassaro and Richard A. Johnson, 27–54. Carbondale: Southern Illinois University Press, 2002.

Gerstenberger, Heide, and Ulrich Welke. *Vom Wind zum Dampf: Sozialgeschichte der deutschen Handelsschiffahrt im Zeitalter der Industrialisierung*. Münster, Germany: Westfälisches Dampfboot, 1996.

Gerstle, Gary. *American Crucible: Race and Nation in the Twentieth Century*. Princeton, NJ: Princeton University Press, 2001.

Gleason, Philip. *Conservative Reformers: German American Catholics and the Social Orders*. Notre Dame, IN: University of Notre Dame Press, 1968.

Goldberg, Bettina. "The Forty-Eighters and the School System in America: The Theory and Practice of Reform." In *The German Forty-Eighters in the United States*, edited by Charlotte L. Barncaforte, 203–218. New York: Peter Lang, 1989.

Golway, Terry. *Machine Made: Tammany Hall and the Creation of Modern American Politics*. New York: W. W. Norton, 2014.

Gordon, Milton M. *Assimilation in American Life: The Role of Race, Religion, and National Origins*. New York: Oxford University Press, 1964.

Goyens, Tom. *Beer and Revolution: The German Anarchist Movement in New York City, 1880–1914*. Urbana: University of Illinois Press, 2007.

Grieves, Kevin. "'It Would Be for the Best to Suspend Publication': The German-American Press and Anti-German Hysteria during World War I." *American Journalism* 37, no. 1 (2020): 47–65.

Gross, Stephen J. "'Perils of Prussianism': Main Street German America, Local Autonomy, and the Great War." *Agricultural History* 78, no. 1 (Winter 2004): 78–116.

Gurock, Jeffrey S., ed. *Central European Jews in America, 1840–1880: Migration and Advancement*. New York: Routledge, 1998.

———. *Jews in Gotham: New York Jews in a Changing City, 1920–2010*. New York: New York University Press, 2012.

———. *The Jews of Harlem: The Rise, Decline and Revival of a Jewish Community*. New York: New York University Press, 2016.

Haberstroh, Richard. *The German Churches of Metropolitan New York: A Research Guide*. New York: New York Genealogical and Biographical Society, 2000.

Haenni, Sabine. *The Immigrant Scene: Ethnic Amusements in New York, 1880–1920*. Minneapolis: University of Minnesota, 2008.

Hammack, David C. *Power and Society: Greater New York at the Turn of the Century*. New York: Columbia University Press, 1987.

Hawgood, John A. *The Tragedy of German-America*. New York: G. P. Putnam's Sons, 1940.

Heinmiller, Gary L., ed. *Craft Masonry in Manhattan, New York County, New York, Vol. IV, Lodges Nos. 512 thru 698*. Onondaga and Oswego Masonic Districts Historical Societies, 2011. Accessed June 19, 2021, https://hobbydocbox.com/70521439-Investors_and_Patents/Craft-masonry-in-manhattan-new-york-county-new-york-approximately-350-lodges.html.

Helbich, Wolfgang, and Walter D. Kamphoefner, eds. *German-American Immigration and Ethnicity in Comparative Perspective*. Madison, WI: Max Kade Institute for German-American Studies, 2004.

Henderson, Thomas M. *Tammany Hall and the New Immigrants: The Progressive Years*. New York: Arno, 1976.

Herbst, Jurgen. *The German Historical School in American Scholarship: A Study in the Transfer of Culture*. Ithaca, NY: Cornell University Press, 1965.

Higham, John. *Send These to Me: Immigrants in Urban America*. Rev. ed. Baltimore: Johns Hopkins University Press, 1984.

———. *Strangers in the Land: Patterns of American Nativism, 1860–1925*. 3rd ed. New Brunswick, NJ: Rutgers University Press, 1994.

Hopkin, Deian. "Domestic Censorship in the First World War," *Journal of Contemporary History* 5, no. 4 (1970): 151–169.

Houghtaling, Ted. "Witness to Tragedy: The Sinking of the General Slocum," New-York Historical Society, *From the Stacks* (blog). Accessed May 24, 2018, http://blog.nyhistory.org/witness-to-tragedy-the-sinking-of-the-general-slocum/.

Hueston, R. F. "The Assimilation of German Immigrants into a Pennsylvania German Township, 1840–1900." *Pennsylvania Magazine of History and Biography* 133, no. 1 (2009): 59–88.

Huffines, Marion L. "Language-Maintenance Efforts among German Immigrants and Their Descendants in the United States." In *Americans and the Germans: An*

Assessment of a Three-Hundred-Year History, Vol. 1, *Immigration, Language, Ethnicity*, edited by Frank Trommler and Joseph McVeigh, 241–250. Philadelphia: University of Pennsylvania, 1985.

Hutchins, John G. B. *The American Maritime Industries and Public Policy: An Economic History*. New York: Russell and Russell, 1941.

Immerso, Michael. *Coney Island: The People's Playground*. New Brunswick, NJ: Rutgers University Press, 2002.

Jaffe, Steven H. *New York at War: Four Centuries of Combat, Fear, and Intrigue in Gotham*. New York: Basic Books, 2012.

Johnson, Charles Thomas. *Culture at Twilight: The National German-American Alliance, 1901–1918*. New York: Peter Lang, 1999.

Jou, Chin. "Contesting Nativism: The New York Congressional Delegation's Case against the Immigration Act of 1924." *Federal History* 2 (2011): 66–79.

Joyce, Simon, and Jennifer Putzi. "Adam Kessel." In *Immigrant Entrepreneurship, German-American Business Biographies, 1720 to the Present*, Vol. 4, edited by Jeffrey Fear. Washington, DC: German Historical Institute, 2016. Accessed February 19, 2019. https://www.immigrantentrepreneurship.org/entries/adam-kessel/.

Just, Michael. *Auswanderung und Schiffahrtsinteressen* [Emigration and Shipping Interests]. In *Auswanderung und Schiffartsinteressen/"Little Germanies" in New York/Deutschamerikanishe Gesellschaften*, edited by Michael Just, Agnes Bretting, and Hartmut Bickelmann, 1–56. Stuttgart, Germany: Franz Steiner, 1992.

Kamphoefner, Walter. "The German Component to American Industrialization 1840–1893." In *Immigrant Entrepreneurship, German-American Business Biographies, 1720 to the Present*, Vol. 2, edited by William J. Hausman. Washington, DC: German Historical Institute, 2014. Accessed May 21, 2019, https://www.immigrantentrepreneurship.org/entry.php?rec=189.

Kazal, Russell A. *Becoming Old Stock: The Paradox of German American Identity*. Princeton, NJ: Princeton University Press, 2004.

———. "Revisiting Assimilation: The Rise, Fall, and Reappraisal of a Concept in American Ethnic History." *American Historical Review* 100 (April 1995): 437–471.

Keil, Hartmut. "German Immigrant Workers in Nineteenth-Century America: Working-Class Culture and Everyday Life in an Urban Industrial Setting." In *Americans and the Germans, An Assessment of a Three-Hundred-Year History*, Vol. 1, *Immigration, Language, Ethnicity*, edited by Frank Trommler and Joseph McVeigh, 189–206. Philadelphia: University of Pennsylvania, 1985.

———. "The German Immigrant Working Class of Chicago, 1875–90: Workers, Labor Leaders, and the Labor Movement." In *American Labor and Immigration History, 1877–1920s: Recent European Research*, edited by Dirk Hoerder, 156–176. Urbana: University of Illinois Press, 1983.

———. "German Working-Class Radicalism from the 1870s to World War I." In *Struggle a Hard Battle: Essays on Working Class Immigrants*, edited by Dirk Hoerder, 71–94. DeKalb: Northern Illinois University Press, 1986.

Keil, Hartmut, and John B. Jentz, eds. *German Workers in Industrial Chicago, 1850–1910: A Comparative Perspective*. DeKalb: Northern Illinois University Press, 1983.

Keller, Phyllis. *States of Belonging: German-American Intellectuals during the First World War*. Cambridge, MA: Harvard University Press, 1979.

Kelly, Joseph F. *The Feast of Christmas*. Collegeville, MN: Liturgical, 2010.

Kelly, Mary C. *The Shamrock and the Lily: The New York Irish and the Creation of a Transatlantic Identity, 1845–1921*. New York: Peter Lang, 2005.

Kennedy, David M. *Over Here: The First World War and American Society*. Oxford: Oxford University Press, 1980.

King, Gilbert. "A Spectacle of Horror—the Burning of the General Slocum." *Smithsonian Magazine*. Accessed May 24, 2028, https://www.smithsonianmag .com/history/a-spectacle-of-horror-the-burning-of-the-general-slocum-104712974/.

Kirschbaum, Erik. *Burning Beethoven: The Eradication of German Culture in the United States during World War I*. Berlin, Germany: Berlinca, 2015.

———. *The Eradication of German Culture in the United States: 1917–1918*. Stuttgart, Germany: Academic, 1986.

Kobbé, Gustav. *The Complete Opera Book*. London, UK: Putnam, 1929.

Koegel, John. *Music in German Immigrant Theater in New York City, 1840–1940*. Rochester, NY: University of Rochester Press, 2009.

Koegel, John, and Jonas Westover. "Beethoven and Beer: Orchestral Music in German Beer Gardens in Nineteenth-Century New York City." In *American Orchestras in the Nineteenth Century*, edited by John Spitzer, 130–155. Chicago: University of Chicago Press, 2012.

Kulikoff, Allan. *From British Peasants to Colonial American Farmers*. Chapel Hill: University of North Carolina Press, 2000.

Lapham, James Sigurd. "The German-Americans of New York City 1860–1890." PhD diss., St. John's University, 1977.

Leuchs, Fritz. *The Early German Theatre in New York, 1840–1872*. 1928. Reprint, New York: AMS Press, 1966.

Levine, Bruce. *The Spirit of 1848: German Immigrants, Labor Conflict, and the Coming of the Civil War*. Urbana: University of Illinois Press, 1980.

Lieberman, Richard K. *Steinway and Sons*. New Haven, CT: Yale University Press, 1995.

Lifflander, Matthew L. *The Impeachment of Governor William Sulzer: A Story of American Politics*. New York: SUNY Press, 2012.

Little, Branden. "Evacuating Wartime Europe: US policy, Strategy, and Relief Operations for Overseas American Travelers, 1914–1915." *Journal of Military History* 79, no. 4 (October 2015): 929–958.

Logan, John R., and Hyoung-jin Shin. "Assimilation by the Third Generation? Marital Choices of White Ethnics at the Dawn of the Twentieth Century." *Social Science Research* 41, no. 5 (September 1912). https://www.ncbi.nlm.nih.gov/pmc/articles /PMC3807942/#R26.

Lowell, S. D. *The Presidential Election of 1916*. Carbondale: Southern Illinois University Press, 1980.

Ludanyi, Renate. "German in the USA." In *Language Diversity in the USA*, edited by Kim Potowski, 146–163. Cambridge, UK: Cambridge University Press, 2010.

Luebke, Frederick C. *Bonds of Loyalty: German-Americans and World War I*. DeKalb: Northern Illinois University Press, 1974.

———. "German Immigrants and American Politics: Problems of Leadership, Parties, and Issues." In *Germans in America: Retrospect and Prospect; Tricentennial Lectures Delivered at the German Society of Pennsylvania in 1983*, edited by Randall M. Miller, 57–74. Philadelphia: German Society of Pennsylvania, 1984.

———. *Germans in the New World: Essays in the History of Immigration*. Urbana: University of Illinois Press, 1999.

Malt, Ulrik F. "Traumatic Effects of Accidents." In *Individual and Community Responses to Trauma and Disasters: The Structure of Human Chaos*, edited by

Robert J. Ursano, Brian G. McCaughey, and Carol S. Fullerton, 103–135. Cambridge, UK: Cambridge University Press, 1995.

McClymer, John. "Of 'Mornin Glories' and 'Fine Old Oaks': John Purroy Mitchel, Al Smith, and Reform as an Expression of Irish American Aspiration." In *The New York Irish*, edited by Ronald H. Bayor and Timothy J. Meagher, 374–394. Baltimore: Johns Hopkins University Press, 1997.

McCrossen, Alexis. *Holy Day, Holiday: The American Sunday*. Ithaca, NY: Cornell University Press, 2001.

Messinger, Gary S. *British Propaganda and the State in the First World War*. Manchester, UK: Manchester University Press, 1992.

Meyers, Stephen L. *Manhattan's Lost Streetcars*. Mount Pleasant, SC: Arcadia, 2005.

Miller, Randall M., ed. *Germans in America*. Philadelphia: German Society of Pennsylvania, 1984.

Millman, Chad. *The Detonators: The Secret Plot to Destroy America and an Epic Hunt for Justice*. New York: Little, Brown, 2008.

Moltmann, Günter, ed. *Germans to America: 300 Years of Immigration, 1683–1983*. Stuttgart, Germany: Institute for Foreign Cultural Relations, 1982.

———. "The Pattern of German Emigration to the United States in the Nineteenth Century." In *Americans and the Germans: An Assessment of a Three-Hundred-Year History*, Vol. 1, *Immigration, Language, Ethnicity*, edited by Frank Trommler and Joseph McVeigh, 14–24. Philadelphia: University of Pennsylvania, 1985.

Moreno, Barry. "Castle Garden and Ellis Island: Doors to a New World." Essay for exhibit *Grüß Gott America, Good Bye Bayern*, Haus der Bayerischen Geschichte, Augsburg, Germany, September 2003. Accessed March 4, 2020, http://www.hdbg .de/auswanderung/docs/moreno_kat_e.pdf.

Morrow, Mary Sue. "Somewhere between Beer and Wagner: The Cultural and Musical Impact of German Männerchör in New York and New Orleans." In *Music and Culture in America, 1861–1918*, edited by Michael Saffle, 81–86. New York: Routledge, 2014.

Moynihan, Daniel Patrick, and Michael Glazer. *Beyond the Melting Pot: The Negroes, Puerto Ricans, Jews, Italians, and Irish of New York City*. Cambridge, MA: Harvard University Press, 1963.

Murphy, Paul L. *World War I and the Origin of Civil Liberties in the United States*. New York: W. W. Norton, 1979.

Mustea, Cristina Stanca. "Carl Laemmle." In *Immigrant Entrepreneurship, German-American Business Biographies, 1720 to the Present*, Vol. 4, edited by Jeffrey Fear. Washington, DC: German Historical Institute, 2011. Accessed February 19, 2019, https://www.immigrantentrepreneurship.org/entries/carl-laemmle/.

Nadel, Stanley. "The Forty-Eighters and the Politics of Class in New York City." In *The German Forty-Eighters in the United States*, edited by Charlotte L. Barncaforte, 51–66. New York: Peter Lang, 1989.

———. "The German Immigrant Left in the United States." In *The Immigrant Left in the United States*, edited by Paul Buhle and Dan Georgakas, 45–76. New York: SUNY Press, 1996.

———. "Jewish Race and German Soul in Nineteenth-Century America." In *Central European Jews in America, 1840–1880: Migration and Advancement*, edited by Jeffrey S. Gurock, 309–325. New York: Routledge, 1998.

———. "Kleindeutschland: New York City's Germans, 1845–1880." PhD diss., Columbia University, 1981.

——. *Little Germany: Ethnicity, Religion and Class in New York City, 1845–80.* Urbana: University of Illinois Press, 1990.

——. "Those Who Would Be Free: The Eight-Hour Day Strikes of 1872." *Labor's Heritage* 2, no. 2 (April 1990): 70–77.

Nagler, Jörg. *Nationale Minoritäten im Krieg, "Feindliche Ausländer" und die amerikanische Heimatfront während des Ersten Weltkriegs.* Hamburg: Hamburger Edition, 2000.

——. "Victims of the Home Front: Enemy Aliens in the United States during the First World War." In *Minorities in Wartime: National and Racial Groupings in Europe, North America and Australia during the Two World Wars,* edited by Panikos Panayi, 191–215. Providence, RI: Berg, 1993.

Nolan, Janet. *Servants of the Poor: Teachers and Mobility in Ireland and Irish America.* Notre Dame, IN: University of Notre Dame Press, 2004.

O'Donnell, Edward T. *Ship Ablaze: The Tragedy of the Steamboat General Slocum.* New York: Broadway, 2003.

O'Donnell, Edward T., and Elke Schönfeld. *Der Ausflug, das Ende von Little Germany New York.* Hamburg, Germany: Marebuchverlag, 2006.

Olson, Audrey L. *St. Louis Germans, 1850–1920: The Nature of an Immigrant Community and Its Relationship to the Assimilation Process.* New York: Arno, 1980.

Perlmann, Joel. "A Demographic Basis for Ethnic Survival? Blending across Four Generations of German-Americans." Levy Economic Institutes of Bard College, Working Paper 646, December 2010. http://www.levyinstitute.org/pubs/wp_646 .pdf.

Peterson, H. C., and Gilbert C. Fite. *Opponents of War, 1917–1918: The Story of the Persecution of Antiwar Groups.* Madison: University of Wisconsin Press, 1957.

Pfleger, Birte, ed. *Ethnicity Matters: A History of the German Society of Pennsylvania.* Washington, DC: German Historical Institute, 2006.

Polland, Annie, and Daniel Soyer. *Emerging Metropolis: New York Jews in the Age of Immigration, 1840–1920.* New York: New York University Press, 2012.

Probst, Nora. *The New York Turn Verein: Finding Aid of the Archival Documents, 1850–2005.* New York, 2008.

Ramsey, P. *Bilingual Public Schooling in the United States: A History of America's "Polyglot Boardinghouse."* New York: Springer, 2010.

Randel, William Peirce. "The Flames of Hell Gate." *American Heritage Magazine* 30, no. 6 (October/November 1979): 62–75.

Ratner, Sidney. *New Light on the History of Great American fortunes: American Millionaires of 1892 and 1902.* New York: A. M. Kelley, 1953.

Reick, Philipp. *"Labor Is Not a Commodity!" The Movement to Shorten the Workday in Late Nineteenth-Century Berlin and New York.* Frankfurt, Germany: Campus Verlag, 2016.

Revell, Keith D. *Building Gotham: Civic Culture and Public Policy in New York City, 1898–1938.* Baltimore: Johns Hopkins University Press, 2005.

Rippley, La Vern J. "Ameliorated Americanization: The Effect of World War I on German-Americans in the 1920s." In *Americans and the Germans: An Assessment of a Three-Hundred-Year History,* Vol. 2, *The Relationship in the Twentieth Century,* edited by Frank Trommler and Joseph McVeigh, 217–231. Philadelphia: University of Pennsylvania, 1985.

——. *The Immigrant Experience in Wisconsin.* Boston: Twayne, 1985.

Rosenwaike, Ira. *The Population History of New York City*. Syracuse, NY: Syracuse University Press, 1972.

Scherzer, Kenneth A. *The Unbounded Community: Neighborhood Life and Social Structure in New York, 1830–1875*. Durham, NC: Duke University Press, 1992.

Schiffman, Harold. "Language Loyalty in the German-American Church: The Case of an Over-Confident Minority." Handout for LING 540, Language Policy. Accessed June 1, 2028, https://www.sas.upenn.edu/~haroldfs/540/handouts/gachurch/index.html

Schneider, Dorothee. "The German Brewery Workers of New York City in the Late Nineteenth Century." In *Labor Divided: Race and Ethnicity in United States Labor Struggles, 1835–1960*, edited by Robert Asher and Charles Stephenson, 189–207. New York: SUNY Press, 1990.

———. *Trade Unions and Community: The German Working Class in New York City, 1870–1900*. Urbana: University of Illinois Press, 1994.

Schniedewind, Karen. *Begrenzter Aufenthalt im Land der unbegrenzten Möglichkeiten: Bremer Rückwanderer aus Amerika 1850–1914*. Stuttgart, Germany: Franz Steiner, 1994.

———. "Motivations and Strategies of German Return Migration." In *Migrations Et Migrants Dans Une Perspective Historique/Migrations and Migrants in Historical Perspective*, edited by Rene Leboutte, 207–218. Brussels, Belgium: P.I.E.–Peter Lang, 2000.

Schrover, Marlou. "No More than a Keg of Beer: The Coherence of German Immigrant Communities." In *Paths of Integration, Migrants in Western Europe*, edited by Leo Lucassen, David Feldman, and Jochen Oltmer, 222–238. Chicago: University of Chicago Press, 2006.

Scott, Kenneth. *Petitions for Name Changes in New York City, 1848–1899, Special publications of the National Genealogical Society, no. 53*. Washington, DC: National Genealogical Society, 1984.

Seifert, Ruth. "Women's Pages in the German-American Radical Press, 1900–1914: The Debate on Socialism, Emancipation, and the Suffrage." In *The German-American Radical Press: The Shaping of a Left Political Culture, 1850–1940*, edited by Elliott Shore, Ken Fones-Wolf, James Philip Danky, and James P. Danky, 122–144. Champaign: University of Illinois Press, 1992.

Seyfried, Vincent F. *The Long Island Railroad: A Comprehensive History*, part 2, *The Flushing, North Shore and Central Railroad*. Garden City, NY: Vincent F. Seyfried, 1963.

Shea, Ann M. *The Irish Experience in New York City: A Select Bibliography*. New York: New York Irish History Roundtable, 1995.

Smith, Zachary. *Age of Fear: Othering and American Identity During World War I*. Baltimore: Johns Hopkins University Press, 2019.

Sowell, Thomas. *Migrations and Cultures: A World View*. New York: Basic Books, 1996.

Soyer, Daniel. *A Coat of Many Colors: Immigration, Globalization, and Reform in New York City's Garment Industry*. New York: Fordham University Press, 2005.

———. *Jewish Immigrant Associations and American Identity in New York, 1880–1939*. Cambridge, MA: Harvard University Press, 1997.

Spitzer, John. *American Orchestras in the Nineteenth Century*. Chicago: University of Chicago Press, 2012.

Stevenson, William. "Charles Pfizer." In *Immigrant Entrepreneurship, German-American Business Biographies, 1720 to the Present*, Vol. 2, edited by William J. Hausman. Washington, DC: German Historical Institute, 2011. Accessed November 3, 2017, https://www.immigrantentrepreneurship.org/entry.php?rec=31.

Tatlock, Lynne, and Matt Erlin, eds. *German Culture in Nineteenth-Century America: Reception, Adaptation, Transformation*. Rochester, NY: Camden House, 2005.

Tolzmann, Heinrich. *The Cincinnati Germans after the Great War*. New York: Peter Lang, 1987.

———. *The German-American Experience*. Boston: Humanities Press, 2000.

Torp, Claudius. "Heinrich Engelhard Steinway." In *Immigrant Entrepreneurship, German-American Business Biographies, 1720 to the Present*, Vol. 2, edited by William J. Hausman. Washington, DC: German Historical Institute, 2013. Accessed July 15, 2018, https://www.immigrantentrepreneurship.org/entry.php?rec=147.

Vacha, J. E. "When Wagner Was Verboten: The Campaign against German Music in World War I." *New York History* 64, no. 2 (April 1983): 171–188.

Vecoli, Rudolph J. *The People of New Jersey*. Princeton, NJ: D. Van Nostrand, 1965.

Venzant, Carol X. *Lawyers, Guns, and Money: One Man's Battle with the Gun Industry*. New York: St. Martin's Press. 2015.

Vernon, J. R. "Unemployment Rates in Postbellum America: 1869–1899." *Journal of Macroeconomics* 16, no. 4 (Fall 1994): 701–714.

Weber, Peter C. "Ethnic Identity during War: The Case of German-American Societies during World War I." *Nonprofit and Voluntary Sector Quarterly* 43, no. 1 (2014): 185–206.

Weir, Robert E. "A Fragile Alliance: Henry George and the Knights of Labor." In "Commemorating the 100th Anniversary of the Death of Henry George," special issue, *American Journal of Economics and Sociology* 56, no. 4 (October 1997): 421–439.

Wiedemann-Citera, Barbara. *Die Auswirkungen des Ersten Weltkrieges auf die Deutsch-Amerikaner im Spiegel der New Yorker Staatszeitung, der New Yorker Volkszeitung und New York Times 1914–1926*. Frankfurt, Germany: Peter Lang, 1993.

"The William Steinway Diary, 1861–1896." National Museum of American History. Accessed August 22, 2012, https://americanhistory.si.edu/steinwaydiary/.

Wilson, Ross J. *New York and the First World War: Shaping an American City*. New York: Routledge, 2016.

Witcover, Jules. *Sabotage at Black Tom: Imperial Germany's Secret War in America, 1914–1917*. Chapel Hill, NC: Algonquin Books of Chapel Hill, 1989.

Wittke, Carl. *The German-Language Press in America*. New York: Haskell House, 1973.

———. *Refugees of Revolution: The German Forty-Eighters in America*. Philadelphia: University of Pennsylvania Press, 1952.

Wood, George S., Jr., and Juan C. Judikis. *Conversations on Community Theory*. West Lafayette, IN: Purdue University Press, 2002.

Wright, Kathleen M., and Paul T. Bartone. "Community Response to Disaster: The Gander Plane Crash." In *Individual and Community Responses to Trauma and Disasters: The Structure of Human Chaos*, edited by Robert J. Ursano, Brian G. McCaughey, and Carol S. Fullerton, 267–286. Cambridge, UK: Cambridge University Press, 1995.

Ziegler-McPherson, Christina A. *Immigrants in Hoboken: One-Way Ticket, 1845–1985.* Charleston, SC: History Press, 2011.

———. *Selling America: Immigration Promotion and the Settlement of the American Continent, 1607–1914.* Santa Barbara, CA: Praeger, 2017.

———. "Wilhelm J. D. Keuffel," In *Immigrant Entrepreneurship, German-American Business Biographies, 1720 to the Present*, Vol. 3, edited by Giles R. Hoyt. DC: German Historical Institute, 2013. http://www.immigrantentrepreneurship.org/entry.php?rec=157.

WEBSITES

Coney Island History Project. https://www.coneyislandhistory.org/hall-of-fame/charles-feltman.

Demographia, "New York Manhattan Sectors Population & Density 1800–1910." http://www.demographia.com/db-nyc-sector1800.htm.

The Elka Club. "About Us." http://elkaparkclub.com/index.php?option=com_content&view=article&id=49&Itemid=44.

Find a Grave. https://www.findagrave.com/.

German Genealogy Group. "The Slocum, June 15, 1904: A Tragedy." http://www.germangenealogygroup.com/PDF/Slocum_Newsletter_Articles.pdf.

Lenox Hill Hospital. "Our History." https://www.northwell.edu/find-care/locations/lenox-hill-hospital/about?id=102.

The Mount Sinai Hospital. "About the Hospital, History." http://www.mountsinai.org/locations/mount-sinai/about/history.

The Political Graveyard. "New York: State Assembly, 1880s." http://politicalgraveyard.com/geo/NY/ofc/asmbly1880s.html.

———. "New York: State Assembly, 1890s." http://politicalgraveyard.com/geo/NY/ofc/asmbly1890s.html.

Political Theology. "Sunday Baseball and Other Sins: America's Pastime and the Decline of Blue Laws." https://politicaltheology.com/sunday-baseball-and-other-sins-americas-pastime-and-the-decline-of-blue-laws/.

Steve Morse. "Brooklyn Genealogy." http://bklyn-genealogy-info.stevemorse.org/Ward/Man.1880.ed.html.

Tenement House Museum, New York City. www.tenement.org, particularly http://tenement.org/blog/a-shop-life-anniversary/ http://tenement-museum.blogspot.de/2010/02/questions-for-curatorial-schneiders.html.

Zion St. Mark's Evangelical Lutheran Church. "Our History." http://www.zionstmarks.org/ourhistory.htm.

Index

About the Author

CHRISTINA A. ZIEGLER-MCPHERSON has a PhD in history from the University of California, Santa Barbara, and has worked as a public historian and museum curator in New York and New Jersey. She is a research scientist at the Deutsches Schifffahrtsmuseum (German Maritime Museum) in Bremerhaven, Germany. This is her fourth book.